DRAWN FROM WATER

DRAWN FROM WATER

An American Poet
An Ethiopian Family
An Israeli Story

Dina Elenbogen

BkMk Press
University of Missouri-Kansas City

BkMk Press
University of Missouri-Kansas City
5101 Rockhill Road
Kansas City, Missouri 64110
www.umkc.edu/bkmk

Financial support for BkMk Press is provided by the Missouri Arts Council, a state agency. This project is supported in part by an award from the National Endowment for the Arts.

Executive Editor: Robert Stewart
Managing Editor: Ben Furnish
Assistant Managing Editor: Susan L. Schurman
Cover Design: Siara Berry
Editorial Consultant: Maureen Hirthler
Cover photo: Dina Elenbogen (above), Cha Johnston (below)
Author photo: Sarina Elenbogen-Siegel

BkMk Press wishes to thank Sabrina Veroczi, Elizabeth Gromling, Marie Mayhugh, Brittany Green, Greyson Honaker, Kristin Pugh, Seann Weir, Alysabeth Albano, Anders Carlson, Rhonda Cooksey, Alicia Vaughn-Bey.

Edmond Jabès, from *The Book of Questions,* translation © 1991 by Rosmarie Waldrop.Published by Wesleyan University Press and used by permission.
Edmond Jabès, from *A Foreigner Carrying in the Crook of his Arm a Tiny Book,* translation © 1993 by Rosmarie Waldrop. Published by Wesleyan University Press and used by permission. www.wesleyan.edu/wespress

Library of Congress Cataloging-in-Publication Data

Elenbogen, Dina.
 Drawn from water : an American poet, an Ethiopian family, an Israeli story / Dina Elenbogen.
 pages cm
 ISBN 978-1-886157-97-2 (alk. paper)
 1. Elenbogen, Dina--Friends and associates. 2. Poets, American--Biography. 3. Americans--Israel. 4. Jews, Ethiopian--Israel. I. Title.
 PS3605.L38Z46 2015
 811'.6--dc23
 [B]
 2015004260
 ISBN 978-1-886157-97-2

This book is set in Dante and Nueva.

for Gil
for Steve
for Sarina
for Ilan

Contents

Author's Note 9
Prologue: In the Beginning 11
Setting Out (1998) 15
Absorption: Jerusalem-Ma'alot (1984-1985) 21
The Place between Two Countries (1985-1989) 79
Five Years after Operation Moses (1989) 99
Operation Solomon (1991) 143
Don't Lose the *Conecshun* (1993) 183
A Garden; A Country (1995) 233
Pockets of Hope (1996-1998) 283
Home: Twenty-five Years after
 Operation Moses (2009) 295
Acknowledgments 307
Readers' Guide 311

Photographs

Laundry at the Haifa caravan by Dina Elenbogen (cover)
Elad by Cha Johnston (cover)
Ma'alot, Israel, 2014, by Sarina Elenbogen-Siegel (p. 11)
Osnat and Baby Sarina, 1998, Cessaria, by Dina Elenbogen (p. 17)
Osnat and sister, Ma'alot, 1985, by Cha Johnston (p. 23)
Elad and friend, Ma'alot, 1989, by Dina Elenbogen (p. 81)
Amnon Yamari, Ma'alot, 1989, by Dina Elenbogen (p. 101)
Diplomat Hotel, Jerusalem, 1991, by Dina Elenbogen (p. 145)
Osnat, Haifa University, 1993, by Dina Elenbogen (p. 185)
Ethiopian Art, Tel-Aviv Market, 2014, by Dina Elenbogen (p. 235)
Ma'alot, 1985, by Cha Johnston (p. 285)
Ilan and Baby Omri, Kfar Saba, 2009, by Sarina Elenbogen- Siegel (p. 297)
Family Reunion, Elad and Family, Kfar Saba, 2014, Steve Siegel (p. 307)

Author's Note

The material in this book was drawn from memory, journals that I kept religiously, particularly during my trips to Israel, and interviews and conversations with people mentioned in the book. I changed a few names and identifying characteristics to protect privacy. I occasionally condensed a few scenes into one, in cases where it had no impact on the substance of the narrative.

Prologue: In the Beginning

There was a Jewish community living according to ancient Jewish law in thatch-roofed huts in the Semien Mountains of Ethiopia, in Gondar province, and the cities of Gondar and Addis Ababa. This community, which called itself the Beta Israel (House of Israel) was isolated from world Jewry, and mostly separated from Ethiopian Christians. There are several theories about how they landed there. Some scholars say they were separated from other Israelites when crossing the Red Sea. Others say they are offspring from King Solomon and the Queen of Sheba, but no one knows their origins with any certainty. Sometimes they were visited by Westerners like Joseph Halévy, a Polish Jew from Turkey who with support of the Alliance Israélite Universelle in Paris, in 1867 led an expedition to Beta Israel communities in Ethiopia. In 1904 his pupil Jacques Faitlovitch, a Polish Jew living in France, followed his teacher's path to Ethiopia and introduced mainstream Jewish practices, bringing the Beta Israel community to the attention of world Jewry. Later they were visited by Christians who tried to convert them to Christianity. Sometimes their children disappeared. Over time they stopped trusting white foreigners. Although the Israeli rabbinate confirmed their status as Jews in 1973, the government was ambivalent about taking action to bring them to Israel.

In Ethiopia the Jews bathed in rivers, and women isolated themselves in huts during menstruation and after giving birth.

They prepared for the Sabbath all week and kept it strictly, eating cold food to avoid building fires and partaking in other work during this holy time of rest. Their religious leader, or *Kes*, prayed for the community in Ge'ez, an ancient liturgical language. They washed when they came in contact with outsiders.

The women wove baskets and from clay created bowls, dishes, figurines. Because they sculpted so beautifully and burned their objects over an open flame, Christians believed they had evil powers and called them *buda,* or devils. Exacerbated by war and the changing governments, they suffered from persecution, poverty, famine. In good times and in bad times they longed for Jerusalem.

In March 2013, in Falls Village, Connecticut, Ethiopian Jews, American black Jews, Caribbean blacks, white Jews, Ethiopianists, *Kessim,* religious leaders, lovers of Zion and lovers of Ethiopian Jews gathered to tell and hear each other's stories and to speak together the language of Ethiopian absorption in Israel. In the dim sanctuary of the Isabella Freedman Retreat Center, Barbara Ribakove Gordon spoke first, returning to 1971, when during a transitional period in her life, she agreed to go on a mission to see the Beta Israel in Ethiopia. The government did not want outsiders to visit or rescue their Jews, so she had to tell many half-truths to get there. She knew that she could not ask for them by name so she asked instead to see the birds that she knew congregated in the Semien Mountains, where an isolated community of Jews lived. She was not a young woman, but she and the other seasoned people on her mission rode mules over mountains and took arduous treks before reaching the Beta Israel. Because the Jews had grown weary of foreigners, Barbara and her cohorts learned some words in Amharic that served as a password to their secret world.

Following her first trip where she had grown enamored of the Beta Israel and passionate about their cause, she formed the North American Conference on Ethiopian Jewry (NACOEJ) which allowed her to begin the work of bringing Ethiopian Jews and Falash Mura, Christians of Jewish origins, to Israel and helping them live productive lives.

She told her story that moved from airplane to mule, to straw huts, to strange bedfellows, through friendships, negotiations, politics and the hard work that would change the course of her life and the face of Ethiopian Jewry.

This trip of forty years ago helped to propel the 1981 operation that brought Jews from Tigray in northern Ethiopia into Israel followed by Operation Moses in 1984 ,which brought 7,000 Jews into Israel, and Operation Solomon in 1991, which during thirty-six hours, airlifted 15,000 people. Before that, Jews had trickled in on their own, escaping through Sudan and finding their way to Israel. In between operations Moses and Solomon there were smaller operations and airlifts of Beta Israel and Falash Mura. There have been other recent triumphs: Miss Israel, an Ethiopian Jew, was invited to have dinner with President Obama when he visited Jerusalem. Educational initiatives under the umbrella of the Ethiopian National Project were successful in helping Ethiopian children do well in school. Balaynesh Zevadia, who arrived in Israel with Operation Moses, became the Israeli ambassador to Ethiopia. Today, thirty years after Operation Moses, there are at least 140,000 Ethiopian Jews in Israel. Each time another man, woman, or child lands in Israel from Ethiopia, the story begins again.

After the conference, on the train ride back to Manhattan, Barbara, who is eighty now, more frail than when she rode a mule over mountains but no less passionate about her cause, asked me to tell my story with the Ethiopian Jews. I had read excerpts of it on Shabbat afternoon, had spoken it over meals, self-consciously read some of it to Ethiopian Israelis in the audience who I was relieved to discover appreciated my perspective, but had never before told my story. I am a poet and a writer. I am not a storyteller. And like the Ethiopian Jews, I am soft spoken, and I tell my most important truths in poetry the way they tell theirs in parables.

But because of Barbara's generosity of spirit, her listening eyes, and knowing nods, I told her my story as best I could spanning twenty-five years. I spoke of my first glimpses of the Beta Israel in Ma'alot, Israel, in the aftermath of Operation Moses, the quick friendships that were formed as I became their English teacher and

teacher of western ways. I described living next door to some families, of returning to America while living with my Ethiopian families in my imagination and during my seven return trips to Israel. I tried to answer for both the Ethiopian community and myself, the not-so-simple question: has Israel become a true home?

I confessed to Barbara the naïveté and idealism I possessed as a young woman, believing there was a truth waiting for me if I only peered into the right set of eyes, asked the perfect question, or visited the most appropriate absorption center or caravan where the newest Ethiopian Jews were being settled.

It has taken me decades of listening to other people's stories, looking into dark and light eyes, taking trains and buses from small towns to major cities in Israel, eating *injera* in Kfar Saba, and now small towns in Connecticut, to understand that the truth doesn't live in one place.

In the beginning there was a mule that took buckets of water from rivers to huts, took Joseph Halévy and Jacques Faitlovitch to the Beta Israel. Took an American woman over mountains. Took the Jews of Ethiopia home. In the beginning there were wandering Jews who, in a promised land, through love and friendship, helped each other find their way home.

Setting Out
(1998)

...how many pages to live, or die, are between you and
 yourself,
 between the book and leaving the book?

—*Edmond Jabès*
from The Book of Questions

July 1998

I carry my daughter through Jerusalem streets. She is asleep on my shoulder. I think of ways to explain why I have taken her to this Middle Eastern country where everything, including time, has been turned upside down, this hot and holy city, where she is light against me, where I push her through stone streets in her blue stroller with American wheels, where she stands up for the first time, weeps next to the Wall, and where in the men's section her father names her: *Sarina Bat Yisrael*, Sarina daughter of Israel.

I have come to finish the story that is always ending and beginning again. I have come to close the book that is never sealed. I have come to walk these streets with Steve, my husband of two years, and our eight-month-old daughter. I have come to see my friends who, fourteen years ago, arrived here from Ethiopia. I have come to see Osnat, my former student, in her home next to the sea, to watch as she and Sarina look into each other's eyes for the first time. I have come to see Elad, Batya, and their family that is growing and spreading throughout the country but always returning to the hearth in Kfar Saba. I have come to see Yael who has been wrapped in secrets these past two years. I have come to hear the story of her mother who has just arrived in Israel. I have come to walk through the

caravans where Falash Mura, whose compound has just been emptied in Addis Ababa, are beginning new lives. I have come to see what, if anything, has been learned from the past. I have come, again, to understand absorption: how a land absorbs a people, how a people absorb a land and then find a way to return to themselves.

When I first arrived in Israel in 1984 the questions I asked were more personal. I did not know the drama that was unfolding. I did not know that during the same spring that I received a master's degree, waited tables, and packed my books for Israel, Jews from Ethiopia were leaving without belongings, trekking through Sudan and in the best of cases, via Operation Moses, making their way to Israel.

While 7,000 Ethiopian Jews were taking their first steps onto Israeli soil, I was seeking a way for my life to fit into the country that was unraveling before my eyes. And my life, too, was unraveling with the landscape that captured me with its harsh, raw beauty. I studied Hebrew on a kibbutz outside of Jerusalem for four months, and when I heard of their arrival, I moved to the absorption center in Ma'alot to teach English and to welcome the new immigrants from Ethiopia.

Osnat, whom I first met as a twelve-year-old student, and her cousin Elad, who was four when I lived next door to the new immigrants in 1985, would ultimately turn my one- year visit to Israel into twenty-five years of returning and retracing footsteps. I would come back to Israel to glimpse the lives of these African Jews and how Israel was and was not becoming the home they longed for. I would come back each time a little older, less idealistic, trying to find the truth about their lives, and about a country that I had dreamt of making my home.

Meanwhile, I was also growing up in America where I would return with notebooks full of impressions, arguments for and against making *aliyah*, going up to Israel to become a citizen, and photographs of the Jews from Ethiopia who reminded me of the purpose of Israel as the country grew less idealistic and

more materialistic. The photographs of Osnat and Elad, hanging on the walls of my writing room in America, keep the question of home alive for me. And the photographs I've taken over the years, of all of us together, remain on their walls and refrigerators, waiting for my next return.

Absorption:
Jerusalem–Ma'alot
(1984-1985)

The water you float on, the water you give in to
Is the water of sleep
The water you wash in, the water you fight against
Is the water of awakening

—*Edmond Jabès*
from The Book of Questions

June 1985—Ma'alot

We know the weather by how quickly our clothes dry on the line, and we know the world continues by the voices in the street. The Ethiopian children are always the first to accept the gift of Shabbat morning: the first to gather the sunlight in their palms, to dig their feet into the earth. They are also the first to greet us on our return from anywhere. Late afternoon or evening, the girls lean out the windows, toward the future. When I return from my monthly visits to Jerusalem, I am greeted by the stillness of the night, the shadows of the mountains, the laughter of the jackals, and then Osnat and Yael, leaning out the window, heads covered in colorful scarves. They softly call my name, "Dina, Shalom, ma nishma?" what's new or what do we hear? And I know then that I am back where I belong now.

October 1984

I arrive in Jerusalem in the dark. Avrahm, who runs our *ulpan*, intensive Hebrew course, is the first person I meet at Kibbutz Ramat Rachel where I will be studying Hebrew and working in the Jerusalem hills. Since the ulpanist's quarters have not been cleaned yet, Avrahm, who only speaks to me in Hebrew, leads me to the guesthouse for the night. Bone tired from travel, I fall into an instant sleep. Before sunrise, awakened by the sounds of dogs, I step out of my cramped room to small lights sparkling from a

distant city. The sky, a beautiful haunting purple, slowly fades to lavender. I wonder why the dogs are barking so early and why there is a certain smell I can't wash from my skin. When the sun comes up, I realize the green-brown landscape of the city in the distance is Bethlehem because the white stone in the other direction is Jerusalem. At this early hour in between night and morning, the country enters my skin. My feet feel solid on the land. A voice from deep within says *welcome home*.

I did not use words like *home* and *dream* when I planned my trip to Israel. On an application for a grant that I never received, I wrote that I was coming to Israel to translate the Hebrew poets into English. But even the poet Yehuda Amichai, on his visit to Iowa City the year before, had told me my plan was too academic. "Just go and experience," he had advised.

I was coming to Israel to learn Hebrew. And I was coming to Israel to see the face of a man I loved who for a year had been exploring this country. I needed to look in his eyes to see that we had no future. I was coming to Israel because, after four years of college and two years of graduate school, I needed to feel autumn apples as I pulled them from trees.

My first day on kibbutz I do not explore the landscape, nor do I inquire as to what work I should do. I take a bus to Beit Shemesh to visit the man I've loved for three years who now lives in this development town called The House of Sun, about forty minutes from my kibbutz. Two years earlier Ben and I had been students together in Bloomington, Indiana, where we had studied English literature, where he had helped me get through astronomy as I explained the poems of the German poet Paul Celan to him. We had been grappling with the Holocaust through its literature and history, and dreaming of the day when we could return to the Promised Land. I wrote poems for him and he received them gracefully. Upon graduation, he told his mother, long distance in Philadelphia, that he would marry me if he could right then. Yet over a long Sabbath meal, he accused me of wanting him to be a professor's husband in America instead of living in Israel. During

my second year of graduate school in Iowa City, he left for Israel. His letters became less and less frequent, but they never ceased.

The man who greets me in the center of town is taller and lankier than I remember. His head is covered with a *kippah*, skull cap, and he wears *tzitzit*, fringes on a prayer garment, around his waist. He twirls me around in the air, and then he lets me fall to the ground.

"I kept looking at my calendar, counting the days until your arrival. As it got closer I'd say, three more Sabbaths until Dina arrives in Israel."

"Really? I thought those huge silences in between letters meant that you'd forgotten me." Ben smiles sadly, refusing to answer my unasked question. In his dorm-like room, I stare at photographs of myself on his wall next to faces I don't know. "Here, Ben, this is for you," I say, handing him my bound collection of poems, my thesis. He opens the cover to make sure the book is dedicated to him. He takes it along on our walk.

As we stroll through Beit Shemesh, a poor town surrounded by spectacular mountain views and populated primarily by Moroccan Israelis, he seems to know each person we pass: older men, young women, and children. When we arrive at the school to meet the English Club he leads for teenagers, the students run up to him screaming in Hebrew, "Is that your girlfriend?"

"No, it's my friend Dina from America." Understanding his simple Hebrew response, I sit in a corner, despondent, not listening to their lesson.

Back at Ben's apartment, visitors come by speaking the same coarse Hebrew I'd heard all evening. As I lean over his porch to escape from the men, I feel the distance that has grown between us and the distance between myself and the ground beneath me. Soon Ben's friend Alon, who describes himself as Ben's Moroccan brother, joins me and as if reading my mind says, "Moshe, I mean Ben, isn't drawn to intellectual American women anymore. He likes wise and simple Moroccan girls. He's no longer the way he described himself in college. He doesn't sit around reading poems. He prays three times a day," he adds with unexpected intimacy.

Looking back down at the soil three stories below I wonder if I am the same woman. I still love him, admire the way he tries to live a Jewish life, how he followed his dream to Israel. But what is my dream? Is he still a part of it? Years before I had chosen Ben over a wilder man, a romantic man who didn't have the same ethical core as he had. I never expected him to go this far. I don't know if he still loves me the same way or not. I sense from his silences that he has decided against me but does not want to completely let me go.

When the apartment empties at last, we get into separate beds. I lay awake listening to him scream "Die!! Die!" to the barking dogs outside. I join him on the balcony and ask why he is so angry, why he wants them to die.

"They are evil dogs who should be fed poison meat, but I'm not telling them to die. *Di* means *enough* in Hebrew."

Back in his bed I weep the rest of the night, unable to articulate my feelings. Ben thinks I am probably just overwhelmed by the fact that we are both in the Promised Land.

On the bus the next morning, on the way back to Ramat Rachel, I think about poet Miguel Hernández's words that I had once recited to Ben when we were still students in Bloomington. "After love, the land, after the land, nothing." Some of my sadness unravels with the landscape. There are so many smells, tastes, faces, and colors of the landscape to absorb.

I enter my small room on kibbutz to be greeted by my roommate Annette, a German Christian, who had come to Israel because the climate was good for her asthma. She had fallen in love with the land, religion, and a Yemenite-Israeli man and was now considering converting to Judaism.

As I fold clothes into a cabinet next to my bed and line my poetry books into a plastic milk container I found near a garbage dump, I look out my window at the other barracks next to ours. I spot a young woman with curls like mine, looking off in the distance. She is wearing a navy kibbutz workshirt as if she has been at Ramat Rachel a while. Occasionally she writes in a notebook

but mostly stares into space. When she looks toward my window for a moment, I see that her face, with furrowed brow and watchful eyes, is familiar although we'd never met before.

Eti, a kibbutz member, comes by to bring me to my first job. "Where were you yesterday? You were supposed to begin working," she whines in heavily accented Hebrew. She is dark-skinned with short curly black hair and smokes Arabic cigarettes.

"I was in Beit Shemesh visiting a friend. I didn't know I was supposed to begin work already."

"Beit Shemesh! Who did you visit there?" she asks with sudden interest.

"My friend from America, Ben... I mean Moshe Levine, he just changed his name."

"Did you meet anyone else?"

"I met some of his friends but the only one I remember is Alon."

Her scowl changes to a warm smile as she introduces herself as Alon's big sister. He had mentioned a sister at Ramat Rachel, but I didn't think she would be the one to hand me a mop and cleanser, instructing me to clean toilets in the guesthouse.

I learn quickly that there is an art to everything, even cleaning toilets. My crew and I open the men's door, spray the room with Lysol, wait for it to settle, run in, scrub the toilets, pick up the fallen tissue, wash the floor with a dirty rag over a wooden stick. Annette works in the rose garden, reaching into thorns, gathering fallen petals. During lunch break she shows me the scars on her arm.

Apple season on kibbutz is short. When I first arrived I had been told that only the men were picking. However, after a week of cleaning toilets, I ask to be transferred to the fields. The young woman with curls like mine, whom I had seen through the window that first day and whom I later discover is Sara, encourages me to join her at the crack of dawn when work begins in the orchard. Sara arrived on kibbutz a few days before I did. After graduating from high school she is taking a year off before beginning her

studies at Harvard. She wants to feel the sweat of hard work and experience life on kibbutz before entering the ivory tower.

On the wagon to the nearby apple orchard, the tall tanned Israeli men give us orders. We then carry bushels from tree to tree collecting the best apples. When I stop to daydream or look at the sky, or when Sara and I sit under a tree to write in our notebooks or talk, someone yells, "Keep going. *Ya la chick chock.*" It is hard physical work. My arms are scratched from reaching into the trees to get the ripest apples, and my shoulders are sore from carrying overflowing baskets.

Soon I am promoted to the guest house restaurant where busloads of tourists arrive from Japan, Germany, and the United States. Within days we can guess that the Asians will order green melon, the Germans strudel, and that the Americans will eat without trays. When they discover from my accent that I, too, am American, they are delighted and ask why I am in Israel. They often mistake me for Israeli. I don't know if the land I am slowly absorbing has somehow changed my look, but I never really did identify with the average American. And when I look at these tourists I feel embarrassed by them and their questions, their gold jewelry, matching sun visors, and voices booming *Why are you here?* When I can't think of a proper answer I say that I no longer remember.

I feel most at home in the guesthouse kitchen when I sing the prayer *"Avinu Malkeinu"* over the loud motor of the dishwasher. After "Our Father Our King" I sing Leonard Cohen's "Suzanne" and translate it into Hebrew for the Arab workers who are intrigued by the bittersweet and sometimes mournful tone. Sometimes a group of us, ulpanists and the younger kibbutzniks, set tables as we sing Dylan songs. When we work together, time flies.

A letter arrives from my father asking for more details about my life in Israel. From what I've written so far, he says he doesn't have a sense of my experience. Today, instead of trying to memorize the new vocabulary words we learned in *ulpan*, I write to my family.

Dear Everyone,

How can I describe my life to you? I can tell you about seven o'clock in the morning in the guest house restaurant—while everyone else is peeling onions, my eyes won't stop watering. I can tell you how I cut to the deepest part of the apple—the toughest but sweetest part—that from cleaning toilets I have come to appreciate slicing lemons and, from washing meat, I cherish the feel of peeling warm potatoes. Some mornings are so cold I wear five layers of clothing. When we return from work we warm our hands and feet next to a small space heater. I remember winters in Iowa City in the old drafty farmhouse where I studied poetry and typed with gloves on, and I appreciate the flowers that have lasted all autumn.

Today in the kitchen of the guesthouse I found an old frying pan that hasn't been used in decades. When I looked at the rust on my palm I thought about how the last time someone used this to fry an egg could have been the day we captured Bethlehem or the week fifteen kibbutz members didn't return from the war. That was 1967. Now it is peaceful. The rattling windows just mean a plane is passing faster than the speed of sound.

The Arab workers are building another room. They think my apple slices are either too large or too small for fruit cocktail. They don't care that we picked these apples with our own hands. They point out bruises on potatoes, and I shave them with a dull knife. Sara and I share our dreams as we pick mint leaves for our tea. The kibbutzniks sip coffee with three lumps of sugar and smoke Time cigarettes incessantly. Some of them appreciate our work but they will never fully accept us. They remind us that this is their home, not ours.

There is a seriousness here that I appreciate—a cause, a land—nourished by strong hands and feet. But where is the idealism now? I don't feel it on this kibbutz. Instead I feel a lot of pushing and shoving to be first on the bus that travels out of this kibbutz and into the city. Only the kibbutzniks get fresh fruit. Once my roommate Annette from Germany stole a bunch of grapefruit and oranges from the kibbutznik's canteen.

She hid them in the corner of our room and didn't share them with the rest of us. Annette is always the first to say that the kibbutzniks don't know anything about socialism.

So what is the seriousness I feel? Survival? The survival of a land and of a people?

What I love about this country isn't logical, Dad. I don't know if I can explain it.

It just feels natural to be here right now. Sometimes I feel like this country is already home, has always been home. Other times I feel that living here would be too much of a struggle. Maybe I don't feel completely at home in either country—not in America with her Christmas trees and the loneliness of New York City, masses of lost souls.

And who am I? An American who speaks Hebrew haltingly, who grew up valuing equal rights, an American who grew up in a Zionist home, whose grandfather was a socialist in Russia. I want to feel at home somewhere.

I sign my name in Hebrew.

The first part of the day is spent working and during the second half of the day we study Hebrew or take long breaks from studying as we dip our bread into vats of chocolate. We are in *kita bet*, level 2, which means that we know some Hebrew from our former countries: America, Canada, Brazil, Germany, Holland, England, and Uruguay. We are Jews, or converts, or people who need to leave their countries for a while. We study Hebrew and dream of the future, not quite sure which landscape will encompass those dreams. Eric went to Jewish day school and is already fluent with a thick Toronto accent. He is fond of telling people I am the first one he met on kibbutz, when I saw him entering one day from the back with a scruffy beard, baseball cap and a heavy green pack. He had just returned from Eastern Europe where he visited the birthplaces of his grandparents. I showed him around the kibbutz that day and brought him to Avrahm. Since then we've discovered his savvy and we go to him for help with our Hebrew, directions

to obscure places in Jerusalem, or advice about where to buy the cheapest film. He is the unofficial leader of our group.

After *ulpan*, Sara and I walk to the Roman ruins on the outskirts of Ramat Rachel with one pair of headsets to her Walkman, listening to Cat Stevens. Everyone, even the Arab workers in the kitchen, calls us sisters because now we are always together and have the same light brown curls. We share poems, love stories, disillusionment. Although I share my days with the other ulpanists, Sara is the one with whom I share my innermost thoughts, the ones that surface while slicing bread or drinking coffee in the evening looking out to Jerusalem. Together we savor the parts of Israel that nourish our dreams: living in a community, hearing the holy tongue, immersing ourselves in history, collecting ancient stone, gathering flowers and placing them in vases next to open windows where exotic bird songs celebrate the beginning of each new day. And together we commiserate over the parts our experience that don't match up to our dreams.

Sometimes the rain, the shift in wind, differentiates one day from the next, and the lime I pull from bushes brings back my exuberance, reminds me of the Israel I visited as a seventeen-year-old, a country where I could pick what I needed from trees.

✿

Moshe, who is still trying to be my friend, asks me to visit Ma'alot with him, a development town in the north of the country. I am reluctant but he finally convinces me to see this remote part of the country and to meet his friends who live in an absorption center for new immigrants and volunteer in the community. I join him and his traveling buddies, still hoping something can be rekindled.

At dusk we arrive in Ma'alot, a small town on top of a mountain. It is Thursday evening, and we will be spending Shabbat with Moshe's American, Australian, and South African friends. After brief introductions we peel vegetables for the Sabbath meal. It is dark so I don't know what lay beyond the plain-tiled, absorption-center apartment where we sit. I don't know that this apartment,

where I lean against Moshe in exhaustion, will become my home only months from this day.

On Shabbat morning I saunter into the main room to find everyone watching out the window in amazement. I lean over the porch railing to see what they're looking at and discover black-skinned men and women in white shawls. I take in their delicate features and the way they greet each other with bows and kisses as they return from the *beit knesset,* house of prayer. A joyful energy emanates from below our window. Our host explains that these are the Ethiopian Jews who just arrived with Operation Moses, which brought 7,000 immigrants to Israel. I am not up on current events. My only source is the English version of the *Jerusalem Post.* I know nothing of these people; I watch them, mesmerized. I cannot put names to these stunning faces, yet these images will return with me to Jerusalem, lodge themselves in my gut.

While the others go to *beit knesset* to pray again before the Sabbath leaves, I stay behind with Avi, an American whose family emigrated to Israel when he was a boy. He declares himself secular and does not want to pray. I am hesitant to stand in another Sephardic shul after having spent Yom Kippur with Moshe, praying behind the callused feet of religious Moroccan women who prayed, heads covered behind the men. I had been lost in the Sephardic service, outside, behind a wall. I also felt uncomfortable when I returned to Kibbutz Ramat Rachel at the end of Yom Kippur, the holiest of days, and learned that everyone had spent the day working and eating. This is when I begin to feel, from the communities I visited, that regarding religion, the water is either burning hot or freezing cold. There are no in-betweens. Yet I am somewhere in between.

In Ma'alot, while the others finish the Sabbath at shul, Avi and I read Amichai poems aloud to each other as the sun set in magentas and purples.

On Sunday morning, while the others pack the car, Moshe and I are suddenly alone. The tension felt on every visit has become intolerable. I do not know how to be his friend. As we sit drinking

tea he says, "I know in many ways I will never find someone as good as you. But we aren't right for each other because of your artsy up-in-the-air temperament. The way you cut lemons. You whittle them instead of slice them in even pieces. You function in your own way but are not so sufficient at daily life. I need someone more grounded."

Instead of laughing in his face or walking out the door, I suddenly want to be that woman, to be better at slicing lemon than at writing poems. I still love Moshe although he no longer reads poems. Can he love me in spite of the lemons? Although I know it is impossible, part of me wants to be that grounded woman, to bring him seven sons.

Back on kibbutz, I decide to let go of the final tattered threads tying me to Moshe. I fall in love with Jerusalem. If during the first weeks I admired her from afar, now I discover her narrow streets, the view of rolling hills from different angles, Yemin Moshe, the Montefiore Castle, the Hill of Evil Council, the Western Wall, the Mount of Olives, the cafés where on cold December evenings Sara and I watch honey melt into our tea after we listen to a rabbi on Jaffe Street lecture on Torah as a way of living. And there are the bookstores where I hold volumes of Hebrew poetry in my hand, measuring how far I am from understanding them without translations. At Steimatzky's Bookstore I ask a soldier browsing in the poetry section who he would recommend. He says his favorites are Yehuda Amichai and Dahlia Ravikovitch. Since I already own most of Amichai's books I decide on Ravikovitch, whose name I'd heard but whose work I was yet to discover. I am determined to understand her by the end of *ulpan*.

I bring my Ravikovitch collection along on a trip to Ashkelon to visit family friends and when a handsome Israeli man sits next to me on the bus on the way back and helps me translate her poems into English while a full moon rises over Jerusalem, I begin to fall in love with him. After a week of drinking tea at the Café Atara, making dinner at his apartment and letting him unravel the pink and blue Israeli scarf around my neck, I find out he already has a

girlfriend. I let him go. I am sad for a few days but relieved that I can have feelings for someone besides Moshe.

During one of the Jerusalem tours that Avrahm gives to our *ulpan*, he shows us our collective losses, Jerusalem's history. We walk along the walls of the Old City, and he points to the green line that separates what was once our land, what we gave up during the 1948 War of Independence and what we won back during the '67 war of victory. But after only four months of walking into Jerusalem's history, it is my short and personal history in Jerusalem that is so difficult to let go of when I begin to prepare for my departure from kibbutz.

I feel as though I am living in history on my walks to the philosopher Martin Buber's former storage room, where the poet and translator Robert Friend has lived since the 1950s. My walks from the #7 bus to his home are just before sundown when the last rays of light shine on the large ancient limestone homes of Rehavia, an old and elite Jerusalem neighborhood.

Robert lives in the basement of one of these grand buildings, and as I walk along Jabotinsky Street to his home, I feel both what is missing in my life on kibbutz and what I will miss when I leave Jerusalem. I dread leaving Robert who has quickly become a dear friend although he is half a century older than me. I treasure the conversations we have about W. H. Auden and other English and Hebrew poets. I relish the gourmet meals he prepares, his friends who join us around the table, his numerous cats, his library spanning centuries and languages, his timelessness, warmth, and unfailing friendship. He reads my poems with a critical and generous eye.

In my translation workshop in Iowa City, my professor had given me Robert's name and encouraged me to contact him when I arrived in Jerusalem. When I called him upon my arrival, he invited me over for tea, greeted me at the door with an old terry-cloth robe over his clothes and served me *lapsang souchong* and descriptions of the Jerusalem poetry world.

As I prepare for my departure from Jerusalem, I mourn leaving our friendship and the potential of getting involved in the poetry

community, going to readings and living and breathing the language of poetry where I am most fluent.

Robert is editing a magazine of English poets writing in Israel. He enthusiastically accepts two of my poems, one of which I imagine would have been described in Iowa City as too Jewish. The other poem was written on kibbutz. If my poetry could find a place here, I wonder, could I?

What is missing in my life on kibbutz is the life of the poet as I had known it—what I had thought I wanted to get away from. After two months on Ramat Rachel I am given access to an English typewriter and a small room to write in which I can only use on the Sabbath. Besides Sara and an occasional volunteer passing through, there is no one with whom I can share poems. Even with my miniature library next to my bed, I am no longer living in the world of poetry—except when I visit Robert.

Although I feel the lack of poetry on kibbutz, I know I need something else to help me discover the country more deeply. I am guarded from something essential. Although from my first moment on kibbutz I felt as though the land had entered my body, I am still removed, speaking English most of the time. The poetry community that I watch from the distance consists of ex-Americans. I am guarded from Jerusalem's stone. I have to pass guards who search my bag, in order to get to the Western Wall. And no matter how many apples I peel in a day or how many new Hebrew verbs I conjugate into past tense, the kibbutz members continue to see me as an ulpanist and so that is how I see myself. My own absorption into Israeli society needs something else to make it complete, or at least temporarily complete.

When a woman arrives at our kibbutz from the Jewish agency to discuss the plight of the Ethiopians in Ma'alot and in other small towns around Israel, something awakens in me. The images in my memory since my visit there some months ago become more vivid as she speaks of the miracle of their arrival, their long journey on foot from Ethiopia to Sudan to be secretly airlifted into Israel, of the many that died on the way. She says the Ethiopian community in Ma'alot needs help learning how to use stoves and sinks, the

essentials of western life. She assures us this will be an experience we'll remember the rest of our lives.

Eric, Sara, and I take the long journey by bus from Jerusalem to Ma'alot to be interviewed by ex-American Elaine Kopp who is running the Ma'alot program. In the program office, we are greeted by her assistant, Elana Gabai, who looks familiar to me as I do to her. We soon realize that we went to the same synagogue and high school in Skokie. She is now a Ma'alot resident, married to an Israeli of Moroccan descent, and the mother of two young daughters.

Elaine, a short dark-haired, middle- aged woman, explains that the Ma'alot program gives one the opportunity to work with the new immigrants from Ethiopia or allows college graduates to work in their fields, give to the community and in return receive a small monthly food stipend, and "an experience that you'll never forget." A chance to help others become absorbed. I look at it the opposite way as well: a chance to absorb Israel into my psyche.

After the interview, the three of us silently survey the town as we walk back to our bus stop. I feel in my body the pain of leaving Jerusalem. Quietly we sit on the bench waiting, looking off at distant mountains. I finally break our silence.

"This is so hard—the program sounds interesting but I'm nervous about working with people after months of cleaning toilets, picking apples, peeling potatoes, folding sheets—and it's so far from Jerusalem!"

"I know what you mean," Sara says distractedly." I'm pretty sure I'll go to Kibbutz Lotan. It's supposed to be this young idealistic kibbutz. I think I want to get to know the desert."

"Well, I'm moving to Ma'alot," Eric says, answering Sara's long questioning stare. "Elaine said I could work as an engineer, and at least I'll feel that my time at university wasn't a total waste."

"I think Ma'alot will be great for you," Sara says earnestly. I, too have chosen Ma'alot.

Beyond all of my doubts I know that I need to live in another part of the country, that the language I long for will best be developed in a place like Ma'alot, where many don't speak English.

And I know that my own private language of poetry could be cultivated not only by living the intellectual life or the life I envisioned in Jerusalem but by being part of a community instead of observing one as I had on kibbutz. I know that by watching these African Jews become Israelis, I will be living in history in a much more immediate way than walking the streets of the prophets.

On Tu Bishvat, Jewish Arbor Day, almond trees bloom on kibbutz. Wherever we walk we are shrouded in a white veil. The air is sweet with future dreams as Avrahm reminds us our days on kibbutz are numbered. We plant trees on the border between our kibbutz and the neighboring Arab village, trees that some day will also bloom on Tubishvat.

Packing our bags and closing up our rooms is bittersweet. Some of us, especially Eric, Sara and I, had come to Israel with the idealized notion of kibbutz. We revered the pioneers who had come to Israel at the turn of the last century to build the land as well as this communal way of living. The immigrants who came after the Second World War continued to work the land. For many, kibbutz was the first home they were able to create in this country. Their connection to the land fulfilled their dreams.

The Israel of 1984 is different, especially on Ramat Rachel. People work for themselves rather than for the larger good of the kibbutz. From the time that we arrived, the doors to the inner kibbutz life have been closed to us. If the connection to the land and the sharing of a mission that I dreamed I would find on kibbutz is lacking, I wonder if maybe it has been replaced by the purity of the new immigrants who would not let their dream of reaching Israel die, who for generations had held onto their Judaism in remote African villages. I wonder if the kibbutz had been replaced by development towns that are absorbing new immigrants all over the country. I wonder if in the Galilee Mountains I could plant new seeds, as I let go of the dreams I carried with me to Israel.

Eric and I drop off our bags at the Ma'alot absorption center and take a bus to the port city of Haifa to spend a few days before our new program begins. Eric stays with some of his friends, and I visit Yossi, the brother of Ilana, my youth group leader during my first visit to Israel in 1977. Yossi had visited me in Chicago and had taken to translating Hebrew poems into English for me. When I arrive at his apartment and slump into a chair, exhausted from so much traveling, Yossi begins his lecture.

"Dina, I don't understand why you like Israel so much given the circumstances under which you've been living. And Ma'alot will be even more difficult. To tell you the truth, I don't understand why you're going there." I look at him for a while before responding, not sure what to say. I recall images of him in Chicago, visiting art museums, dining at the finest restaurants, attending symphonies, trying to hold my hand.

"Yossi, I didn't come to Israel for an easy life—I came to experience the country. I'm going to Ma'alot to help the Jews from Ethiopia. To get involved. I don't expect it to be easy, but what I really need right now is support, not criticism." I am so busy defending my choice to Yossi that I forget my own fears about entering this unknown world on top of a faraway mountain.

The support comes the next morning when Yossi's mother, Ora, visits me while he's at work. Ora arrived from Vienna in the 1930s with the other *halutzim*, pioneers, and is now a scientist at the Weitzmann Institute. She tells me how she envies the work I will be doing and that she had wanted to volunteer in a development town for a long time. After listening to her passion and the careful way she pronounces each English word in her gentle accent, I feel redeemed. Unlike her son, Ora understands that home is not always about comfort.

๛

I arrive in Ma'alot in layers. Everyone warned how cold it would be up north. I have a vest that Tamarah, a former ulpanist, had knitted on kibbutz, the sweater that Boaz (the Israeli man I'd met

on a bus in Jerusalem) had given me, and now a sweater that Yossi's mother had knitted for him and which he never wore. It is huge on me. I have no place to carry everything except for on my body.

Eric and I explore our new home, climbing set after set of cement steps before reaching the center of town, on top of the hill upon which Ma'alot is built. There is a market, a falafel stand, and a few other shops. Next to the market, a man with swarthy, wrinkled skin sits on his knees selling mint leaves. In the center of the business district, another group of elderly men play *shesh besh* (backgammon) arguing in Moroccan and smoking cigarettes. Mint leaves sit in the bottoms of their empty tea glasses. Most of the buildings surrounding the town center are cement slabs like the absorption center, but from our previous visit, we know there are unique and beautiful homes as well. One level down we stand on a ridge overlooking the mountains and villages in the distance. The clouds are thick and dense. Soon we can no longer see into the distance.

In the morning I find the Galilee Mountains outside my window, still green from the winter rains, and the Ethiopian women hanging their clothes to dry on their back porches. On my first Sabbath I watch them again in their white *shammas,* traditional shawls, a few of them outside with the men and children. Others I see from behind glass: my window looks into their window. They are standing in front of the stove warming the afternoon meal. The fire has been on since before sundown, the night before. The men are outside the building in white shirts, *kippot* on their heads, prayer books in their hands. They've just returned from the *beit knesset.* Each time one man greets another there are three bows and four kisses. The children are in light colors, running and falling on the sidewalk, grass and dirt mounds, digging up roots outside their windows.

On my first Sabbath I also meet Jackie who spends her mornings with Ethiopian children in a *gan,* literally garden, similar to a day-care center, where they stay while their parents study Hebrew in *ulpan.* Since the religious school where I am scheduled to teach is on Purim break, Elaine Kopp suggests that I join Jackie in her garden.

When I stop merely watching my Ethiopian neighbors through the windows and join Jackie in her *gan*, I meet Elad. He is the bald child, head shaven for lice. He is the child who slides down the slide again and again yelling *ani, ani*—my turn, my turn. He squats in the dirt with a large floppy sun hat falling in his eyes and a mischievous and endearing smile. He plays alone, full of laughter and secrets.

March 4, 1985

Sometimes, like this morning, I look at these beautiful children and their small dark hands, their running noses and their smiles, and I can't believe what a miracle it is that almost forty years after the White Paper that barred European Jews who were dying at the hands of Nazis from this country, we can open our arms to Jews from Yemen and Morocco, and now these Jews from Ethiopia escaped from their own Egypt. Now they are trying to build lives and I am here to welcome them into a country that was new to me just five months ago.

Of course it isn't simple. There are still limits on immigration. Operation Moses was stopped in the middle when word of it leaked and now families are broken. There is a distance between the Ethiopians and their Israeli neighbors. There are rabbis who are trying to tell them that they are not yet Jews. But they are here, they will live, and as I discussed with Jackie today, perhaps they can learn to love Israel and at the same time, love who they are and not lose it.

Jackie's love for them is infectious. She reaches out her arms, and the children come to her. We call her the Pied Piper because she is always followed by a group of children. I have a tape of her in her apartment with the sharp screams of children playing in Hebrew with Amharic accents. Jackie is repeating, in a sweet yet stern voice, "This is my house, it isn't your garden. Be careful, Elad; don't stand on the table. This is my home. This is my home."

I return every morning during Purim break, sit with Jackie, and play with the children, especially Elad. As the kids circle us, pull our hair, take our hands, and stop for us to tie their shoes, Jackie gives me their stories, how many family members they

had lost on the walk from Sudan. Elad plays with a wooden beaded necklace. When Jackie asks where he got it he says sadly that his father made it for him. When he runs off to play, Jackie whispers that his father had not arrived with the rest of the family. I would learn later that when word of Operation Moses was leaked to the press, it was then halted. Half of the Jews who were escaping to Israel from Sudan were stopped in their tracks and sent back to Ethiopia.

I leave the children's garden to teach the older kids, but my conversations with Jackie, red-haired, freckled and passionate about her work, continue on walks through town, as we pick poppies in the Galil, and between our two *marpesets*, or porches, two floors apart. And my games with Elad continue as we play soccer in the street or walk hand-in-hand to the center of town or play patty-cake/baker's man in front of our buildings at dusk.

<center>❧</center>

After Purim and before Pesach I begin teaching English in the religious school and in the "Ethiopian *ulpan*." In the religious school, the Israeli kids, mostly of Moroccan descent, are wild and disobedient; the teachers seem tired. They spend most of their time disciplining children who come from large poor families and crave attention at school. I enjoy speaking simple Hebrew with some of the girls but mostly I feel like a babysitter.

Teaching the Ethiopian students is different. I take one student at a time from a group of nine thirteen-year-olds who meet in a building across from where the Israeli students learn. The principal of the school, Eli Shitrit, wants to get the Ethiopian students into a classroom as soon as possible. The first step, he says, is teaching them English.

In the beginning, my students are silent. On our short walk from their classroom to the library, I ask them in Hebrew how long they've been in Israel. Some of the students do not know enough Hebrew to understand or answer my questions. Some just smile and others reply *ken, ken*—yes, yes—to whatever I ask.

These students are so similar to each other in their variations of silence but from the moment I see Osnat, I know that she is different. I do not have to go into the classroom to get her because she is sitting in the hall waiting for me, her head buried in a book. She is very thin, with large sad eyes, a short Afro, and hand-me-down Israeli clothes that modestly cover her arms. Her skirt falls past her knees. She understands my questions and although her eyes focus on the ground, she gives me pieces of her story beginning with how she arrived in Israel five months ago along with her mother, father, sisters, and brother. She skips over their arduous trek and the horrible conditions in the transit camps where they waited to be airlifted into Israel. She tells me instead how she and her oldest sister Yael learned some English in the public school in Gondar and how many of her classmates had come from villages where they had not been exposed to any written language.

Osnat falls into long bouts of silence, but this does not stand between us. We understand something essential about one another that is hard to define. We are both shy on the surface. We love the sad melodies of Hebrew songs. We share a thirst for learning. Something in our essences touches one another and although it will take a decade to define, I feel it on our walk from her classroom to the library where I present her with the English alphabet.

After a few weeks, most of the students know the alphabet, but they tell me very little about their lives. They only speak when spoken to and answer my questions with as few words as possible. Osnat, with deep brown eyes and a soft yet sad beauty, absorbs everything I tell her and asks to learn more. We move from letters of the alphabet, to numbers, days, and months of the year.

Osnat and her fellow classmates live in the absorption center next door to my building. Outside of the classroom they drop some of their silence and run about joyfully like other Israeli children. And every time I look at Osnat, her shy smile, her downcast eyes, her girlish laughter, her delicate hands choosing the perfect fruits for the Sabbath meal, I am reminded again of the miracle of her survival, and the survival of her people. In Ethiopia, the Jews lived with the belief that they would make it to Jerusalem

someday and Osnat, walking her cousin Elad home from the garden each day, is the realization of this dream.

On a Friday, when the boys have shop and sports from ten o'clock until noon, I teach the girls. This is my favorite part of the week. All classroom formality is dropped as I run from student to student, each one at a different level in the book. We learn Hebrew prayers as well as English words. Yael, Osnat's older sister who is fifteen, chubby, and usually smiling although she claims to dislike school, asks, "Teacher, can we learn one of your songs?"

"One of my songs?"

"Yes, the kind of song you sing in America."

My mind goes blank. The only English song playing in my brain is the biblical psalm "By the Waters of Babylon." I write it on the board. Although they do not understand all the words, even after I clumsily translate them into Hebrew, they absorb the longing, the beauty, and the sadness of the melody while repeating each word until they pronounce it correctly. Ever after that, one of them always runs up to me on the street, grabbing my hands and singing, "Byyy the Waaaterss, the waaaterss of Babylon. We lay down and wept, and wept for thee Zion. We remember, we remember, we remember thee Zion."

The next week I arrive at school to find my students swinging on swings and playing in the grass instead of sitting at their desks in the classroom. Asher, one of the boys, says they are on strike until the principal takes stronger action against Israeli students who had been throwing stones at them. I had seen other girls walk by Osnat as if she were invisible, but this was the first I had learned of stone-throwing. I am enraged at the bullies and impressed with the Ethiopian students for organizing this protest. They had learned the concept of *shvita* (strike) from their parents who learned it from the Israelis. The garbage collectors, postal service, and the nurses have all recently gone on strike.

The Ethiopian community had gone on strike against the rabbinate by walking across the country from the north to Jerusalem. The rabbis were asking the Ethiopian men to undergo circumcision

again and for the women to dip in the *mikvah*, a purified ritual bath, to make sure they were kosher. This policy was the ultimate insult for the Ethiopian Jews who had held onto their religion against centuries of persecution. Now that they were in Jerusalem, the place for the ingathering of exiles, where they believed they could freely be Jews, their own purity and authenticity were questioned. They arrived in their Promised Land to see many Jews not behaving like Jews and the religious leaders of the country telling them that they are not Jews because their rituals are pre-Talmudic. This is how they told their story, man after man, woman after woman after child. Their strike was brave and graceful. They walked and stood carrying signs of protest written in Hebrew. The children are now protesting in the same way. They will not attend a school where they are not protected. The principal is impressed with their chutzpah, and he controls the Israeli children.

§

Spring arrives in the Galil bearing gifts of white anemone and red poppies. If the winter was the coldest I had ever lived through, sleeping in three layers of clothing and holding vigil over a small kerosene heater, the spring in and around Ma'alot is the most exquisite. On Shabbat, Shimon, whose family left Morocco for Israel when he was three, leads a group of us volunteers on a hike. When Shimon first started visiting my room and stayed after everyone else left, he felt like an unwelcome guest with his hungry eyes. But in this landscape, I appreciate his expertise and enjoy his company. We hike until we discover a clear stream on top of a mountain that we never thought we'd reach or a new wildflower growing in the heart of a valley. We carry bottles of mineral water, and the Israelis carry guns. We hike past Arab villages and then into a landscape that is neither Arab nor Jewish. We stop by a wadi to rest, and my back fits perfectly into the crevice of a stone.

In the evening, Shimon introduces us to Memunah, a Moroccan holiday that ends Passover. During this festival, the doors of all of the Moroccan homes are open, and people enter to find banquets

of fruits, nuts, macaroons, cakes, whiskey, soda, and one whole fish for good luck. The women are dressed in traditional gowns, and the homes are filled with dancing, howling, and a celebratory mood. Charleen, my new South African roommate, Eric, Shimon, and I are hungry from a week without bread, our sustenance, we are golden and drained from the sea.

Shimon takes us first to his family home. His mother is warm and welcoming. She has deep black hair, and her wild laughter reveals her toothless mouth. She looks more Arab than Jewish with her dark brows that sit over her slanted eyes like two great mountains. Shimon's father sits in a corner, silent and drunk. Charleen, Eric, and I stand back and watch like anthropologists. The henna- colored hands and howling bird-like sounds are too strange for us to absorb immediately. Every home we enter has the same exotic racket of joy.

Tired and full, the four of us return to the absorption center, Shimon's arm gently around my shoulder. Eric returns to his apartment and Charleen packs for an archaeological dig she is to leave for the next day. Shimon and I sit in the dark living room, listening to my one American tape, Bruce Cockburn. Shimon sings along not understanding the words. I sit across the room from him until after much discussion, he convinces me to sit next to him. Part of me wants to let go and explore the growing electricity between us. The other part wonders what Eric or Charleen would think. Would the person whom I thought I was and the person whom I need others to think I am approve of this? When I first met Shimon, I didn't take him seriously. But now I know that beneath his boisterousness, his monologues, and his despair is a warm, tender, and wise man who lives close to the earth with a huge heart and a storehouse of passion. I see it in the way he dances, the way he sings, hikes along unmarked paths; and finally, I feel it in the way he touches me.

April 21, 1985

*Just when I decide to keep my distance from Shimon, I find myself on the
way to the sea with him. He carries me over treacherous pathways, me
in my blue-and-white-print dress and blue tourist clogs, that's what he
calls them. I feel so wild with him, so free. The view of the sea from the
top of the craters is magnificent, just as I remembered it from seven years
ago. I read Shimon a poem by Carolyn Forché from Gathering the Tribes.*

*I try to translate it into Hebrew, and we both laugh from deep in our
bellies. We rest behind a rock near the shore. The waves reach up toward
us and wash away what we have known in each other.*

*The next morning, Eric, eight other volunteers, and I dig at the
archaeological site at Hamat Gader. We don't know if we're digging a
city, a church or a home. Under the sometimes unbearably hot sun we
shovel dirt, finding floors, pillars, pieces of pottery, coins, and teeth. We
are trying to find another civilization. It is important to dig gently, our
leader warns us, not to destroy the beauty, just beneath the surface.*

April 22, 1985

*We mistake stone for skull, a wall for what's beyond the wall. We lift
stones, toss out anything that doesn't tell us something new. The glass
we find is modern; the dirt we remove is tossed to the wind. My body
aches, all our bodies, for knowledge of how they lived, the places their
doors opened and closed, the benches they sat on, how large their walls
were. We collect teeth and coins. Mostly we want to know when. We know
already, from books, how they baked their bread. Our hands are blistered
with the desire to touch what they touched. We dig until our shovels hit
stone. Stone doesn't, wind doesn't, rain doesn't, sun doesn't stop us from
going one more layer under. I keep beating the same ground over and over,
because I know something is underneath. Everyone else has moved to
another corner.*

On the fifth day the rain falls hard, and we soak in mineral baths.
I am anxious to return to the people I am beginning to discover,
especially Elad and Osnat. Yet no matter how much I dig, they

don't have the language to bring me into the world they escaped in Ethiopia. I see Elad's absent father in his eyes and a sorrow in Osnat's eyes that I still can't name. Even if we did share a language, they can't afford, at the earliest stages of their absorption, to look back. They need to keep their eyes glued on the present; that's how they'll survive.

I feel strong from days of beating the earth and elated knowing worlds wait for me that I can still enter by walking through doors and taking the small hands of children.

I return to Ma'alot in time for Yom Ha'atzmaut, Israel Independence Day. There had been a municipality strike, and the ground in front of our building is littered with garbage. Ethiopian boys whom I had never met before are throwing stones at us. They are just children playing around, yet I am shocked, have never seen that behavior from Ethiopian children before. Disappointed by my homecoming, I walk to the center of town where I run into Shimon, who greets me with open arms and convinces me to return to his apartment where some new volunteers will be cooking spaghetti for everyone. I am struck by how dressed up he is for the holiday and how handsome he looks in a suit and tie.

After a festive meal, we return to the center of town to join the rest of the Ma'alot community in singing, dancing and skits performed by children. It is a celebratory night that as Americans we feel slightly removed from. The people dancing have sons, brothers, fathers, husbands, lovers, or friends who fought for independence. And everyone dancing—those who were born in the country and those who had been here for two decades—have lost someone in his or her family or community to war. And as Americans we had cheered the country on from the other side of the world. Our parents or organizations sent money. We did not build or defend this country with our own hands.

When the festivities quiet down, Jackie, a new volunteer named Amy, and I stand on a ledge singing American songs. I have spent months discarding my American identity and here I am, laughing arm in arm with my American friends. Some women soldiers

approach us and say we are standing on their soldier's memorial. We get down apologetically, overtaken by a shameful silence.

Sara writes from the desert, "Can you meet me in Tel Aviv after Yom Ha'atzmaut? Am returning to America. Must see you." I had seen Sara on my last visit to Jerusalem in April where she had come from her kibbutz to greet me on my twenty-fifth birthday with a bunch of pink roses and the writer Amos Oz's *Stories from the Kibbutz*. I had been impressed by how fluent her Hebrew had become. We were able to pick up our conversation where it ended, just before I went to the northern tip of the country to live and she to the southern tip to work the land.

Now we are walking along the sea, quiet at first because there is too much to say. Sara will be returning to America for her sister's wedding but isn't ready to leave the kibbutz. She is already deciding when she will return and is trying to describe to me why being in Israel feels essential for her.

"In America," Sara begins, "first I have to fight to be who I am and then for what I want. Here, I just have to fight for what I want." I quietly take in her words, amazed as always by her youthful wisdom. She continues, "Dina, I think you won't make *aliyah*. You are too out of this world to make a commitment to a country, with all of your dreams. You'll come back to Israel a lot but you'll never live here." I am taken aback by her prediction. It feels like a slap in the face. Israel is my country, the country for dreamers and poets. And after three months in Ma'alot I can't imagine any other life.

"So tell me about Kibbutz Lotan, the real kibbutz experience," I ask, trying to forgive her prediction and to mask my hurt feelings.

"Well, first of all, it is such a small kibbutz. Most of the members are just slightly older than me and they all really believe in the purpose of kibbutz and in the Reform Movement. People work hard. I'm so tired but look at these muscles! I just feel a part of things, like what I do matters."

"Sara, I'm so happy for you—that's exactly what you were looking for!"

"Yeah and now I have to go home," she mutters looking out at the waves and twisting her curls into a bun on top of her head. "And you, my dear? Your skin is so brown and your curls are almost as blond as mine are. I thought you were teaching, not working in the fields!"

"It seems like we are always on break from teaching. We hike all of the time." I pause for a moment, trying to contain my emotions while explaining the reality of my life to her, a life I have mostly been living rather than analyzing. I continue: "I'm still trying to swallow what you said about all of my dreams because what I love so much about life in Ma'alot and in Israel in general is the richness of daily life. It's not an abstraction. When I take the time to stop and think about it I am amazed that I am here to help the Ethiopian Jews. But on a daily basis it is simply the smells, textures, immediacy of daily life—going to the market each day for fresh pita and ripe tomatoes. Tomatoes never appealed to me in America. And the view of the mountains from my window, and the children next door. Elad brings up all of my maternal instincts. And, well... I'm involved with someone, a Moroccan-Israeli guy," I add sheepishly.

Sara looks at me smiling, "I knew there was something you weren't telling me."

"Actually, you're the first one to know."

"Darlink, I'm so happy for you. Just be careful. But what do I know? I'm so innocent when it comes to men."

The sun sinks toward the sea. We part with reminders of how precious our friendship has been to both of us. I know we will see each other in America and Israel but that never again will it be the winter of 1984 in Jerusalem. As I run to catch my bus home, I look back at Sara with blond curls in a Tel Aviv café, in the spring of 1985, the year I turn twenty-five, she eighteen.

On my way back to Ma'alot I think about all of the words Sara and I shared. I haven't spoken this much English in months. I have new English-speaking friends with whom I share thoughts and

feelings, but I realize that my most important friendship, the one growing between me and Osnat, is beyond language and how much I enjoy the gestures, silence, and wordless understanding we share.

I return to more strikes in Ma'alot. This time it is the entire town against the municipality. Everything is shut down: schools, gardens, stores, post offices, banks, and factories. Outside our building is covered with twice as much garbage as the week before. During difficult times like these, people pull together and heroes reveal themselves. A group of Ethiopian children, including two eight-year-olds, Elad's sister Batya and Osnat's sister Liat, gather up all of the garbage in front of our buildings and burn it.

The stores are closed, and it is the beginning of May; our monthly checks are delayed due to the postal strike. One check barely lasts a month so we have no left over money with which to buy food anyway. Elana Gabai from Skokie, who now runs the program because Elaine is abroad, goes to her house on the other side of town and gathers all of the vegetables from her refrigerator. Many of us gather our few remaining carrots or tomatoes, and we put all our food together to make a big stew.

With full stomachs, Jackie and I return to my apartment. Osnat soon joins us. On the couch listening to Joni Mitchell, squinting at each other against the late afternoon sun, Osnat holds each of our hands as she slouches into the sofa. The school year is coming to an end. When Osnat had first started visiting us she was shy but now she seems comfortable, listening to our music and singing for us in Amharic.

Our restfulness is soon interrupted by Shimon's knock at the door. Because he now works as an electrician, his company is also on strike. Osnat's posture grows tense with his arrival. Usually we are not confronted with the men in each other's lives. It is always Osnat, her sisters, and her mother, draped in the traditional white gown, sitting in front of the apartment together. During the day, Osnat's father and brother are at work or in *ulpan*. Sometimes the men gather near the steps that lead to the center of town, but they

are never a part of our conversations or of our silence. Osnat is sometimes confronted with American male volunteers, but Israeli men are still more foreign to her. So when Shimon starts arguing with Jackie, as has become their habit, Osnat runs for the door. I go down the stairs after her but she vanishes into the safety of her own home.

When Osnat leaves, Shimon and Jackie's argument intensifies. Jackie is trying to convince Shimon that it isn't acceptable to use the word *Cushim* to describe the Ethiopians. *Cushim*, which means black, is a derogatory word. Shimon insists he is not using it in a negative way. Jackie says it is hurtful and still unacceptable. We decide that Shimon is just too selfish to understand other people's pain. Tension continues between the three of us all weekend. Yet I can't give him up.

I tried to hide from him in the ancient stone of the cities we dug up in the north, in the disapproving gazes of my liberal-minded friends. I've tried to hide from his recklessness behind the purity of Osnat's perfect posture. But little by little he has devoured all of my defenses until his pain and his passion have become inseparable from my own.

That Saturday night at the Beit Ha Te, the tea house that the soldiers who are stationed in Ma'alot put together for themselves and for other young people in the community, Shimon describes me to some of our friends. "She seems very quiet on the outside, but inside she is full of passion." Everyone laughs and Jackie says, "The cat's out of the bag." It is a relief to stop hiding.

As usual, a large group of us share a table: Shimon, his best friend Aron, South African Dave, Charleen, Eric and others. We've fallen in love with our lives and with the people who surround us daily, the joy and fear, the tension on the border, the contradictions clashing and rubbing up against each other causing bursts of laughter.

The next day Charleen sits on our living-room couch surrounded by cardboard boys and girls that she is decorating for the children in her garden. Unlike Jackie and myself, Charleen has made no

connection with the Ethiopian community. But the four-year-old Israeli students with whom she works bring great pleasure while uncovering her artistic skills. I've also discovered that she is a poet and in possession of a beautiful wardrobe with long, flowing skirts. I borrow a white shirt and flowery skirt to wear to the event that Jackie and I are incredibly proud to attend: the Bar and Bat Mitzvah of my Ethiopian students.

In the cultural center that evening, I feel the excitement in the air. The room is filled with new immigrants and long-time members of the Ma'alot community. Unfortunately, we were given the wrong time, so Jackie and I arrive when the ceremony is over and Eli Shitrit is ending his speech about how pleased he is to have the Ethiopian families join the Ma'alot community. Other teachers describe it as the first time they've seen the Ethiopian community embrace the richness of modern Judaism and incorporate it into their lives in a positive way.

The young women are in yellow cotton dresses and the boys in brown shirts with white satin vests, radiating youthfulness and accomplishment. After the meal there are songs and more speeches in Hebrew. I am honored to be a part of this celebration and to see Osnat with her arm around her friend Ora's shoulder, large beaming eyes, a buried smile, elegant in yellow cotton.

The B'nai Mitzvah of the Ethiopians is followed the next day by a hike to the Tel Dan waterfalls at the northern tip of the Galil. I walk hand-in-hand with Osnat, whose stride suddenly seems more deliberate and confident. Sometimes Yael, who has not participated in the B'nai Mitzvah ceremony for unexplained reasons, joins us and other times runs ahead to walk with the other girls.

It has turned hot, and we are thrilled to be in the cooler north of the country and to soak our feet in the falls. I had first visited these falls when I was seventeen and had described them to my friends as the closest I had ever been to paradise. I am still amazed by the exhilarating rain of water against stone. But now I've been absorbed by the more subtle beauty of the land around Ma'alot, which I've come to know intimately: the way the sun lands in

crevices of stone, the varying shades of green each hour of the day, the wadis that appear as out of nowhere.

As Osnat and I walk slowly back to the bus behind all of the other students, I look at the beads hanging from her ears and wonder how Jackie and I have changed her. We removed the thin sticks she had worn in her ears by giving her Israeli earrings. Now she is different from her friends who envy the gifts she receives from her American girlfriends. She has seen pictures of our country and now dreams of visiting someday. Before, her dreams didn't reach beyond Israel. How else have we changed her? How has she changed our lives? We've fallen in love with a country by helping her learn how to live in it and by encouraging her to remain herself at the same time. But at this moment, walking along the landscape that so firmly holds my feet, it is too early to know how profoundly she has changed me.

❦

"Even in their most private moments, they do not forget the headlines of the paper." A translator used those words to describe Israelis and to shed some light on the political nature of the work of some of the younger Israeli poets.

This becomes the truth about our lives.

I return home from an afternoon of tutoring Efrat, the principal Eli Shitrit's daughter, to join Shimon in front of his TV where we hold vigil listening to reports about the release of Israeli prisoners from the Lebanon War. On May 21, 1985, three Israeli prisoners were released in return for approximately 2,000 Arab terrorists. "This is how much we value each life." I hear that again and again. There are still four Israeli soldiers captured, no one knows where. As we sit glued to the news, watching the reactions on the faces of freed Israeli soldiers, the tears and the joy, Shimon tries to explain what I've missed in the translation. And every hour after that when the news comes on the radio, we stop what we are doing and listen in silence. I imagine the entire country at a standstill the way they had been when the siren declaring silence went off on Holocaust

Memorial Day. We are on our way out of Lebanon, after the longest, bloodiest, and, arguably, the most nonsensical war.

Udi Sufad, the principal of the high school in the Arab village of Tarshiha which is co-governed with Ma'alot, contacts the volunteer office looking for an English teacher. Elana chooses me as her delegate.

This village, a fifteen minute walk from Ma'alot, is like entering another time and country. One main road leads into town. The houses or villas have three floors to accommodate three generations. On the roofs, laundry hangs in purples, greens, and reds over mostly uncultivated land. The center of town is a pharmacy, a bakery, a bank, and a school. Where the main road ends, small dirt roads lead through town. As in Ma'alot, the streets are filled with children on bicycles or playing soccer.

Friendly Arab men drinking coffee greet me at school. Although I don't drink coffee, I know it would be an insult to refuse their offer. I down a glass of Turkish coffee: a peace offering.

"I'd love to teach English literature to your students," I assure them.

Udi counters, "They need to learn English conversation, and you'd be meeting with a group of students after their regular school day. And don't worry that you don't have a worker's permit; we will be able to pay you a small stipend for each session. Because this is a Christian rather than a Jewish town, your volunteer status doesn't transfer—but it is no problem." I accept his offer. "Before you leave let me show you my home," he says.

We sit on the balcony overlooking the quiet cool green of his town. In the distance are the modern buildings of Ma'alot, buildings that went up overnight to accommodate the new immigrants from Morocco who arrived in the fifties, including Shimon's family. Udi, a poet as well as an administrator, tells me that his grandfather was also born in Tarshiha. "This village, this land we live on is older than time." Below his house is a potato garden, purple snapdragons and roses in pink, white, yellow, and salmon, growing toward the sun. Like the town, the flowers feel natural and

uncultivated. There is an ancient beauty and longing in the air of Tarshiha. I am amazed by how far away Ma'alot feels though just across the road.

The next week I walk back to Tarshiha to teach my Israeli Arab students. As long as it is light, I am told, it is safe to walk there alone. Sheep graze in the hills nearby. When I get into town, all eyes are on me. They know I am a foreigner. Women stop hanging their laundry to watch me. They do not smile back. Before I enter the classroom I do not know which language I will speak in.

Twelve students silently sit around a long table. I know I can get lost in their faces, but I take control, assuming a teacherly stance that I am not familiar with. As they go around and introduce themselves, I take in their faces. I have grown used to all of the shapes, sizes, and colors of faces in Ma'alot. The blond Ashkenazi students, the dark-complected Moroccan students with large brown eyes, the mixture of east and west, blue eyes next to dark skin and the exquisite Ethiopians, black skin and eyes of blue, brown, and green. The expressions on these faces are different: neither open like the Israelis nor modest like the Ethiopians. These faces are constrained; holding something back. Eyes are shaped like almonds. The women's hair is long, falling way past shoulders.

When the students describe themselves, their faces open slightly; the girls giggle with one another. I ask them basic questions in English about their lives. We only use Hebrew as a bridge when falling into the abyss of silence for lack of an English word.

"Why don't you ask each other questions?" I suggest. A bright and articulate sixteen-year-old boy asks another boy across the table how he feels about life in Tarshiha. The boy answers, "I'm living in a tragedy circle."

"A what?"

"A tragedy circle. We need to strip ourselves of our customs in order to progress, but without our customs we are nothing."

A severe-looking woman with a ponytail that falls past her waist chimes in, "We must keep our customs, they are beautiful. I was born into Tarshiha. It is my life and I treasure it. We can

progress scientifically without giving up too many things. I am proud of my village."

"Which customs are important to hold onto?"

"A woman should keep her honor. She should not give herself to a man simply for pleasure."

She reminds me of an orthodox Jewish woman with whom I rode the bus on my way home from visiting Moshe at his kibbutz the last time I saw him. She was engaged to be married and spoke proudly of how she and her intended had not yet touched.

"It is beautiful when a woman doesn't touch a man until he is her husband."

I wonder, with envy, what it would be like to step into their veils of purity. I think about my Ethiopian students and the purity of their religious practice in Ethiopia. What will they be able to hold onto and what will they have to give up?

Walking out of the classroom, I am excited by what transpired. In my teaching in Ma'alot, I am working on words and simple phrases. It is difficult to have real conversations with any of my Israeli students. The students in Tarshiha have the English vocabulary to tell me about their lives. I can't wait to return the next week.

The sky darkens and in the distance I spot a young man with blond hair and blue eyes, waiting for me in a blue Chevy convertible. He offers to drive me back to Ma'alot. I've seen him in Udi's office before so I assume he is safe. Yet I enter his car with trepidation, as if I have no choice. We are silent the entire ride from his country to mine, just across the road.

When I return to the Arab village to teach the next week, I discover that my students' politeness was a façade. Today they speak out of turn and I spend so much time disciplining the boys, I feel as if I'm back in Ma'alot with my Israeli students. I wonder if they are testing to see how far they can push the first Jewish teacher ever to step foot in a Tarshiha classroom.

During discussion session a young man talks about how difficult it is to be an Arab in Israel. "The Israelis, they get everything and we get nothing. I think they should all be thrown in the sea."

Somehow I manage to remain calm as I tell them the other side of the story beginning with pogroms in Europe and ending with the Holocaust and the need for a Jewish homeland. The girls listen carefully, now and then nodding their heads. The boys get quiet with smirks spreading on their faces. One student quickly changes the subject, telling his group about his ambition to study in the university. He does not have to do army service like Jewish Israeli men so his studies will begin the next year. Most of the class members share his goal. Some want to return to Tarshiha to work after they receive their degrees, and others want to live abroad.

I end our class with Rudyard Kipling's poem "If", and this is where we join, as we discuss why the words of an English poet move us. It is for moments like this that I continue to teach them. I am no longer certain how much of their lives I want opened up to me. The student's words, which echoed Yasser Arafat's—throwing Jews into the sea—stay with me long after I leave the village.

The young Arab man continues to drive me back to Ma'alot. Our silence has grown to few words. When he asks how my classes are going, I complain about the boys' behavior, which is quickly becoming more rowdy. "What did you expect?" he answers unsympathetically. One day I tell him not to wait, that I need to stay and speak with Udi Sufad. He waits anyway. I enter Udi's office without the usual pleasantries but instead inform him that I'd now been teaching in Tarshiha for a month and have not received the weekly salary that was promised to me.

"I'm sorry, we cannot pay you because you do not have a worker's permit."

"But we discussed this last month and you said it wouldn't be a problem."

"I don't remember that we discussed this."

When I report the situation to the Ma'alot officials the next day, they are outraged. An American expatriate, who works for the Histadrut, labor union, that governs both towns, looks into the situation for me. After many weeks and discussions, they agree to give me credit at the grocery store that is jointly owned by both towns, instead of a salary. They allow me to take forty shekels or

twenty dollars' worth of groceries. I am used to working without money but I'm angry about their deceit. My intrigue turns into suspicion, and I am unsure of whether I want to continue teaching for them or not. I am tired of the eyes that devour me, tired of the boys who now hit each other and make too much noise for our lessons to proceed. I am running out of poems, and the library in Ma'alot doesn't carry poetry in English or Hebrew. It is a pleasure, however, to go to the market and purchase things that have become luxuries because of their expense and my small monthly stipend. I fill my cart with lavender soap, toothpaste, body lotion, shampoo, wine and delicacies for the coming Sabbath.

Although I am disillusioned about my work in Tarshiha, I don't reveal this to Eli Shitrit, the principal of the Ma'alot school. One afternoon while I am at his home tutoring his daughter Efrat in English, he invites me into the kitchen to have coffee with him and a friend of his. This is an unusual occurrence. Usually I exchange greetings with his wife and then spend my time with his daughter, leaving the house without seeing Eli. This time, seated around his large wooden kitchen table, I accept his Turkish coffee. Eli had gotten word that I was teaching in Tarshiha and that is how he introduces me to his friend in an animated and agitated voice. "Aren't you here to help Jews? Doesn't it bother you to work with Arabs? Don't you have enough Goyim in the United States?"

The truth is that when I enter the classroom in Tarshiha, I miss my Ethiopian students, their silence, their grace and their respect. But this is not the time to share this fact with Eli Shitrit. I am also at a disadvantage, two Israeli men against one young American woman arguing in Hebrew.

"They are people." I answer him in simple Hebrew. "They want to learn English, and I thought I could help them. Of course I'm here to help Jews, but I am also here to learn about the life, and the Arab people are one aspect of life in Israel."

"Why do they want our land? They have so much of their own land. This is all we have." Not expecting me to answer his question Eli pours me more coffee, impressed that I down it in one gulp. I

do not tell him that his Arab neighbors across the road taught me how to drink strong coffee.

I understand Eli's mistrust; he lives with the constant fear of his neighbors. In 1979 there had been a horrible massacre. A group of Israeli students who were on a field trip were spending the night at Nativ Mayer, a religious school in Ma'alot. That evening, Palestinian terrorists murdered almost everyone inside the school. Thirty children were killed. When someone mentions Ma'alot in Israel, that is the first image that comes to mind. Eli, like other residents in Ma'alot, believe that the residents of Tarshiha were somehow accomplices to the massacre, that they reported to the terrorists on the visiting children. For months after the massacre, no Arab from Tarshiha entered the gates of Ma'alot.

I do not share this history; I am still an observer. I do not tell Eli of their hatred. I do not tell him about the students who said all Israelis should drown in the sea. I want him to understand their side instead. I tell him about the boy who described his life as a tragedy circle. Although Eli does not see my point of view he listens to me while exhaling smoke from his Arabic cigarettes and patiently waits for me to express myself in his language. He cannot speak a word of mine.

"Dina, will you come here to live?"

"It is a possibility." I answer him, suddenly shy. When he tells me about the four soldiers in Lebanon who were released I ask, "How many more of us do they have?"

Eli decides to extend the Ethiopian ulpan into the summer in order to help the students catch up. We have the school to ourselves; the Israeli students are on summer break. Myself, sometimes the new volunteer Amy, and a small group of girls—Osnat, Yael, Talia, Limor, and Ora—sip our tea and eat fresh pieces of melon that the Moroccan cleaning women cut up for us. I arrive with my hair curly and wild from the summer heat and leave with it in many intricate braids on the top of my head from my students' diligent hands. The distances between us are vanishing; the differences remain a constant source of fascination. There are days when our

friendship and our laughter get in the way of our lesson, but I know they need affection more than a few extra English words and phrases. What I don't know at this early stage is that Eli Shitrit's plan to teach the new immigrants English and get them into classes with other Israeli students is what would allow them to succeed in ways kids sent away to "special schools" would not.

On the way home from school one day, Amy, who has been a volunteer in Ma'alot less than a week, complains to me about Eli Shitrit and the fact that he is teaching religion to the Ethiopian students. She thinks the country is doing a poor job of integrating the new immigrants. Although I agree with some of her criticism and said some of the same things when I first arrived, her words disturb me. Suddenly I see her as an outsider, an American who doesn't have the right to criticize what she doesn't understand. I feel like an insider when it comes to the Ethiopians, still married to the ideal of their arrival. I want to stay in that place. I do not want to dwell on the work ahead of us but want to live instead in the moment of them rooting themselves in Israel and to the time of us rooting ourselves to each other.

"Amy, they need to learn the basics of survival first. Do you know how difficult it is to bring a new group into such a foreign way of life, into the future? Everyone is doing the best that they can." I realize suddenly, that I am preaching back at her, calling her an American intellectual who can only analyze things from the outside instead of feeling the joy in them. And when I get home I realize it is not only Amy who I am scolding, but the part of myself that I want to put to rest. Later that afternoon, I go to Amy's apartment two floors below to apologize. Together we plan the next day's lesson.

One day I complain of a headache and the next day do not come to class. I am suffering from what we named "Ethiopian cough." The symptoms are exhaustion, a sore throat, and a continuous cough that echoes all night from the rooms in the Ethiopian homes. That afternoon, Osnat comes by to see me, remembering that I had had a headache the day before. I am touched by her concern. We sit quietly, drinking tea with mint. I

give her another pair of Israeli earrings with red beads that I bought at the shuk in Jerusalem during my last visit and a similar pair to take home to her sister Yael. Upon leaving, she looks deeply into my eyes with sympathy that I feel exceeds my condition. "Rest, Dina, let it pass through you."

It isn't until sometime later that I learn why Osnat had been so concerned. In Ethiopian culture people used the term headache to describe any number of serious ailments. In addition, to them a headache means that an evil spirit had entered the body. It was not something that could be cured with a few aspirin and some rest. It had much deeper reverberations.

On other summer afternoons, Yael and some of the other girls join Osnat on her visits. They study the photographs of America on my wall and everything from Lake Michigan, the large body of water from where I was drawn, to the Chicago skyline, to my family and friends is *yafe* or *yofi*—beautiful or fantastic. I want to see images of the landscapes where they grew up, the body of water from where they were drawn, but they could not bring pieces of their other countries with them to Israel. They are still unable to tell me the story of their trek from Ethiopia to Sudan, from Sudan to Israel.

When I hang laundry, Osnat wants to help rather than listen to music in the next room with the other girls. On Thursdays or Fridays, I often see her at the shuk near our building, carrying a basket filled with vegetables home to her mother who is busy preparing for the Sabbath. Many of Osnat's thirteen-year-old friends, especially those from Gondar and other villages in Ethiopia, are already married and run their own kitchens. Sometimes I tease her by asking if she has a boyfriend and if she wants to marry. She responds, "Perhaps in twenty years."

June 1985

Lately, Jackie and I have been mingling with our neighbors. They take our hands and lead us into their homes. Last night we were taken to Elad's mom's apartment, little Elad, star of the family, ball of fire.

There is a warm feeling with all of the women bringing in their special bread, injera, with some spicy substance that I guess one must acquire a taste for. The apartment is empty, and the sun comes in, a soft color, late afternoon. Gaveret Yamari (Mrs. Yamari, Elad's mom) smiles a lot but doesn't speak Hebrew. She has a green tattoo on her neck like other Ethiopian village women, and she wears a white gahbi with yellow and red embroidery. Often she is in another room. Batya, Elad's older sister, tickles Elad; soon everyone joins in, the room full of laughter. We listen to the new words he learned in the garden: yadayim, reglayim, rosh, lev, hands, feet, head, and heart). We listen to Ethiopian music, chants, as they ply us with injera and juice. On the wall is a picture of Israeli soldiers; there is nothing much else, just a lot of love and closeness.

Today, Jackie and I went to Osnat's for lunch. Osnat took me by the hand, Yael took Jackie, and we walk up four flights to their home. Osnat's view is like mine, the mountains, the windmill, and beyond. The inside of their home is also barren. The walls are empty except for two drawings that Liat, the eight-year-old, made with Hagar, a soldier friend: a gun and a bird, and a green girl, and again, like Elad's home, there are soldiers cut out from magazines. On the bookshelves there are bottles of medicine and two golden Sabbath candleholders, the sustenance of their lives. Osnat serves us tea, bread, cookies and two whole potatoes without silverware. We hold them in our hands and eat them as if that was the way we always ate potatoes. They sometimes slide between our fingers onto the plate but we pick them up and continue eating until we are finished. Osnat is gracious, and we eat happily because of the light it brings to her dark eyes.

During the summer Ma'alot is surrounded by a dry heat and a breeze that comes from the mountains. The Galilee Mountains and the Arab villages surrounding us are more clear and inspiring than ever, as the sky is a bright blue and we can see all the way to the sea. The headlines of the paper read *Yatznu*, we are out, meaning out of Lebanon. Yet my Israeli friends are being called for their army service that occurs once a year or as needed. On Sunday mornings, the beginning of the workweek, all of the men are in uniform giving their children final hugs. Planes speed by on their way to the border of Israel and Lebanon, shake the windows,

disturb my breakfast of Wizotsky tea, pita, tomatoes, and cheese, shaking me a little. We clean, dance on top of and later read poems inside the bomb shelters.

The summer nights are cool and clear, a relief from the heat of the day. Early evenings, the children play outside in the parking lot that their building shares with ours. When I walk to the *mercaz* to make a phone call, Elad joins me. We walk hand in hand stopping for *chatoolim* and *clavim*, cats and dogs, or any intriguing objects we might have found on the way up those never-ending steps that lead to the center of town. I am amazed by how much Elad has grown over the months that I've known him. He tells me stories in complete Hebrew sentences, no longer just the silly and sometimes forlorn child with his father's beads around his neck, but the curious and sensitive child as well. Elad cherishes the world around him: the streets, wild flowers, animals, and cars. He is no longer afraid of these things as he was when he first arrived. When I walk with him, I look at the world through his eyes, stop to notice, more than usual, the textures and colors of the streets we walk along.

Once in a while, Elad climbs the five flights of steps to my apartment, and we make bubbles out of soapsuds, or watch out the window where the other children play. One evening we sit on the bench in front of our building playing clapping games and chasing cats. Elad invites me into his home to have dinner with his family, pulling my arm in the direction of his apartment. Although I enjoyed my lunch with his family the other day, I can't bring myself to follow him. I have not shared anything with Elad's mother besides brief smiles when our paths cross; I don't know how to determine if she is up to company or not. She was mostly absent or quiet the other day when we came for lunch. She's been ill, her coughs echoing into our rooms at night, and she has not been outdoors for weeks. I can't explain this to Elad so we sit there until Charleen arrives and asks me to join her to town. I accept Charleen's offer although I'd rather stay with Elad. I walk him to the door of his home and sadly walk away.

June 1985

My clothes tell me how fragmented, disparate, or diverse my life has become, how many different people I am in one day. In the morning, as I dress for the Ethiopian ulpan, I wear a long skirt and long-sleeve shirt. I cover as much of myself as I can for the religious school. I follow the kids into the room and kiss the mezuzah on the doorpost as they do. I have bought these clothes from the WIZO thrift shop for ten agarot. The girls wear T-shirts, hand-me-down Israeli skirts that fall past their knees. The boys' heads are covered with kippot. Later in the day, when I tutor Efrat, also twelve with pale white skin and dark freckles against her dark straight hair, I keep the long skirt on and change into a short-sleeved shirt for the heat. Later in the day, dressing for Tarshiha, I try not to look too American or too Israeli. Sometimes I change clothes five times and am late because of this. I usually settle for slacks and a casual blouse, comfortable shoes for the walk over. In the afternoon, playing with Elad, I am in blue sweats, a blue and white striped T-shirt, and my hair pulled back in a blue clip. Later in the evening, I wear shorts and a sleeveless shirt like an American or secular Israeli girl. When I am with Shimon, in Brazilian sandals and a long skirt, I feel like a woman.

One afternoon as a large tour bus pulls up in front of the *mercaz klita*, I say to Jackie, "Oh, look, Americans, I bet I know someone on that bus." Sure enough, among the middle-aged American tourists is a rabbi and his wife from Skokie. I had met them before at the home of mutual friends. As they get off the bus I greet them with my hair on top of my head in a clip and like other shoppers in Ma'alot, a plastic basket hangs from my wrist. They do not recognize me. Their tour group has come to view the Ethiopians. Their matching caps and their eagerness embarrasses me. "What do they need?" each tourist asks us. *Money*, we repeat, *money*. Instead they hand us giant packages of Wrigley spearmint gum, razors, and shampoo. We do not tell them that the immigrants from Ethiopia do not chew gum, shave, or use American shampoo. They take pictures of themselves with a group of Ethiopian children and push me into the center.

"What is it really like living next to them," the rabbi's wife asks, vulgarly.

"It is absolutely wonderful," I say, grabbing Jackie's arms and excusing ourselves.

Jackie and I sit outside on her *marpeset* and watch the bus pull away. It is so easy to criticize the ignorance of the other Americans, but what are our blind spots? We wonder aloud if there is a way that we could be more useful to the Ethiopian community.

"Would it be more helpful if I were more "scientific" in my understanding of them?" I ask.

"There is a selfishness to the life of the anthropologist. Often their work is for their own interest. How does it help the people they are studying? Wouldn't it be better to be a nurse and treat those who are still suffering in Ethiopia?" Jackie wonders. We sit silently. I dream of returning as an anthropologist as if that would give me a truer understanding of the Ethiopian community. Jackie dreams of becoming a nurse and curing the ill who wait in Gondar Province. She is selfless. Instead of asking continuously how I could better help them the way that Jackie does, I wonder why more poetry is not coming out of my experience.

Poems of Ma'alot, love poems, hordes of images, stop me in my tracks in the center of town and insist on finding a home. My poetry has taken on a new life here. But where are all the words to describe the miracle of this exodus from Ethiopia? Where are all of those poems?

July 1985

The lights on staircases going out in the middle of a conversation, blurring out a final smile. He asks where my eyes are, but finds my lips—we kiss twice before the lights come back on. I go the rest of the way, in the dark, alone.

Hiking on Mount Meron, on a clear day, I can see Lebanon or Lake Kinneret. There are so many different barks of trees that I could put my hand around, so many scents of flowers; I step carefully, try to destroy nothing. In the woods, not too far from the road, I am

*awakened by the grunts and wheels of cars that remind me of a life
I've left, a life I must return to. Letters arrive with questions I can't
answer, "When are you coming home?" Voices are calling me back;
my feet are caught in this earth.*

 *Shimon and I are lying in the pines, needles prickling one leg and
one arm. He wants to hear the history of my heart. I tell him about
Moshe and suddenly I feel nothing, only that I am describing someone
else's life. I tell him I was walking a straight line through my life in
America: six years of higher education. I come here and now everything
looks different. Where do I live? How can I be far from the people I love
yet how can I leave the new home I've found, the home that feels true?
We look at each other for a long time. It has become real between us.*

It is Shimon's last night in Israel before his trip to America with a
one-way ticket. We gather at his family home where his mother
begs us to eat and breaks into tears while his father sits silently.
She is a simple woman with eight sons and one daughter. The
youngest son, about four, has a drippy nose and dirty face. The
oldest son, Shimon, is walking out of her house with an American
woman who says *shalom* and *todah,* hello and thank you. His mother
is at the table making bread. Later she stands at the door watching
him walk away, wondering where she lost him. The American
woman doesn't understand why he can't sit still at his mother's
table. His mother screams after us that she wants to go to the
airport. Shimon says no, that she will make a scene. I look at the
summer clouds that suddenly seem white and wintry and think
there will be some comfort in being alone again.

 Back at my apartment, sitting on Shimon's lap with his hands
around my belly he says, "If I were well, I'd marry you. I have so
many problems; I'm nothing. You write poems and have two
degrees. I can't love myself and my love for others is complicated."

 I am moved, suddenly, that this simple and wise man can love
the poet in me, that over the past few months he struggled to hear
my true voice by understanding my poems against language and
cultural barriers. I think back to how Moshe's friend Alon had
described him as only liking Sephardic women. Through Shimon,

I am developing the same preference. Suddenly all of the American men around me pale next to him.

The next afternoon I wait for a bus to Tarshiha, and Shimon waits for one to the airport. I hand him a new poem written in Ma'alot called "Leaving."

"You are going to miss Shimon," he announces.

"You are going to miss Dina," I answer.

"Yes I will," he says during our final hug. When his bus arrives he yells after me, "Keep yourself."

❧

For the first time, I feel impatient with Osnat. She, like me, is sad about Jackie's imminent departure and visits with more frequency. She is still modest and graceful but not as shy, asking for more and more, even for things I can't give to her. She sees a pair of mother-of-pearl earrings on the dresser in my room and with large eyes asks if she could have them. Moshe had given them to me before he left for Israel, and they were my favorite and only elegant pair. I say no to her for the first time; we're both embarrassed and ashamed.

Although someone is always leaving, it is painful to say goodbye to Jackie. She was my original link to the Ethiopian community and with her I was able to share, day after day, the miracle of their arrival. With Charleen, my roommate, I share poetry, fears about returning to America, dreams hidden in the mountains of Ma'alot; she is most connected to my inner life. But when the inner life takes over the outer, a day can become very lonely.

On the Sabbath after Jackie's departure Osnat and I make plans to take a walk together. She usually spends the Sabbath with her family, but on this particular day, we need to mourn Jackie's absence together. Although it is already unbearably hot on this July morning, she wears a long cotton skirt and a T-shirt that hits her elbows. A large flowered scarf covers her hair. The other volunteers watch from their balconies as we walk hand in hand toward the forest on the other side of town.

The shade of pine trees and the soft chirping of birds welcomes us.

"Dina?" Osnat gently asks. "Do you think Jackie is in America yet?"

"Yes, I think she arrived by now."

"What do you think she's doing?"

"She's probably sitting with her mother and drinking a large mug of coffee and showing her pictures of you and talking about how much she misses us." The loud chatter of Israeli families picnicking on some benches interrupts our conversation. They, too, stop what they are doing and stare at us; our pace picks up rapidly. Osnat looks at the ground and I stare back at them until they turn away.

The rest of the afternoon I read under blankets or look out the window. My home has become too lonely with Osnat's deepening sadness, without Jackie drinking coffee on the *marpeset*, without Shimon's heat. I put on a heavy purple sweater my aunt sent from her trip to Mexico, as if it could somehow warm me.

<p style="text-align:center">❧</p>

I spend more hours at my desk, in front of the English typewriter that Elana Gabai lent to me. In Ma'alot, I do not need a writing room. Poems grab me as I walk through town and I rush over to the nearest hot boulder, park bench, and kitchen table to write them down. Most of the time I am too caught up in life to find language for my experience. But the place I had begun to call home is changing, losing its clarity like the thick white clouds of late summer.

Language has always saved me from my alienation. It has been my shelter. As a thirteen-year-old, I'd be lost out the window as my teacher lectured about grammar or even as she tried to introduce us to metaphor. My inner life would take over, a life only the poets spoke of and a life I couldn't speak of to others until I started to craft my own poems. That year the poet Langston Hughes saved me. His words gave me solace when I couldn't

express my own thoughts. His poem "Hold Fast to Dreams" became my mantra. In art class I painted his words onto glass and hung them on my wall: "Hold fast to dreams / for if dreams die / life is a broken winged bird that cannot fly." Dylan lyrics and Joni Mitchell songs carried me through high school. After my first visit to Israel, Amos Oz novels that I borrowed from the Skokie Public Library, spoke most deeply to me. His characters spoke from the heart like poets. I loved his books, then, because they spoke of a place that had now become not only the landscape of my dreams but of my memory as well.

In college, as an English major, I could not relate to Chaucer or Milton like my peers, and I never felt compelled to learn Latin. Rather Hebrew, and the Jewish poets, especially Yehuda Amichai, spoke to me of ancient dreams, brought that landscape of my youth to life, nurtured my longing for Jerusalem. Poetry brought me into other worlds. It allowed me to sort, beautify, and understand the truth of my own experience, the subtleties of my own landscape.

So now I sit with my images of Israel, with my "spontaneous overflow of deep emotion" and try to form them into perfect poems. I begin to think of my audience because Elaine Kopp has asked Charleen and me to organize a bilingual poetry reading and to somehow involve the poet laureate of Ma'alot, Elana Aviel.

Elana Aviel's house, set back from the street on top of a hill, is luxurious by any standard. I join the poet on an overstuffed couch as we exchange pleasantries in Hebrew. "What a beautiful home," I say taking in the art that adorns her walls, the elegance of her décor, the uncultivated beauty outside her window. There is a youthfulness in the pale blue eyes of this sixty-something woman, the long,, heavy Eilat stone earrings and the intensity of her engagement.

"I'd love to listen to your poems," she says and I reach in my bag for my newest work. It is difficult to converse; her Hebrew is fancier than the language I hear in the streets; I exhaust my entire Hebrew vocabulary just to get through our brief meeting. I read the first few stanzas of my poem "Leaving," and she listens, nodding her head.

I have nothing else to tell you,
we finished all the bread,

even the hard part, the part
I break off and save.

The mountains have become my only sustenance
beyond a thin pane of glass

and a table with only two
tomatoes and all of the words eaten.

"Dina, that's lovely. I didn't understand all of it but I can feel the rhythm and the mood. Let me read you something that I wrote about leaving." Lost in the rhythms of her words, I know I am listening to the voice of a poet.

Elana tells me about another poet in the community, David Kesos, and I tell her about Charleen. We promise to contact them and plan a reading for later in the month, a major triumph to bring poetry into this community.

On the day of the reading, Yossi, my friend from Haifa who months before had tried to discourage me from living in Ma'alot, arrives at my door. Yossi still doesn't understand what I am doing in Ma'alot but is always supportive of my poetry; I am touched that he came for the reading. While Charleen decides upon the right dress to wear, Yossi and I drink mint tea and speak of my imminent departure. After much deliberation, I booked a flight for the sixth of August, one month before my ticket to America expires.

"I feel that in order to return to Israel to live, I have to first go back to America to make that decision from the other side of the world. And I've run out of money. It's been an amazing year."

"Dina, in other ways you've grown tremendously. You're not so emotional as you were before—you're more down to earth and rational."

"Well, I'm still frustrated that I can't read Elana Aviel's poems in Hebrew." I say.

I speak Hebrew all of the time in Ma'alot, can conjugate my thoughts into the past, present, and now I am almost able to think of the future in Hebrew. The language I speak in Ma'alot is the language of daily life. My relationship with Shimon is shaped by this directness: we are together or we are apart. I do not have the language to discuss the in-between with him. I cherish the directness and simplicity of our communication; we've come to know each other beyond language. My relationships with the Ethiopian children are the same. We express our feelings by taking each other's hands, sitting together silently, braiding each other's hair. They still do not have the language or the inclination to tell me about their lives in Ethiopia. And so we live in the moment together in Israel.

Reading my poems means revealing my inner life in the language in which I am most fluent: poetry. I am about to give this part of myself to the community, and I am afraid.

Charleen, with her long silky brown hair and flowing satin dress walks with me to the bomb shelter. Soon the room fills with volunteers, soldiers, and members of the community. Chaim, our English emcee, introduces Elana Aviel who reads a poem by Yehuda Amichai, "My Son," a poem that Yossi had discovered in Haaretz newspaper and that we, along with Eric, translated into English a month before while sitting near Lake Kinneret. Elana then reads a group of her own poems in Hebrew. Chaim introduces me by saying, "This is the first time Dina ever read in a bomb shelter." I read a series of poems about leaving Jerusalem, strikes in Ma'alot, Shimon's family. I am sad that he is deep in an American life now, not with us in the bomb shelter of poetry. Charleen reads a group of her poems about returning to Jerusalem, drawing clowns with Israeli children, and the distance she has kept from the Ethiopian children. A guitarist performs while people order tea and pastries. Just when we think the reading is over, David Kesos, our closet poet, reads some of his poems in Hebrew. He says he is so moved

by the event and so grateful to us for organizing it that his reading
is his gift to us.

And our reading is our gift to the community. We are told by
David and Elana that we've given birth to the tradition of poetry
readings in Ma'alot and are promised this tradition will continue.
For once, I am able to bring all of the disparate parts of myself to
one event that involves people I love and a community of which
I now feel a part. And now it's time for leave-taking.

One day, while Osnat braids my hair, I tell her I will soon be leaving.
Although she already sensed this, she begins to cry.

"Osnat, I always want to keep in touch with you. I always want
to know how you are and I want to know when you get married."
She looks down at her hands bashfully. "But let's not talk about
my leaving anymore." I add.

It is not as difficult to say goodbye to the other students. On
my last day of tutoring Efrat, we share how much we enjoyed
working with each other and then shift our conversation to her
father, Eli Shitirit, and the Ethiopian community.

"My father is good and not so good to the Ethiopians. He does
a lot for them but needs to do a better job of bringing them together
and getting them involved in the community."

"Perhaps it would be better if they were in the same classes
already so that there isn't this feeling of us against them," I add.

"Yes and there should be more social groups and field trips for
both the Israeli and Ethiopian kids so they can get to know each
other." Impressed by the perceptiveness of this twelve-year-old
girl, I hug her and tell her how right she is.

On my final Sabbath in Ma'alot a peaceful hush descends on
everything. The shuls fill with prayer, the homes with song. As
Charleen and I walk to Elana Gabai's home for the Sabbath meal,
we stop to absorb this view in our memories—the breasts of
Ma'alot, as the mountains are called—the far away lights on the
hillside. We dream about our future lives in Israel and the places
that will house those dreams. We dream, for a moment, of Charleen

married to Dave, a South African artist who paints bomb shelters and now shares her single bed, and me married to Shimon. I dream of beautiful dark children. She dreams a job in art therapy, and I dream a teaching job at the nearest university. We envision a stimulating group of people living near us like the poets we've just discovered on Rehove Iris.

We gather around Elana and Yehuda's table, which is already set with a traditional Moroccan Sabbath meal: plates of hummus, fish, chicken couscous, challah and Jerusalem salad of chopped tomatoes, cucumbers, and onions. Elana lights the Shabbat candles with her young daughter Shani as her baby daughter gurgles from her highchair. I relish the warm home they've built together—Elana with her blue eyes, light hair, and Skokie roots, and Yehuda with his olive skin, dark hair, and Moroccan heritage. We welcome the angels with *Shalom aleichem malachei hashalom*—the prayer that floats from one home to the next on Shabbat in Ma'alot. After Yehuda finishes Kiddush, the blessing over the wine, he says, "Dina, you must return in a year to live here among us. You are more Israeli than American now." At that moment, like so many others, I want to believe that I will please all of the Zionists, all of the dreamers, all of the people I love in Israel—that I will assuage the deepest part of my longing and return.

When the Sabbath ends I go to Jerusalem for more farewells. It is almost August; the stone smolders, and the number of tourists overwhelms me. On Kibbutz Ramat Rachel I find a cool breeze and warm greetings from Avrahm, my former ulpan leader; Meir "the Zionist," and most heartily, from the Arab workers with whom some of my friends are still working. I leave my luggage in the volunteer's room where I often stay on my monthly visits to Jerusalem and jump into the pool—swimming back and forth between Bethlehem and Jerusalem.

Life continues on kibbutz. Bellies protrude with new life. A South African immigrant died of a heart attack. In the dining room men and women fill their plates with cucumbers, tomatoes, and sour cream. Toddlers run around freely as older children chase

after them. I sit with some volunteers. Meir, who has just lost his
wife, Sarah, soon joins us.

Meir is a Zionist in the old-fashioned sense of the word. His
skin is tanned from the fields. He has white hair and blue eyes
that match his kibbutz shirt with red strings that represent his
movement—Habonim, the same movement my parents are
involved with in America. He still believes that working the land
is the most important work one can do and that all Jews should
live in Israel. Numerous evenings, when I was still on kibbutz,
Meir would join our table and our discussions as soon as all of
the cigarettes had been extinguished. Today, Meir is trying to talk
me into *aliyah*.

"Dina, why do you have to return to America to make your
decision? Just stay and the decision will be made for you. What do
you have in America, anyway?"

"My family is there. And if I follow the path I've envisioned, I
would teach in a university, publish my poems..." Meir looks at
me long and hard as my words dissolve on my tongue.

On the floor in the volunteer's quarter where I sleep, the same
dreams confront me, the dreams I've wrestled against all month.
I would be returning to America and crying hysterically. Or I am
pregnant and about to give birth. Sometimes Elad is my child like
in the dream I had that night.

I was caring for him although he had parents in the same village.
One day he came running home, very sweaty, full of water. Another
woman and I told Elad's father that he needed a shower. The father refused
and started yelling about how hard it is to care for his son. I implored
him to give the boy a shower or to give him to me. The father started
complaining about a doctor bill for his son. I said that I would pay it and
kept repeating "I love him, I love him."

I awake from the dream and realize how much I already miss
Elad and Osnat. Although this is a short separation, soon I will be
oceans apart from them, not knowing if they are okay.

My other home in Jerusalem, where my spirits are always lifted, is Robert's dinner table where I've sat for hours on all of my return visits. Robert serves gefilte fish, chicken, and a Jerusalem salad. "I hope you don't mind that I sprinkled sugar on top of it. I think it adds the perfect touch."

"Oh, no, I think it's wonderful with sugar," I say reassuringly.

We dine with Arthur, another expatriate and one of Robert's first students at Hebrew University where he taught literature before his retirement. Nasri, Robert's cook and Arabic teacher, joins us as well for a festive meal with robust conversation about poetry, my life in Ma'alot, and Robert's early days in Israel.

"Robert, remind me of how you ended up here—weren't you a kibbutznik when you first arrived?" I ask.

"You know I was on my way home from Europe, from the Second World War. I wasn't religious or a Zionist but I was curious to see this new Jewish State." His eyes sparkle and his complexion is rosy and smooth, only his white hair suggests his seventy-something years. He refills our wine glasses, tightens the frayed belt of his terry-cloth robe and continues.

"I worked on a kibbutz for a while, and I just remember how sweet the watermelon was when we stopped to devour it in the fields. It was like each fruit had its own internal cooling system when you sliced it open and had a piece. Anyway, when I left the kibbutz I ran out of money so I rented Martin Buber's storage space, where we are sitting today, and I got a job teaching at the university. The rest, my friends, is history."

After our dessert of chilled cherries with yogurt, Robert reads us a poem he's been working on called "Two Deaths":

Lying in the arms
of my big death,
shall I be thinking
even then
of breathless lovers
dying/even then
their little deaths?

Arthur is the first to applaud. "It always amazes me, Robert, what you can do in such little space." Nasri and I, fans of Robert's work, quietly praise it as well. Suddenly I'm aware that I'm the only woman in the room.

"Dina, have you brought us some new poems?" Robert asks.

"Here are my Ma'alot poems," I say reaching into my bag. "But please read them to yourself." Robert reads quietly as Nasri and I clear the table. I am nervous, putting up all of my defenses knowing that Robert always finds something to fix in my poems. But this time, he beams at me. "This is your best work. Go home and send them to the best American journals."

"Home? I'm not sure where that is anymore but thank you, Robert. Those words mean so much coming from you." And then privately, as we walk to my bus stop he says gently, "Dina, I would love for you to come back to Israel to live but it isn't an easy life. Do whatever is best for you." I thank him, grateful for such generous advice. He isn't telling me what would be best for the country or for him. He is the first one who is wondering what would be best for me.

The Association for North American Jews in Israel is helping me look for a job for my potential return. They arrange a meeting with the translator and poet Betsy Rosenberg who meets me on Jabotinsky Street and walks me back to her apartment where fresh fruit and flowers fill vases and bowls. Betsy had left America thirteen years before and was afraid to return, even for a visit.

"You'll find a job if you decide to come back. Let's just talk and read some of our poems. We'll learn more about each other that way." We settle into her living room and she reads some of her shorter poems that are rich and spiritual. I read her some of my "Israel poems" and try to describe the poems I wrote in America.

"There was always a yearning to be elsewhere. I was always longing for Jerusalem, like the Ethiopian Jews and so many other Jews in the Diaspora. It's funny now how much I longed for a country that I didn't really know," I tell her.

When she discovers that my original family name is Katzenellenbogen, Betsy grabs my arm and leads me next door to meet... the Katzenellenbogen family. Mrs. K., an elderly woman with hair pulled back in a scarf, greets us warmly when Betsy tells her my family name. She apologizes in a very high Hebrew for the fact that her husband, Moshe, is at work at the Jewish publishing house that they own. She shows me Moshe Katzenellenbogen's portrait on the wall and the portraits of his father and his father's fathers—all of them Jerusalem rabbis. I see my father's blue-gray eyes in their eyes, and my grandfather's eyes that I had only seen in photographs. Their home is laden in talmudic literature. In Hebrew, it is too difficult to figure out where our ancestry connects. Mrs. K. assures me, on my way out, that we are family. Standing outside the doors of their homes Betsy says, "You see, it's in your blood —this religiosity, this Jewish longing. I guess in America, the rabbis turn into poets!" We hug goodbye like old friends.

I return from Jerusalem with swollen feet and aching shoulders from carrying gifts for my friends and family in America: earrings from the shuk, Armenian pottery, simple Hebrew books, Shabbat candle holders. As soon as I approach the absorption center, Elad runs up and takes my hand. Osnat appears as if from nowhere and carries one of my bags up to my apartment. The flies and bees have invaded. We run circles away from the *devorah* (bees) laughing and slamming the terrace door each time another one escapes.

There is no easy way to say goodbye. I hand over clothes to Osnat and her sisters and promise that I will return in one year and that we'll all know where to find one another. To Elad, I say goodbye as if I will see him again the next day. I give him bubbles to blow, reach for, and chase after. I do not know how to tell a four-year-old boy whose mother is often ill and whose father is still in Ethiopia that someone else is leaving. I let go of his small hand and watch him run into the distance.

August 4, 1985

The cough and the blue light in the distance, the lights slowly going off on the top of a faraway mountain. The coughs echo down many long staircases, from window to window. We are all turning in our sleep, the fog over the blue window where I imagine Ethiopians turning down their beds. They love us because of the sweet smell of our skin. They love us for what we give them, the white pearls dangling from Osnat's ears, the red beads from Yael's ears, the blue tourist clogs, the quick kiss on the cheek. They love us for what we can give them, not knowing of those things we can't give. When one of their babies cries he cries in all of our dreams. The fog is covering my stars and the tip of one of my mountains. I can leave now, I can, it's just that my bags are not yet large enough to carry the weight of everything I've found.

The Place Between Two Countries
(1985-1989)

*My language is my fatherland. Hence the country
of my language has become mine," he said.
And added: "Two countries share my soul.
"The first—the one I came from—speaks to me of
my native absence. The second—the one I went to—
has given me the habit of turned pages from which my
words will dawn.*

—Edmond Jabès, from The Book of Questions

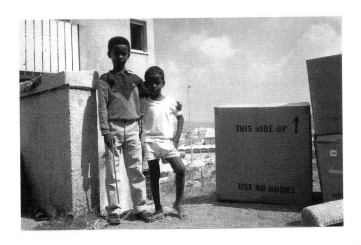

April 21, 1986—Chicago

Lately I think about my backpack sitting in Yossi's apartment and that rainbow quilt rug in our apartment that Elad sat on to blow bubbles. I think of the blue clogs I left with Osnat. I think of these things sitting in apartments in Ma'alot and I lie back and dream that everything will wait for me, that the red anemones in the valleys of the Galil will bloom and then wait for me to return before they pass on. Other times I know that orange blossoms will perfume the air and fade away, that hands of beggars will freeze and swell, that there will forever be a hand reaching out, there will be that hand in Jerusalem that is forever in the air, forever asking, forever begging—that hand will open and close again and open. I know too that the rains will fall that people I love will huddle in front of heaters. Bellies on kibbutz will be full and then empty. Someone will spend a winter knitting a blanket. And there will be things, too, that could never be covered over no matter how many layers are worn. I know this will happen and things more severe, before the next time I return. I know these cycles will not halt, they will not wait for me although I dream they do. And maybe when the right moment comes I can jump into the cycle and feel it carry me along with the red anemones, the orange blossoms, the sound of far-off gunfire. And the yearning hand will wait for me to place something inside of it.

August 1985

When Israelis leave Israel they are described as being *khootz l'aaretz*, outside of the land. As I fly over the long rivers and red-roofed buildings of Europe on my way out of Israel, that is how I feel: One is either inside or outside of the land; there are no in-betweens. At first glance, nothing outside of the land holds any meaning. There is black tar from the sea on the bottoms of my feet; my hair is sun drenched and my skin brown: silver Yemenite earrings dangle from my ears and a loose salmon-colored Israeli dress hangs from my body which has grown slighter during my year away. Over my shoulders I carry the knit blue-and-white sweater that Tamarah, a fellow ulpanist, gave me on kibbutz. I wear it like a mourner's cloak to protect me from the chill I fear will greet me as I rudely awaken in America.

I am shielded from the most intense culture shock when I land in New York. Jackie, already back in America a month, greets me at Kennedy Airport. I spend a few days on Long Island helping her buy clothes for Middlebury College, the next chapter in her life. Particularly when I'm by myself, I find the New York of 1985 overwhelming and cannot look beyond the disparity between the lives of the wealthy and the beleaguered.

On the way to upstate New York to visit Shimon at a Jewish camp where he is a counselor for teenage boys, I look out of the window at rain. I did not miss anything about America except rain. So as I watch the water pound furiously at the windshield I think, *Okay, I've seen the rain again, I can leave now.*

Shimon greets me in the center of the small town surrounding his camp. As I run into his wide-open arms I whisper conspiratorially in Hebrew, "I hate it here, so big and empty." In his cabin where he lives with nine boys, I point to my picture next to his bed. "Shimon missed Dina."

He smiles and adds, "Yes, and Dina missed Shimon." My deep kisses tell him that he is right. Amazed by how much his Hebrew has improved in two months, I play him the tape of our poetry reading in Ma'alot and when he hears the first words of "Say a

Prayer But the Sea Wind Blows Them Out" he understands it is about him and his family.

You say it's easiest to embrace the dead
easier to stand next to your grandmother's grave
easier to light her candle...
easier than your mother crying over dinner... You said once,
the world is mostly
 darkness, that is why we need these things: candles
menorahs and bulbs
that is why you tell me just before the first three stars appear to
light candles for the sabbath....

Still we speak Hebrew in the center of the small town of Monroe, New York, as I hand him shekels and Israeli cigarettes. He eats a carton of shrimp from a Chinese take-out restaurant and chews Bazooka bubble gum. The bubbles explode in my face as he rants. "This country is not healthy. There is a giant absence of meaning—real spiritual earthly living. People eat and live for no reason."

"It feels that way from the outside—doesn't it? But my life here once had meaning. I just can't remember what it was." We walk hand-in-hand through the quiet town as the sun begins to set and prepare for another departure.

On the bus trip back, my mind races. Shimon, now with long wavy hair and a distinguished beard, still has my heart. He promised he would come to Chicago at the end of the month when camp ends. I do not know how he will fit into my life in America, a life I can no longer imagine.

I have used up every last penny and shekel in Israel. I do not have enough money to get to Chicago. I tell my parents that if they want to see me again they need to send me a few hundred dollars for a ticket.

August 10, 1985—Glencoe, Illinois. Home of My Parents

It is the simple things that are most difficult to digest. The lightness of American coins in my pocket, how quickly they are chewed up in telephones, asking directions in English, no excuses for my inability to know in which direction to go. I am walking around the Port Authority humming "Hatikvah," the Israeli national anthem. I am in upstate New York handing Shimon shekels, Time cigarettes, Hebrew words, Mideast passion.

At home the pillows are so large and fluffy I can't sleep. Mail comes on Saturdays. The absence of Shabbat in America as I knew her in Israel, the weakness of the sun.

The small shocks continue—looking in the mirror, concentrating on my newest image here: my skin lighter, eyes darker, hair cut and curls controlled. I look at my bookshelves. The poetry that was with me in Israel sits on a separate shelf. Amichai is the only one who reaches me these days with his longing. James Joyce, Gertrude Stein, William Faulkner, Camus, Nietzsche, Plato, and even Spinoza stayed behind in America. Have I read all that? None of the books jump out at me like they used to. None of them can save me. Walter Jacobson on the ten o'clock news reports on a young black boy who was killed on the South Side. His family and his community mourn. In Israel, his country would mourn.

Sara and I had promised to write each other about our first impressions of home. She kept her promise to me in a letter she had sent me in Ma'alot describing her first Sabbath in America. After she cleaned her home, baked challah and then looked into the blank stares of her mother and sisters when she asked them to bless the wine with her (her father was in Germany on business) she had concluded, "There is no place for Shabbat in America, we'd just dirty her up."

She also wrote about her ambivalence about beginning her studies at Harvard. She was excited but also anxious to return to Israel, and begin army duty with people her age.

Sara,

 In Chicago the shock is quiet, creeping and heavy. In the suburbs it is the largeness of everything, the spaces between houses, the spaces between people. I cannot lean down my porch and smell what someone is cooking for dinner. I cannot lean down and invite someone up for tea. There are no children in the street that want to be hugged by me.

 How long can I rest against this emptiness? There are things I have to give up, things I am dying to keep.

Eric, one of the few remainders of the group in Ma'alot, writes to say that Elad came by to look for me and the bubbles I used to give him. I cry when I read it. It had been too painful to say goodbye to Elad and too painful to bid farewell to Eric. Eric and I had been comrades since the beginnings of our journeys in Israel. Although we did not count on each other as much once we got acclimated to life in Ma'alot, we always had a strong connection. I had dreaded our goodbye. Eric, who was never good at showing emotion or at separation, was nowhere to be found on my departure day. Eric was now preparing to return to Jerusalem to study in a Yeshiva. He writes:

 When Elad realized you were gone he seemed so sad. I told him you are writing stories about him. When Dave returns to Chicago he'll tell you what a brat Elad has become since he had his head shaved. But lately he's been better.

Jackie writes from Middlebury:

 I cried when I read your letter about Elad looking for the bubbles. I can't explain the feeling of emotion that came over me. The experiences feel so far away yet the feelings are so deep inside of me that it is painful when I allow myself to think about it. When I think about the children that I love so much I am overwhelmed by the pain and there is no outlet, no way to express it. And here I am living this non-existent life. I love my

classes and I know I need a degree and all that but I feel so self-centered in my existence here that I feel non-existent.

 Many times I dream I am in Israel. I dreamt that the Syrians were attacking and I was helping to reload supplies for the soldiers. I could see them attacking from over the hill.

 I woke up wanting to be in Israel, I know there is no life for me in America. I know for sure I don't feel like an American. But an Israeli?

While Jackie writes about letting go of her memories because there is no way to express them, I do the opposite through writing. I write down my dreams about Osnat and Elad, which arrive with more and more frequency. I paste their pictures to the wall and play the tape of Osnat singing in Amharic, Jackie playing with the children, a group of us singing on Shabbat, then sitting in a room debating and laughing.

One day while writing down dreams, I begin an essay about Osnat and Elad called "Dreaming of the Children." Poetry, my first language, is unable to contain what I want to say or discover about the Ethiopian children. My connection to the children and my desire to know them and understand the truth about their lives is coming out in prose where I have more room to explore and more space to tell their stories. "Dreaming of the Children" is my first published essay. I send a copy to Jackie.

Dina,

 Thanks so much for sending me the article. I read it about five times the first hour that it was in my hands. It helps so much when I feel alone with my experiences in Ma'alot. I saw a movie here called Falasha—it was about the Ethiopian Jews and how for so long the Israeli government wouldn't let them come into Israel. It was the saddest thing I've ever seen. I felt so naïve and angry. The film was made right before Operation Moses that brought in the people that we know. They had an update at the end saying that after they showed their film to the Israeli government, "Operation Moses" took place. I am

confused about the truth. The filmmakers went to Ethiopia and interviewed the Falashas in their villages. I swear some of the people that I saw in the movie were people from Ma'alot. To see how Elad must have lived was incredible. The movie also informed me of the difficulties caused by prejudices against Jews in Ethiopia.

I put the letter down for a moment and think about how naïve I still am about my friends' lives in Ethiopia. In Israel, it was as if their past was erased and they were reborn with Hebrew names. I could not imagine their lives before Israel and they did not have the desire or the words to tell me their stories. Only once, Ora began to tell me about a ceremony that she was attending for a cousin who had died on her walk from Ethiopia to Sudan. She had told me this without emotion and did not want to elaborate. There were other moments when I would be suddenly reminded and profoundly aware of their pain, but they were only moments. The lives I shared with them existed only in the present.

Jackie's letter continued:

I have a collage of nine black and white photos of Ethiopian eyes, and noses, bald and bushy heads. I stare at them. The picture you sent of me and Osnat is the most beautiful of all I own because I can see in front of me Osnat as she was and the love she gave to me. It's scary because I just sink into the past and I know that it is just all wrong. I can't be there; I couldn't have stayed yet there is something... I don't know what it is.

I am comforted by Jackie's feelings. Yet I know that she will soon take down the photos and place them in a drawer as she gets deeper into her studies and into college life. The intense feelings are something she wants to give up. I hold onto them like a raft in a choppy green sea.

Charleen writes from Ma'alot, describing the changes in the sky, how lonely she feels as she walks to the back porch to watch the sun set. In a few days she will leave for South Africa with plans

to return a few months later to study at Haifa University and live with her boyfriend, who we still call South African Dave, in Ma'alot. Charleen, the least Zionistic among us, is returning to live; Jackie is closing the book. I am somewhere in the middle.

I am most surprised when a blue aerogram arrives with Moshe's handwriting. We've been out of touch for several months, but I had written to tell him I had returned to America. He writes about the difficulties of being a soldier, how at Yad Vashem, the Holocaust memorial museum, when he looks at photos of even German soldiers, he wonders how heavy their packs are and for how long they have been standing.

"But I do it out of love of G-d and country," he writes. "And when are you coming to Israel to live? You know, there are no Zionists in America."

Moshe's is the only letter I cannot answer. In his eyes I am no longer Dina, a woman he once loved. Instead I am the generic Jew, whose mission it is to live in the Promised Land.

In September, when Shimon comes to visit, I live again in Hebrew, which is still the language of my quickest thoughts. Where are my shoes? What time is it? Is it raining?

It's Indian summer. On the beach in Glencoe we listen to the Chaim Moshe tape I'd brought back from Israel. On Shabbat, we sing Hebrew songs, breaking the suburban silence as we walk the mile from my parent's home to Lake Michigan. When we visit Impressionists at the Art Institute, culture shock waits on a bench across from me, reminding me how clean, how strange, and how foreign my city still feels. Caught in a heavy rain, we laugh at our reflection through the train window.

Watching the dexterity of Shimon's hands as he builds a wall in the living room with my father, I remember back to the weeks in Ma'alot when he had had surgery on those fingers and I became his hands: washing him, preparing his meals, carrying things. That same week, I was his witness at the American Embassy in Tel Aviv when he went to get his visa. After speaking briefly with Shimon, the embassy worker asked to speak with me. Shimon had described me

as being a poet. This avuncular man called me over for an interview and asked, first, "How are you going to support yourself as a poet?" I can't remember how I answered, as stunned and amused as I was by this stranger turned father and the audacity of his question.

I had all of the time in the world back then and all of the energy to give and help Shimon find his way to my country. Things are different in Glencoe America where Shimon is growing more and more comfortable and I am feeling suffocated by his demands. I am helping him find a job, an apartment, and a driver's license. Sometimes he flirts with my friends. When I take him to a café for a good Israeli meal, within minutes he has discovered the Israeli underground—men working illegally, living in this country without citizenship or visas. I don't have the energy to build two lives and I don't know if even tentatively I want to make this my home.

When my mother calls me from work and asks how much longer Shimon will be staying, I know she has also reached her limit with this friendly but boisterous Israeli occupying her home. When I hang up the phone I suggest to Shimon that he go to Minnesota where his best friend lives, an American former volunteer in Ma'alot. He silently fills his duffel bags with clothes as I pace the empty rooms in my parents' home. The next morning, when I watch his Greyhound bus pull away, I sit on the shore of Lake Michigan and weep. I gather small stones and toss them into the waves, letting go of the last piece of my life in Israel and the dreams we had together. I know that the dreams Shimon once had about me have turned into American dreams. I return to the lake again the next morning and then I close the book.

I try to find my own life again by looking for work. I go to Truman College to see if there are any openings in the English department. On the way out of the maze-like building, I run into a sign that says Refugee Department. I peer into the office to discover Ruth Lambach the director, a strong-looking, forty-something woman whose walls are covered with Hmong pieces. Ruth invites me to sit down and tells me about her program—teaching English as a

second language to refugees from all over the world, particularly from Cambodia and Vietnam.

When I tell Ruth about the work I had done in Israel with the Ethiopian immigrants she says, "I detected an accent in your voice. Is it Israeli?"

"I don't think so." I answer a bit confused. My friend Sandi who I had met in Iowa City and who is becoming my best friend in Chicago, likes to say I have an Eastern European accent, that I am carrying the voices of my ancestors. Ruth likes the way I enunciate my words and the way I respond to her short story. If I pass the paperwork with the administration, she promises me a job the next time a position becomes available.

As I ride the train back and forth to do paperwork, from the suburbs to Uptown, a rough neighborhood of refugees and the homeless where Truman is located, I think about the voices of my ancestors. My grandparents came from Russia in the early 1900s. Cossacks had shot my great-grandfather, Yehuda Leib Katzenellenbogen of Lithuania in front of his wife, simply for being a Jew. This was 1904. In 1905, his son Saul, who had been imprisoned for socialist activities, came to America where he gave up half his name. Saul Elenbogen settled in Chicago, and then Humboldt Park, at the time a neighborhood of immigrants from Russia, Italy, and Poland.

Saul married my grandmother, Ida, an observant Jewish woman who had come to America from Russia when she was fifteen, leaving behind her parents and several of her siblings. Saul endured Ida's rituals, he even helped her carry boxes of kosher dishes up four flights of steps for Passover, but didn't follow any of the rituals himself. He believed that religion only separated people from one another. However, this began to change at the end of his life. In America, a not always so welcoming country to Jews, he came to realize that he would be seen as Jewish regardless of how he saw himself and, more importantly, he came to see himself as Jewish and to respect the moral qualities of the Jews he met in America.

Saul and Ida's youngest child is my father, Gershon David or Gilbert. He married my mother, Irene Kaplan, also a first generation

American, and part of the illustrious family from the rice fields of Kaplan, Louisiana. My mother's parents, Molly and David, emigrated from White Russia at the turn of the century. I grew up in my parents' Zionistic home where for the first nine years of my life my grandmother Ida lived with us. Saul had died years before I was born.

In our suburban home, Ida washed clothes on a washing board and in the summer hung them in the backyard to dry. She cleaned with a vengeance for the Sabbath. Each Saturday morning her sister Libby would join us. The sisters would sing Russian or Yiddish songs and when they grew angry at each other or wanted to speak of private matters their heavily accented English would shift abruptly to Yiddish.

When Ida died in 1969, the Old World faded a bit from our lives. I stopped hearing Yiddish and began to study Hebrew. The Sabbath no longer pervaded our home. But my grandmother's rituals of lighting sabbath candles, changing dishes for Passover and keeping kosher stayed with us as well as my grandfather's socialistic values and his humanism.

When the paperwork is complete, a job opens up and I begin teaching English to refugees. How strange it sometimes seems. Here I am, a second-generation American, welcoming refugees from Vietnam and Cambodia as my grandparents had been welcomed two generations before. But I do not feel American. I am still reeling from my love affair with Israel, particularly my connection to the Ethiopian refugees, and looking for meaning in an American life. I miss the sense of community I felt in Israel with my fellow volunteers, friends in the community and particularly with Osnat, Elad and their siblings. Sandi and I sometimes organize Sabbath gatherings but the spirit isn't the same.

I am teaching level 1B: words, sentences, paragraphs all related to daily life in America. I am teaching them how to go to the post office, bank, library, and supermarket. My students are adults, some illiterate in their own languages. Although my task is difficult and sometimes frustrating, I grow attached to the Vietnamese, Cambodian, Romanian, Eritrean, and South

American faces. But they do not become a part of my life outside of the classroom the way my Ethiopian students in Israel had for me.

I had felt more comfortable teaching the Ethiopian children about Talmudic Jewish holidays like Hannukah and Purim than I do teaching these refugees American holidays like Halloween, Thanksgiving and Christmas. I want them to live fulfilling and productive lives in America but we do not share a greater mission. Teaching them deepens my thinking about what it means to be an American, not to take that freedom for granted.

After nine months, I get burnt-out as an ESL teacher. I am ready to teach writing and literature to college students, to move back to the path that I had once planned to follow. It is time to give up my refugee status and I take a job teaching part-time at two universities in Chicago.

Unlike my refugee students, I have the luxury of living in the place between two countries all year long. I can function in America and dream in Israel. Even after I move out of my parent's home to Greenleaf Street in Chicago where my friends live, where Ehran, a new Israeli friend, found me an apartment across from his, there is still the echo of my footsteps, landing on Israeli soil. Living across the courtyard from an Israeli, and calling *boker tov* (good morning), helps.

March 23, 1986 — Chicago

I have gathered beautiful stone from a broken country, stone that sits on the sill and collects dust and sun. I call out good morning in your language to your window across the way. Our Chicago windows change from fog to rain to sun to fog again, quickly, like the currency in your country. Here, neighborhoods change, color and food smells, so many expressions of hunger. I hold onto ancient artifacts of a Promised Land: a chip of lantern I dug up near Eilat, a stone from a cave in Rosh Hanikra. I hold onto these stones like a life preserver—these beautiful stones from a breaking country— toss them back and forth between our broken lives, shine them each spring before the holidays, the way the Moroccan women

*hang their rugs out the window before Pesach. No matter how crystal-like
they seem, no matter what shade of blue they've become all these centuries
later, no matter how smooth they are in our palms, we cannot put them
away—yet they are not heavy enough to lead either of us home.*

Letters from Osnat have now been coming for a year. During my
first two years away from Israel I had received only words and
drawings from her, enough to know she was thinking of me but
not enough words to know how she was doing. In 1987 she left
Ma'alot to study at a *pnemia,* a religious boarding school near Tel
Aviv where many of the Ethiopian students were being sent. She
was now able to write in Hebrew.

6/10/87
Dear Dina,
 *Greetings! Dina, how are you? How do you feel? Dina, how
are you getting along with your girlfriends in America? If you
meet Jackie, if you find her send greetings from me. Everything
is okay with me, thank G-d. My studies are just a little difficult
for me but I'm doing well. Dina, do you want to come to the
Land of Israel to return? If yes, write to me, okay Dina? I
wrote you a letter but you didn't write me. I thought maybe you
moved.*
 *Dina, I want you to write me a letter and send me money
if you can if you can't don't send it, okay? Dina, I will say
goodbye to you now and good luck in your studies.*
 *From me, Osnat Melesa. Ps. Send me a picture of you. After
I finish studying I will visit you in America. I love you- Osnat .
Good Bye My sister.*

I am taken aback by her request for money. Teaching part time, I
struggle to make rent each month. And I do not have Jackie's
address. She had stopped writing more than a year before. I don't
know if she is still in Vermont or not. I did not go in search of her;
I assumed her lack of response to my last letter meant that she did
not want to be found.

Yet as I prepare to leave for Iberia with my boyfriend Jonathan, a doctor I've been dating for a year, who has invited me to join him on this expense-paid journey, I feel guilty. I try to forget about Osnat's request but in North Africa, I see her sad eyes in the eyes of a young African girl begging for money. I did not know how to explain to Osnat why I would not send money. I think of the Berber rugs that Jonathan bought in the Medina in Marrakesh and how we should have sent that money to Osnat instead. And I feel uncomfortable. Does she need the money or does she still think of me, of us, as rich Americans who have more money than we know what to do with? Soon I see her sad eyes everywhere. Shortly after I return from North Africa I receive another letter from her.

9/14/87
Dear Dina,

How is it to be in America? I really, really miss you. I want you to come visit me in Israel. Dina, my family remains in Ma'alot. I told you that I study in a pnemia in Tel Aviv. At the school in Tzfira, I'm alone. I travel to my family once a month or every two months because they don't give me much money. It is very difficult for me because I don't have money. If you can help me, tell me, and also tell Jackie. I was very happy to receive your letter. I want you to write me more and more. That also helps me. I love you. Elad sends his love, too and my whole family, Osnat.

What could I say to my friend who I so want to protect? I had dreamt of giving her old jackets, worn jackets, things I didn't need anymore. I had given her small gifts from the market. Decades later I still wonder. Why didn't I ask my doctor boyfriend who had paid for my ticket to Spain to send her money? Why didn't I insist? What if she really had needed it? Did I somehow feel too close to her begging? Did I still feel too much like a refugee myself to be thought of, even for a moment, as a rich American? I had wanted to give her language, self-esteem, friendship, confidence and shelter. But money?

It takes me a long time to write back. My Hebrew is deteriorating and my letters to her are as simple as her letters to me. Silenced by her request: I cannot find the Hebrew words. I revert to my private language and I write a poem instead.

"The Letter I Wanted to Write, the Letter I Wrote"

In the Medinah, in Marrakech
a veiled girl tried to sell me a basket
she wove in greens, purples and the color of wheat.
Heavy lipped, black alabaster, like you
she stumbled through my language
pleading 20 dirham, 15 dirham . . .

Everything is fine in America.
I am teaching at the university.
I just got back from a vacation far away
Not far from where you were born.
Yesterday it rained so hard
There were rivers in the street.

The veiled girl grabbed my wrist
with her slender fingers
chanting 10 dirham, 5 dirham . . .
When I walked away I saw your eyes
large wooden bowls, waiting
to be filled.

Are you happy in your new country?
Are you studying very hard?
Are your brothers and sisters still with you?
Does your mother feel better
Now that the rains have passed?
I am sorry. I cannot send money.

In the Medinah there were rugs
the colors of mountains and sky

and baskets in the bony arms of girls
like your thin legs that carried you
from Ethiopia to Sudan
and then to the place that was promised.

Has the dream come true?
Can you write in three languages? Sing
"By the Water of Babylon" in English?
I have not stopped humming the words.
My students are learning poetry
but do not take it outside the room.

My students have golden pens.
They do not braid my hair in summer.
They run circles not knowing
of smaller countries
empty plates, washing in rivers
the sun asleep in fallow fields.

Do you still wear the blue beads
I gave you?
Everything is okay in America.
I hope you are well.
Please excuse my language.
I have almost forgotten it.

I bought the basket from the girl
whose eyes shone through her white veil.
She wanted me to have another
but it was dusk
my arms were full
I pressed the coins to her palm.

I am sorry.
I cannot send money.
It is not easy.

It does not grow on trees.
I promise I will visit.
Never stop writing.

I filled the basket
with dirty clothes
and brought them back to America.
In the basement I hear them spin
and dream of rivers
cleansing orange against wheat.

Friday, April 15, 1988

Dina, How are you? How do you feel? Dina, how are you
getting along in America?
 Dina, how are your parents? How are your friends getting
along with you?
 Dina, do you still know Hebrew or have you forgotten?
Dina, I'm fine, thank G-d and everything is good with Yael.
Dina, I really, really miss you—outside of that I have no
problems. Dina, will you come to the Land of Israel to visit?
I really, really want to see you. Why aren't you coming? Dina,
if you meet Jackie, if you find her, tell her to write me a letter.
Dina, why aren't you writing me a letter? Dina, I love you very
much. Yours, Osnat Melesa
 And with that I finish my letter.

Spring 1989

Dina, I was very happy that I received your letter especially
when you said that you were coming to Israel. Dina, I'm very
happy that you are coming and I will be happy to see you soon.
I wait for you. Dina, I think that we are moving in the month of
July to Ramat Eliyahu (next to Rishon LeZion). If we are not
still in Ma'alot I'm sure that I can visit you there. If you want
you can see my pnemia but we will probably be on break.
 I love you, Osnat Melesa.

After four years in America I have not decided to stay here or return to Israel to live. I still live with this question like an extra bag of luggage I carry wherever I go. What has kept me in America thus far is circumstance: family, fear, and the Jewish doctor with whom I share everything except poetry and my passion for Israel. And now our relationship is over. When people ask me why it didn't work out with Jonathan I return to the moment when we looked into a valley in Toledo, Spain, and I said it reminded me of Tzvat. He said that all of his years have held the same significance or lack thereof. He found it curious that my year in Israel had been so pivotal and had become how I frame the world around me. He knew then that I would not be the conventional doctor's wife and I understood that he didn't have his own convictions. We held on for several more months and then painfully broke apart.

It is time to return—for a visit. Even Osnat has given up on my permanent return. If at first she asked, "When are you coming back?" in recent letters her question has shifted to "When are you coming to visit?" I know that I will not discover the answer to the question of home from American shores. I need to be in Israel again, even if it is only for the six weeks between my summer and fall courses. And perhaps I will not find the answer just now but I will be able to deepen my understanding of the question. I need to see Elad and Osnat, to discover who they are becoming. I want to know, as I had asked in the poem that I had written to Osnat when I returned from North Africa: Has the dream come true?

I don't have money for a ticket so I apply for a grant. On the application I write that I want to discover how the Ethiopian Jews in Israel are fairing five years after Operation Moses. I propose to write an article about my discoveries. To my delight I receive enough funding to cover plane fare. I pack my bags.

Five Years after Operation Moses
(1989)

"When they sleep in Ethiopia, we wake up in Israel."
—Elad Yamari

My family arrived in 1979 (with the first large wave of Ethiopian emigration to Israel from the villages of Gondar province). We went straight to an absorption center/ulpan in Beer Sheva and then we came to Ma'alot. And that's it. Now I go to pnemia. There are about 700 students and we study, eat and sleep together.
—Ofer

When you walk down the platform at Ben Gurion Airport, alongside the throng of people waiting, you feel like a celebrity. One-by-one or two-by-two people pass, and the crowd outside anxiously awaits the arrival of their loved ones. I expect to be greeted by Eric, but there is no sign of him. I soon realize that he has not received the fax I had sent him from Amsterdam to tell him my flight was delayed three hours. Ehran, my neighbor in Chicago, is visiting his family in a suburb nearby; I take a cab to his home.

Osnat had written me, "Do you know Hebrew or have you forgotten?"

I wrote back: "I am forgetting." But as I ride to Ehran's home along orange groves and the sweet smell of a Tel Aviv summer, suddenly my Hebrew comes back fluidly.

Like my first morning in Israel years before, I awake some hours before the sun to new sounds and smells. I love this early hour when the sweetness of the land seems to rise above the distant murmur of traffic. The sun is not yet unbearable. As a cool breeze comes in through the open shutter, I remember some of the more unpleasant smells of Ma'alot that had not returned in my memory with me to America: the incinerator burning garbage, smoke, specks of refuse, flies everywhere, dirty faces, large boulders unlike Jerusalem stone next to cement buildings with plastic porches. Where have all of these images gone during my four years in America? I want to go back to Ma'alot, and I fear being isolated in

the Galil; I want to embrace the entire country. Once, Ma'alot was where my home was. Now, Ma'alot is where I have an apartment and where not only my friends wait for me but where my work is, where I can continue the search for an answer to the question of home.

The *mercaz klita* that four years ago housed Osnat, Elad and next door Charleen, Jackie and all of the other volunteers, the building which I remember glimmering in sunlight, looks drab in the harsh reality of 1989. No girls lean out of the windows; they are closed and the area is infested with garbage and remnants. The parking lot is empty of soccer games and young voices. The remaining Ethiopian families are indoors, hiding from the heat. Garbage laces the bushes in front of our building, and there is feces on the steps leading up to my apartment.

Elana Gabai, now running the Ma'alot program, generously agreed to let me stay in my former apartment on the fifth floor.

As I saunter over to my building, which has changed from my crystallized memory to a harsher reality, from castle to absorption center, a tall Ethiopian man greets me in English with "Welcome to Ma'alot." This teenager, Ofer, offers to help me carry my luggage up the steps; I drop my American pride and allow him to. I begin asking him questions about his life in Ma'alot and Israel, keenly aware that I only have six weeks to discover how the Ethiopian Jews are getting along five years after Operation Moses. Ofer becomes my first victim.

Unlike my other Ethiopian friends, Ofer, at seventeen, has already been in Israel a decade. Standing in front of the absorption center, his broken English shifts to fluid Hebrew. "Life in Israel is okay, except the Jewish Agency is trying to separate us from our families. They won't allow my family to move to Netanya, near the seas, where we want to live."

Exhausted from jet lag and the heat, it is difficult to absorb all of Ofer's complaints about housing and jobs. I suggest we meet the following morning to finish our conversation. Ofer does not have a calendar, and mine is wide open.

I am alone at night in Charleen's and my former apartment. Outside my open window the Galilee mountains welcome me home, but the deep red sunset can be mournful alone. I am no longer the woman who tried to throw her American identity out the window that separated her from her life. Yet my American identity has shifted to contain the part of me that grew up in Israel four years ago and the hand that continues to reach toward Jerusalem.

I feel exhausted and shocked by the poverty of the Ethiopians, the smell of fire, the ugliness of this barren apartment that was filled with warmth and color. I look out at the building across the way—not the *mercaz klita* but some apartments that were given to the Ethiopian families who first arrived in 1979. All lights are out except one or two. Through the window, a woman is vigorously washing clothes in a bucket while others stand by watching. I can still hear a baby cry as if it has not quieted down from the time I left four years ago. In front of the building it is much quieter. There are Israeli-born toddlers who look like children I had known before. Young Ethiopian men hang out and quietly stare. Israeli men still hassle. I hate that there are still fly-infested dirty children on the street. These buildings are physically depressing, but they can change depending upon who lives inside of them.

The next morning there is no knock on my door at ten, my designated meeting time with Ofer. I find him outside, seated on a bench in front of our building, common territory, waiting. I sat on this bench four years ago with his cousins and friends while he had been away at boarding school. We would be singing Hebrew songs, learning English words, looking into each other—infatuated by our different rhythms and fragments of stories told in our common second language. We would not be preparing for an interview.

I invite Ofer up to my apartment, and he seems bashful and perplexed, especially when he sees the tape recorder on the couch, waiting to steal his words.

"My Hebrew is rusty," I apologize, "and it is difficult to take everything in at once. That is why I am using the recorder." The Hebrew word for recorder, *klita*, derives from the same word used to describe the building where Ofer lives—*mercaz klita*—center of absorption. I was now absorbing his words.

Seated on the absorption-center couch with flat brown-and-black-checkered cushions, he grows quieter. The privacy of my apartment, the black box absorbing his words and the sudden intensity of my listening makes him answer me this time with facts. The feelings that he had released so candidly the day before are now buried beneath his simple answers.

Everything else about Ofer is very Israeli: the way he clicks his tongue in disagreement, his cotton blue slacks and white unbuttoned shirt, which reveals his broad chest, his tennis shoes and curly dark hair. And I treat him like an Israeli with the directness of my questions.

It is summer break so Ofer is with his family in Ma'alot where his mother stays home with his younger siblings and he and his father work in the factory.

"What have the changes been like for your family?" I ask, putting down my tea with mint leaves and leaning into the corner of the couch.

"My father never knew what a grocery store was: now he goes and shops there every day. When we came we didn't know anyone, now I have many friends." When Ofer finishes school he will become a soldier. He tells me this in the same matter-of-fact way that other Israeli men would. It is not something he questions but considers it his duty. "When I finish the army I want to go to the university to study biology. I love biology, and I think there are many jobs in the field. But I do not want to return to Ma'alot to live. I'd rather live in Netanya."

When Ofer mentions Netanya again, I think about our conversation the day before on the steps to my apartment. He had complained that the agencies who were supposed to make life easier for the immigrants were not good to them because they asked to live in Netanya but were sent to Ma'alot. Today,

however, Ofer doesn't have any complaints. Despite the cold that comes to the mountains in the winter and the crowded conditions in Ofer's family's apartment, he has grown to love his small world: the Ethiopian community in Ma'alot, his best friend Michael, a Moroccan-born twenty-five year-old who has lived in Ma'alot all his life, and the North American volunteers whom he hangs out with in the evening. He is especially attached to the view outside his western window of the mountains of the Galil and the small white rooftops of homes in Arab villages and, on a very clear day, the sea.

Ofer opens up when he asks me about my life in America. He is more interested in talking about basketball, especially Michael Jordan, than he is in talking about his life. He is incredulous that, as a Chicagoan, I've never met Jordan, let alone been to a Bulls game. He is even more disappointed that Jordan (with such a name) is not a Jew and that most Blacks in America are not Jewish.

At the end of our conversation, Ofer promises to help me find Elad—whose name I've wanted to scream at the top of my lungs since my arrival—and Osnat's family's new address in Ramat Eliyahu. I had been looking for her address since I arrived, but the absorption center officials and the few people I've run into have no idea who might have it.

A few minutes after I part from Ofer, Elad whizzes by on his bicycle, having received word of my arrival. My eyes fill with tears when I see the bashful smile of eight-year-old Elad, his eyes studying the ground.

"Do you remember me?" I scream over to the boy on the bicycle.

"Not so much," he answers, circling the parking lot.

When he returns to look me over again, I hand him a photograph of himself as a four-year-old standing with his cousin Osnat and me. As he studies it, his memory of me connects with the woman who is now standing next to him, and the mischievous smile blossoms on his face, showing me that since the last time I saw him, half his life ago, his baby teeth have fallen and his new teeth have grown in with a little space to insert Popsicle sticks.

In the photograph, Elad is wearing scuffed red sandals that are on the wrong feet, a white sweater with red and green stripes, and soiled sleeves that climb towards his elbows. It had been August. Around his neck was a piece of leather with small wooden red and yellow blocks, the necklace his father had made for him before Elad left Gondar, the city where his father remains. As Elad, who is now a tall and thin eight-year-old boy in blue jeans and a clean white shirt with blue stripes and I study the photograph, we giggle at his wide-open eyes that had been staring at Osnat in her flowered head scarf and hand-me-down Israeli clothes. She had been blowing bubbles, but it was hard to tell if his eyes were following her or what she was making with soapsuds. I try to imagine him as the boy he had been, the boy that I imagined he still was.

I had expected to find the same darling, everyone's darling, but instead I find a sometimes sad-faced and sometimes grinning Elad, always in motion. He is no longer the youngest; there is now a new generation of Ethiopian sabras. It is impossible to find Elad without his bicycle beneath him or next to him. He speaks to me briefly and then speeds off into the not-too-far distance, quickly circling back to the parking lot. In my memory, there was often an older sister's arm around his shoulder. Now Elad is the tallest among his peers; he stands guard-like as he watches over the sabra children. He also spends many afternoons playing soccer with the teenage boys.

The next morning Elad peers at me through his window on my way to the market. "Shalom Dina, *Ma nishma?*"

"Shalom, Elad! I have a present for you. I'll give it to you later today." When I see him on his bicycle, circling the abandoned parking lot later that afternoon, I invite him to come to my apartment and receive his gift. I wait as he carries his bicycle down the steps and hides it behind my building. Climbing up the steps behind me, I ask Elad to guess which floor I lived on; he remembers on the third try.

In my apartment, he sits bashfully on the edge of the couch, where he sat eating tomatoes four years ago, and unwraps his gift. He smiles at the book with a picture of the large fish on it. It is the

story of a young boy who grew up in a family of butchers and subsequently turned into a fish. We look at the pictures as I translate the story from English to Hebrew. Every now and then Elad corrects my pronunciation, and when for the second time I confuse the words *happy* and *joy*, he brusquely corrects me with more than a trace of impatience in his voice. If Elad has to adjust to a new perception of me from his somewhat faded memories, it would be my lack of fluency in Hebrew. Because of the very basic level at which we both spoke four years ago, it never dawned on him that Hebrew was not my first language. Elad now understands that the book I gave him came with me from America and was written in my native language.

At the end of the story Elad says, "When it is day in Israel it is night in America. When we wake up in Israel, they sleep in Ethiopia."

"Yes, how wonderful that you are learning about time." I walk him outside where the younger barefoot children run and scream in the parking lot, where the older women still sit in their traditional gowns, holding their sabra children and grandchildren. Elad runs to the other side of the building and pushes the youngsters spinning on the merry-go-round.

Although Elad is no longer the same child who always wants my attention, it is gratifying to see him as the leader of the sabra Ethiopians, as a bridge from one generation to the next. Elad also runs around with Ethiopian kids his own age as well as the occasional Moroccan-Israeli who lives in the same area, on the lowest part of the mountain.

Hanging laundry to dry on the back porch late one night, I see in the distance what appears to be a lonely man standing on a rock. After I am able to separate him from the night, I realize it is Ofer, looking off at the white lights from the Arab villages and the slopes of the Galilee Mountains. He turns around and waves sadly with *Ma nishma?* that echoes into the distance.

The next morning, when the screams of children and the moving of furniture from Ofer's family's apartment awakens me,

I understand the sadness and solitude I had witnessed the night before. The Jewish Agency informed Ofer's family that an apartment was available for them in Hadera, a small town outside of Haifa. The tiny lot that separates their building from mine is now littered with bright pink blankets that the excited children use as trampolines, delivered by the Jewish Agency as gifts with which to begin their new lives in larger and allegedly more integrated homes.

A blue truck arrives with what resembles a paddy wagon or cage for horses with large white letters that spell Transport. The workmen help three generations of Ethiopian men load the substance of their lives into the truck: a large aluminum tin with which the women still make *injera*, smaller plastic tubs into which they still peel garlic and let it dry in the sun. And on the grass lie blankets, the older worn ones next to their newer ones. As the men lift these things into the truck, the women stand in the shade, chatting among themselves in Amharic.

Although Ofer's family does not have a telephone, word spreads quickly throughout the community and by late morning, cousins, uncles, and brothers arrive from different parts of the country to help with the move and to bid the family farewell.

I sit on a large rock, one of many behind my building, and watch. Through the lens of a camera, I see my loneliness in their faces. Our sense of home is shifting. They are about to leave Ma'alot, the first place they put down roots in Israel. And I have just returned to Ma'alot, and to the question of home that sometimes speaks in shouts and other times in whispers.

An older man with graying hair and a long beard poses next to his cane in Western clothing, Israeli sandals, and a wristwatch. Behind him, in the shade, his wife in her white shamma and three heavy beaded traditional necklaces around her wrinkled and tattooed neck, speaks Amharic to her daughter, also in traditional garb, and to another young mother in hand-me-down Israeli clothes.

The elderly man's great-great-grandson, a young boy, poses next holding with both hands the cane that looms above him. Next to him is his tricycle, which Elad gallantly watches over. Against the cement light posts are larger bicycles belonging to older kids

(Elad's bicycle was put away for moving day) and ten speeds, the last items to be packed. Things that they did not even have names for five years ago are now essential parts of their lives. What remains when everything else has found a place on the truck is an empty stroller. The women still prefer carrying their babies on their backs.

A shy girl approaches me with a warm and familiar smile. "I remember you, but your hair was shorter and blonder," she says in Hebrew. After a few seconds I realize she is Batya, Elad's older sister who was a skinny and wide-eyed eight-year-old when I'd last seen her. Jackie and I had taken her and Osnat's younger sister Liat to the sea in Nahariya one day. I had carried her into the waves as she cried in terror and in joy as the first sprays of salty water reached her. Now she is a plump and cheerful twelve-year-old.

We walk to the playground like old friends and sit on the swings as the smaller children circle on the merry-go-round. "So Batya, how is school going? Are you in the same class as all of your friends?"

"School is okay. I have lots of friends. Ethiopian and Israeli," she says looking away. "But this summer a lot of my friends are in camp and, you know, running around town. But I'm at home, helping my mother, cleaning, shopping. There is so much work to do."

Batya's family, from a village in Gondar province, did not have western conveniences like ovens and refrigerators. The women would spend their days preparing food as the men were out hunting and gathering. I wonder, but do not ask, how these things have changed their lives. Was it difficult to find the ingredients they need for *injera*? Did the market confuse them with all of its ready-made dishes?

"How is your mother? I've seen Elad, as you've heard, but I haven't seen your mother."

"She's over there," Batya says pointing to a group of women in traditional garb sitting on a bench next to the absorption center.

Batya accompanies me to the bench to greet Gaveret, Mrs. Yamari, who stands up when she sees us coming. She bows shyly and takes my hand, smiles, and nods but still does not speak Hebrew. In Amharic, Batya tells her who I am, but I see that she

recognizes my face and is pleased to see me. She looks heavier and healthier than the last time I saw her. She had been suffering from Ethiopian cough, which in her case I later learned is asthma. She is still a handsome woman with green etchings across her neck and warm eyes.

Batya and her mother sit with the other women waiting for the family's truck to pull away. They are interested in the move but not too invested. The family who is about to receive a new home is a 1980 family originally from Tigray in northern Ethiopia and Batya and Elad's family, the Yamaris, is a 1984 family from Gondar province. They are neighbors but not necessarily friends.

A tall teenager approaches the women on the bench and greets Gaveret Yamari with kisses on each cheek. "That's my older brother, Amnon," Batya announces proudly. He has long curls and Elad's sweet smile.

"Shalom, nice to meet you," I say shaking his hand. I don't think I met you the last time I was in Ma'alot."

"I was in boarding school four years ago, but I've heard all about you. Welcome to Ma'alot"

When the truck pulls away, I stand there by myself trying to absorb the morning. The sweet side of the bittersweet move has to do with imagining this family living in their own larger home, near Ofer's school and his best friend Asher, also from Ma'alot. Hopefully it will be easier to find work and to integrate more fully into Israeli society. The bitterness or sadness has to do with the breaking of community, the separation of families, which to the Ethiopians is the loss of an integral part of their identities.

The Ethiopians are going on with their lives, only looking back when I ask them to. If I had stayed in Ma'alot, I would not have thought so much about the changes either. If I had stayed in Israel perhaps my Hebrew would be good enough to understand everything that was said. But was it language that was getting in the way? Was it a lack of words standing between me and the real truth I had been seeking? Or was it that I no longer had the patience,

the inner peace to sit still and wait for the truth that comes in between words or when all of the words have failed?

I feel lost because without language I have no map. I had always understood the world through texts. When I asked my mother difficult questions, she handed me books. When I first wanted to know Israel, find an entrée into her landscape, I proposed to translate the lesser-known Israeli poets into English. I wanted to crack open the secret language, to listen to the whispers of the poets in order to discover the essence of Israel. But as Amichai, the wisest of the poets, had instructed me, I was not coming to Israel to explore her libraries. And it would take years, if not a lifetime, to gain the intimacy with Hebrew I'd need to translate the Israeli poets.

The Ethiopian Jews, by a twist of fate, have become my next enigma. They are my text: their wide eyes, sealed lips, the rhythms of their Hebrew, their secrets, the distant echo of their footsteps trekking through Sudan. I'm still not sure what I need to translate this text. Hebrew is only one of the tools. And what would knowing their lives tell me? I had asked Osnat in the poem I wrote to her: Has the dream come true? Can you write in three languages? If their dream comes true, I can believe in the purpose of Israel, not to swallow her immigrants but to truly say to them, welcome home.

In my mission to discover if the Ethiopian Jews have really come home to Israel, language is getting in the way. Once I was their teacher, friend, and comrade. In America, I did not stop dreaming of the children. I never forgot the shy smiles of the Ethiopian women in white *shammas*, deep green scarves, babies on their backs. I did not forget these women who were unable to use the language that their children were just starting to master. Now I walk among them with a blank notebook and a thick black pen. And I am armed with questions, so many questions. I am becoming the anthropologist that Jackie and I talked about on her porch. Instead of absorbing their lives into my own, I am watching again, through a window. I'm not speaking their language of silence but am giving straight and difficult questions to a private and gentle

people who speak their most important truths in parables. But I
am on a mission and have six weeks to find an answer. And I am
relieved, I think, that sometimes my question shifts. I no longer
constantly ask: *is Israel my home? Should I have made aliyah? Can I
live here now?* Instead when I speak to my Ethiopian friends all of
my questions, large and small, can be translated into one simple
one: Has Israel become your home?

<center>❧</center>

One 1980 family was now on their way to a new home. In order
to discover the remainder of that community, those who have
already been in Israel a decade but who have moved out of the
absorption center and rented apartments in Ma'alot, I climb halfway
up the large hill to view their homes: run-down yellow buildings
similar to the absorption center. I do not have an appointment so
I walk past the two buildings where they live, but there are no signs
of life. A few blocks away is the home of Shimon's sister Rimonda;
I know her door will be open.

Within minutes we are seated at her kitchen table drinking
soda and discussing Shimon. She devours the stories about her
brother in Los Angeles, working as an electrician, making more
money screwing in light bulbs and making other repairs for the
residents of Beverly Hills than I am from teaching in a university.

Over the years that we have been back in America, Shimon
and I stayed in touch. Every once in a while he asks me to marry
him, but mostly we've remained close friends, helping each other
with our various struggles. He calls every Jewish holiday with wise
words; we still share a genuine concern for each other.

While Rimonda tells me how much she and her mother miss
Shimon, a tall handsome Israeli man with a blue pack on his back
enters the apartment. I'd met Prosper, one of Shimon's brothers,
a few times in 1985, but I would not have recognized him with his
shaved beard, thinning hair and slender physique. We, too, share
a joyful reunion; for the first time in many years, Shimon's absence
is palpable.

I tell Prosper about my work, and he volunteers to help. "Let's spend some time together; we'll begin tomorrow. I'll take you to Gideon's house, the leader of the Ethiopians."

The next afternoon Prosper escorts me back to the pale yellow stucco buildings. This area is often referred to as the Ethiopian Ghetto because it is one of the poorest buildings that houses six Ethiopian families. Besides the smallness of the place and the neglect (it could use a good painting), it doesn't look much different from the other four-story buildings in town. Lower income families, mostly of Moroccan descent, inhabit the buildings next door.

Boys playing basketball in the small courtyard in front of their building greet us. Sabra Ethiopians. Produced in Israel. They wear *kippot* and lime-green T-shirts with the name of their *choog,* social group, painted in white letters.

Prosper and I sit on the steps leading to their entranceway, tossing the ball back and forth with our questions. When Prosper asks how school is going for them, one of the boys replies, "School is fine, and yes I have some Israeli friends. But when our friends get angry they call us *cushim.* At home, in the summer, we don't play with Israeli children except maybe a neighbor," he says pointing to the merry-go-round in the cement park next to their building. "We play sports in the cultural center in the afternoons. It is only on Fridays, when the other Israeli kids aren't using it, that we get to play soccer in the large field next to the exit out of town."

We ask the boys if we can speak to their mother, and a few minutes later Rifka's eight-year-old son leads her to us. This thin twenty-nine year old mother of four boys leans against the wall of her building, posture slightly slumped. She wears a t-shirt, cotton blue skirt and gold chain around her neck. She listens to Prosper's questions and answers in whispers. Regarding the Intifada, or Palestinian uprising, one of the first topics discussed in 1989 after "how are you," Rifka says, "I understand how the Palestinians feel wanting to return to Israel, wanting to return to their country. But I am not concerned with the Intifada right now. I care about having a bigger house and being in a community where I feel comfortable." Although her body language is hesitant,

her answers are definite and honest. She invites us into her home and serves us juice and cookies. She sits next to me on the couch and tries to answer my questions.

"I work as a cleaning woman in Telrad, right near Ma'alot. I was hired instead of the Arabs. I make less than minimum wage. Now I am cleaning schools. My husband worked in the factory. He stopped when he got sick from [overexposure to] chemicals. We live on his welfare check and my small salary from part-time cleaning." Besides the injury to her husband's pride, Rifka's salary is not enough for the family to live on.

"We pay for school, and we pay for our children's *choog*. We do not have enough money for our own *choog*." Rifka looks down sadly at her long, thin legs and her feet that cross at the ankles. "We live among ourselves. We want to live closer to our family and friends, but there have not been apartments available and we have no money. My parents live in Ashkelon with my younger brother and sisters. When we said yes to living in Ma'alot, we didn't know how far away it was from Ashkelon."

On the wall of their apartment are photographs of two of Rifka's brothers, soldiers who remain in Ethiopia. Another brother, she tells us, is a soldier in the Israeli army.

Rifka continues, "I feel that we are much poorer than the 1984 people. When we arrived we slowly gathered things, but the process has slowed down. We still live as we did in 1984—while the people who arrived in 1984 are progressing—moving out into other cities." Rifka's family of six lives in a small two-bedroom apartment. Fortunately, there is great harmony among them.

"My cooking is still of two worlds," Rifka continues. "I still make *injera*, but I'm beginning to learn some Israeli dishes as well. I like to make *cholent* on Shabbat. So in cooking I have held onto my own culture. The menstrual hut has been my biggest loss." Rifka explains that in Ethiopia, when a woman was menstruating, she would be separated from her family inside a small hut where people would leave her meals so as not to have direct contact with a woman bleeding. No one was to touch what the menstruating woman touched or walk where she walked. When they arrived in

Israel they used the back porch for that purpose, but it became complicated; they ended up crossing paths anyway. As a result, many families gave up that ritual. Now the women go to the *mikvah* in town with other religious Israeli women.

This ritual was profoundly difficult to give up. Purification rituals have always been an important part of Ethiopian Jewish culture; they washed whenever they came in contact with outsiders. As a result, Ethiopian Christians described the Jews as smelling of water. I think of them as having been drawn from water, taken from the purity of their religious practices in Ethiopia to Israel where their customs are sometimes questioned, other times a challenge to maintain.

The boys return from their room where they'd been playing with Prosper and join their mother on the couch. She reads them a book. She doesn't understand many of the Hebrew words so she looks at the pictures and tells them stories in Hebrew. Because Rifka is unable to help them with their homework, a tutor comes for the older kids who in turn teach the younger ones.

Most evenings, Rifka and her husband move from one Ethiopian family to the next drinking black coffee. They do not mingle outside of their building. Rifka says she is bored. When she and her husband are not visiting and commiserating, they watch their large color TV, larger than any Israeli family had before the Begin era.

Our next meeting is with Dani, the brother of Alemu, a local Ethiopian artist. From the moment that Dani peers out at us, I can see that he is depressed. He doesn't attempt to change his humiliated and angry expression while he explains that his wife supports the family by working in the factory in Ma'alot, a job she hates. In Ethiopia, most women did not work outside of the home. It was especially humiliating for a husband to be supported by his wife. In Israel and especially in this home, the dynamics are changing, and Dani isn't taking it well.

Dani doesn't waste time with pleasantries like inviting us to sit down or offering us drinks; he gets right to the point. "The situation for the Ethiopians is unbearable: the unemployment, low wages, crowded conditions." And then, looking into Prosper's eyes

"If the government doesn't take it into their hands, I will take it into mine." At that statement, Prosper gets up to leave and I follow. Helpless, and not sure if it's a suicide threat or not, we head next door to the apartment of Gideon, the leader of the Ethiopian community in Ma'alot.

We are welcomed graciously by both Gideon and his wife. When we tell Gideon what Dani said and ask if he could be suicidal, Gideon chuckles a little, "Dani always complains. If the Ethiopians act a certain way they will be accepted by Israelis; it's up to them." He will not tell us what a proper way of acting is. He tells me instead that there are many things he cannot say because he works for the Jewish Agency.

"I can tell you that I want a bigger apartment but would be pleased to stay in Ma'alot—even with the cold winter. I can also tell you that when I go to the mayor, Shlomo Buchboot, to complain about housing, he talks to the Arabs first, even if I was before them in line. But let's change the subject."

His young daughter with curls finds her way into my lap. She points to her kindergarten picture on the mantel, a mixture of black and white faces. Gideon returns with traditional Ethiopian wedding garb that he invites us to try on. I enjoy the proud way he shares these artifacts with us. I photograph Prosper in the groom's garb: a heavy, long, white cotton cloth without trim that wraps around the body. It is not so different from the *shammas* that the oldest and some of the middle generation wear. However, now when the Ethiopians get married in Israel, they dress as Israelis do. Prosper then photographs me in the women's gown, similar to the male's, but with red, gold and blue tapestry-like trim.

In a further attempt to share pieces of his heritage, Gideon says, "We know when Yom Kippur is coming by the shape of the moon, not from a western calendar. A month before the holiday, we cannot see the moon at all and then it becomes a sliver." I am amazed suddenly, like eight-year-old Elad, that it is the same moon in Ethiopia and Israel. Gideon pauses and then continues, "Our food is still the same, we've only picked up a few Israeli recipes. Some day there are so many things I want to tell you."

❧

I feel the weight of Shimon's absence again when I enter his former apartment the next day to have lunch with his family. Prosper and Shimon's mother, Gaveret Perez, left her husband shortly after Shimon left for America. Since Israeli law dictates that the one who leaves loses the rights to the home, Gaveret Perez moved into Shimon's old apartment. I was anxious to return to the small apartment that had become home to me four years before, but it was unrecognizable. The absence of Shimon's things, the crowd of family inside, the green walls that have been painted white, erased Shimon's character.

As I sit in Gaveret Perez's small apartment among this large, warm family who still speak to each other in Moroccan Arabic in the presence of their mother, I feel as though I am in another time and culture as much as when I am inside the Ethiopian homes. Prosper's mother, who emigrated from Casablanca thirty years ago, speaks less Hebrew than many of the Ethiopian women who have been in Israel ten years. In the large Moroccan community of Ma'alot, Gaveret Perez can speak Moroccan at the bank, post office and clinic; she can get by very easily without Hebrew in her insulated world. When she has to conduct business or pay bills in Hebrew, she relies on one of her sons or her daughter. The Ethiopians, on the other hand, need Hebrew for their daily survival.

The poverty of the Ethiopians who arrived in 1980 is also not unique to them. Prosper learned to eat one meal a day from when he went to school and had little money. He then became a teacher in a Ma'alot high school and earned as much as he would on unemployment. In the late afternoon, however, Gaveret Perez, who is on welfare, prepares a festive meal in the Moroccan style of pepper salad, fried fish, bread, and hummus. She always makes extra in case there is a guest.

In another room, she and her daughter Rimonda yell at each other in Moroccan while the men wait for their food. When the

matriarch returns with tears in her eyes, Prosper throws ice down her dress to make her laugh. And it works.

Mishoo, the second oldest son in the family, skipped the afternoon meal. He is waiting for his own family to return from Germany, his wife's homeland and where she recently gave birth to their first child. After the meal I go to his apartment, a hill away from his mother's home. Although I'd only met him once before, he greets me with a warm hug.

"So Dina, you are here on some mission Prosper tells me?"

"Well it isn't exactly a mission. I'm studying the lives of the Ethiopian Jews. Seeing how they've been getting along in Israel over the past four years since I've been away."

Mishoo sets mineral water on the table, sits next to me on the couch and begins his spiel. "Israelis and Europeans care more about other human beings than Americans do."

"They do? What about the way the Israelis are treating the Ethiopians?"

"The Moroccans were treated the same way. We were washed with DDT to remove the animals that they said grew from our hair. We were thought of as barbarians, and we were made fun of. Fortunately, we had our own large community in Ma'alot. Whenever I was around an Ashkenazi I felt alone. Still, today, when I go into offices where I have to deal with them, I feel alone. Ashkenazis wear ties and sit up straight and listen to Bach. I lie back and listen to Um Kaltoom, a popular Egyptian singer.

"Um Kaltoom! That's the singer I heard in a friend's home. I love her voice. I've been looking all over for her music. Can you play something of hers?" I am thrilled that we have a common passion; I am hoping that when he talks about Ashkenazim, he only means Israelis, that he isn't referring to me.

"Sure—I'd love to," Mishoo says, surprised and impressed by my request. He continues his lecture with Kaltoum's passionate voice in the background.

"During our first decade in the country we were told *we built the country*. The Ashkenazim told us how many sons they had lost in defense of their country. However the Yom Kippur War was

also the Sephardim War. We lost our sons; we fought to defend our country. We built the country, too. Thank you very much for building the country, but it is my country, too. I can't help it if my mother was born in Morocco," Mishoo says to no one in particular.

I am saddened by the transformation that has taken place in our discussion. Mishoo began by speaking as an Israeli, defending his country's treatment of the Ethiopians and criticizing Americans. As soon as it became personal and he began to identify with the new immigrants, he spoke as a Moroccan, the previous black sheep of the family.

August, 1989

I am more shy with the Ethiopians. I no longer want to discard my American identity, only the parts of my personality that get in the way of being with them.

All of the time Elad spins around on his bicycle. Sometimes the other kids get a turn but usually it is just Elad—circling, circling. Sometimes he rides with an older Israeli boy. Sometimes Batya gets a turn. They call to each other in their Hebrew names, not their birth names, as if they were born again with new names and Israeli clothes.

Yesterday Batya, Elad, their cousin Ora, another boy without shoes, and I went for a walk to the center of town. We watched South African Dave paint bomb shelters and wrestle the boys to the ground. We walked through the forest to Rehove Iris. Elad had been there before with his class, but it was Batya's first time in this fancy neighborhood, and she was amazed by the large houses. Elad was always running ahead of us, climbing up hills as we climbed steps. Once I knew how to make him listen by taking his hand. Now I don't know how to be his guardian. I bought everyone ice cream that melted on their faces.

They became shy when we went to public places, especially when we returned to South African Dave's office, outside of their own territory. Dave seems sad as if he never recovered from Charleen's decision not to return to Israel to live but to stay in South Africa with her new love, Ferdi, who will be the father of her child.

I sleep next to August sky over dried mountains. It has not rained in months. The sky is empty of planes on their way to the border. The fighting now is on ground, the border between Jerusalem and the territories.

<center>❧</center>

It is time to leave for Jerusalem and places in between, but I do not have Osnat's address. During my weeks in Ma'alot I asked numerous families if they had this information. Some said they did but never came through with it. Others sent me to their neighbors whom they thought might have it but to no avail. Knowing I cannot continue my journey without a map to Osnat's home, I call Aviva Zohar, a woman who had worked with the new immigrants in the Ma'alot absorption center from 1984–1986. Aviva, now home with her own children, apologizes for not having the address, much to her chagrin, since she had known the family well, but she offers me her opinion on the state of the Ethiopian community.

"The Ethiopians have been given more than other groups. A mistake that has been made is that they are all put together with their own problems and are for the most part separate from other Israelis. The Israeli families do not like when blacks move in; like in America, the property value goes down."

"Osnat's family, the Melesa family, is a success story—not a typical one. They were educated in Gondar—they come from the city. The reason some families like Osnat's make it to university is because of their smarts and the help they receive. Many have a strong will to succeed. It is more difficult for those that came from the provinces, like many of the people who came in 1979 and also the village people who arrived in 1984—like the Yamari family."

On the way out of the Ma'alot office where I'd spoken to Aviva, I begin to lose hope until I see that the door to the absorption center office is ajar. During a good week, this office is open maybe once for a few hours. I peer in at an Ethiopian man speaking with the director, a middle-aged Israeli woman. I do not wait for an invitation to enter.

"Shalom, it is so nice to see someone in this office. It has been closed the entire time that I've been in Ma'alot. I am looking for an address of a family who left the *mercaz klita* a few months ago—the Melesa family." The Ethiopian gentleman repeats, "Mishpacha Melesa?"

"Yes, the Melesa family. Do you know them?"

"Yes. My name is Reuven, and I'm a friend of the family. I've heard about you—that you are looking for their address. I live in the absorption center next door."

Reuven, who arrived in Ma'alot in 1980, copies down their address from his phone book that he carries in his shirt pocket along with directions to their new home.

"I will also be visiting them next week," Reuven adds with a warm smile. "I'll let them know you are on your way."

"Thank you so much. I was lost without this address."

Reuven turns back to the absorption center worker to continue their talk.

Now the barriers between Osnat and me are intangible. I have the map and the numbers that will lead me to her, but what will I find when I reach her?

The next day as I run for the bus Batya, Elad and Amnon call out, "Have fun in Jerusalem. We'll see you when you get home."

At the Haifa station, Ethiopian soldiers and groups of teenagers move with an air of self-assurance, blending into mainstream society in their army uniforms, stylish dress, and their determination to reach their destinations. I want to approach a soldier sitting on his duffel bag, but his straight-ahead stare and the quiet and privacy that surround him stops me.

Arriving in Jerusalem, that magic moment when the green landscape changes to white stone that glistens under sun or stars is bittersweet. Some men bend down into their prayer books, thanking G-d for a safe trip and others from America, Morocco, Ethiopia, Yemen, Iraq, Europe, Israel, and the territories gaze out

the window not only at the landscape, but at the place that marks a recent tragedy. A bus had been run off the road by a Palestinian terrorist, and many people had fallen to their deaths.

In Jerusalem, the political situation is on the forefront of everyone's mind and no one, not even Sara, has an opinion about the absorption of the Ethiopian Jews. Although it had been two years since our last visit together in Chicago, Sara greets me casually at her office where she is helping an organization run programs for American teenagers in Israel. She runs to the radio where everyone listens to the latest news about the American volunteer on Kibbutz Lotan who was kidnapped. She hands me her keys, and I head to her apartment on Rehove Avidan, the center of town, not too far from Robert's home.

As the harsh afternoon sun moves lower in the sky, Sara arrives home to find me spellbound at her desk.

"Oh my G-d, what a day. I just want to forget everything. So Dina, what do you think of this place?"

"I love it. I've totally fallen in love with the view of the Old City from one *marpeset,* and Independence Park from the other. What a great place to write!"

We walk through the park early that evening, trying to unravel the past two years of our lives for each other. Sara has fallen in love, and men and relationships are her favorite topics outside of the political situation. It isn't until Sara and I discover that we've been reading the same Israeli writers that we really connect again and both of our moods lift.

We spend long mornings on the porch drinking coffee and telling stories while she slices a pepper into long strips, fills a bowl with plump purple grapes and another bowl with cheese. We bring out the loaf of bread that I pick up from the bakery each morning and eat it quickly, before it hardens. Some mornings I am able to distance myself from the tension in Jerusalem. I have become a master at finding respites.

Drinking mugs of strong black coffee with sweet milk, Sara says, "The old elements of our friendship have come back and now there are new elements as well. The colors are all swished together."

"That's true. And we each have our own relationship with Israel now. I am envious of your Hebrew, though."

"I became fluent in *ulpan*. I can't believe I'm reading Oz novels in Hebrew."

"That's amazing. I still can't read Amichai in Hebrew without a dictionary," I confess.

"But your language has grown as well. It's great that you can do your research in Hebrew. And you seem calmer, more centered, your eyes are deeper—although you still have this intensity."

I don't ask what she means but silently take in her words. She goes inside for more grapes and then adds, "My mother said that poets have to be shattered every day."

At Robert's apartment conversations about poetry continue over a three course meal, surrounded as always by cats and books divided into genre, century, and language. I give Robert the box of tea that Nasri, his Palestinian friend and former housekeeper had given me during a recent meeting in Chicago. Nasri had left Jerusalem to join his brothers in Chicago where they own a liquor store on the South Side. When Nasri heard that I was coming to Jerusalem, he called and arranged for me to bring a gift to Robert. Our meeting had been bittersweet; Nasri was longing for Jerusalem but due to visa complications he could not return. Robert placed the tea that Nasri had sent with me on the table and ran his fingers through what was left of his white-gray hair.

"I understand that Nasri wants to come back here, but maybe he's romanticizing things—life is not so easy for Palestinians now—not that it was ever easy." Robert's new Arabic teacher, Ollie, lives in the West Bank and is often detained by curfews. Another Palestinian friend was accidentally shot by Israeli soldiers—mistaken for a terrorist.

"The country is going down the drain," Robert says leaning into his favorite wicker chair, "I don't even know what to say anymore. But it's strange, somehow. I worry about my Arab friends, but my own life is unchanged. I write in the morning, go for a swim, take a siesta, and visit with friends in the evening."

Arthur and another poet arrive in time for Robert's chicken served on a bed of salt. Over dessert we discuss some of Robert's translations of a Hebrew poet and laugh about new trends in American poetry. As I walk out the door at the end of the evening, I know for certain that Robert's bohemian basement apartment is still my home in Jerusalem.

❧

After days of wandering Jerusalem, where I and throngs of other pedestrians had to clear the street at least five times for suspicious objects, it is time to get back to work. I want to move beyond my own families and my own observations of the Ethiopian community to see if I am getting close to understanding the truth about their lives. I've spent hours on the phone trying to make appointments with Ethiopianists. The first one I reach is tired of speaking about the Ethiopians. She directs me to someone at the ministry of absorption. He invites me to his office, asks me to tell of my observations, and then looks at his watch and like a good psychotherapist says our time is up.

I walk down King George Street, gazing in the window of Steimatsky's bookstore, on my way to meet Ayelet, a sociology student who worked with the new immigrants. At the Atara Café on Ben Yehuda Street, over our first sips of cold coffee, when I tell her I am observing the progression of the Ethiopian Jews she blows up at me.

"Dina, listen to the word you used. *Progression.* Are you insinuating that they are barbaric? The Israelis' approach to the Ethiopians is terrible. Not any better than the way they treated the Moroccans. Here read this article from *Haaretz*, the major Israeli paper," she says pulling a clipping from her backpack. "It says that when the Ethiopians are given new clothes 'their eyes light up'. This makes them sound like children. And the work they are forced to do… it's beneath the Arabs. How many of them are doctors or lawyers?"

"Doctors or lawyers? In five years can anyone learn a language and a culture and become educated enough to succeed in law or medical school?"

Back on Sara's balcony, where I try to absorb the words I collect each day, she leans into her white metal chair, sighing.
"I'm so glad this week is over."
"Yeah, me, too. I'm beginning to feel overwhelmed with all of these different truths."
"So what is the word on the street?"
"I haven't found too many words on the street and in my meetings with Ethiopianists. I don't feel that anyone is really looking for the truth. Instead, everyone seems to be looking for who to blame for the fact that the Ethiopian community isn't doing so well. They are being forced to give up what is sacred to them yet they haven't found ways to contribute to society. Language is difficult. Housing is difficult. Socially they are among themselves. They still have such a long way to go."

"*Baruch haba'ah*," Eric calls out, welcoming his two weary travelers as Sara and I climb the four flights of steps to his apartment. Our pre-Shabbat bus ride was long and draining although Petah Tikvah is only an hour from Jerusalem.
"Eric—it's so good to see you—my G-d you're a citizen now—there is so much to catch up on," I say, dumping my bags on the couch. His bachelor apartment has dirty tile floors and a chair with an absorption center-like checkered cushion in front of a large television. The walls are covered with photographs of friends and family; above his table, prominently displayed, is a group picture taken at Ramat Rachel at the end of ulpan. Eric is now working as an engineer for the army.
"Let me show you your room. Shower. Relax. Do whatever you need to do. I have dinner completely under control. We can talk later. Let me *daven*, pray, *Shabbos* is almost here."
Daniel from Uruguay joins us for the evening meal. He had been on Kibbutz Ramat Rachel with us, a wild seventeen-year-old,

forced to leave his country. Now he's a new immigrant and will soon become a soldier. We sing the prayers at the top of our lungs, joyful to all be together for this rare Sabbath meal. And although Eric could never utter the words, we could feel his love in the festive meal he prepared, course after course of good Jewish food.

Sara and I tell Eric stories of how difficult it had been for us to return to our American lives. And yet after having been away from Israel four years, it takes only a day or so to reacclimatize. Eric, who had not yet returned to Canada, listens curiously.

"I just can't imagine what that would be like. I'm almost afraid to go back. Maybe when my sister gets married. Meanwhile, my family will visit me next month." Eric, like our Ethiopian friends, felt Israel was his home long before he set foot on this soil.

"Eric, I really admire your commitment to staying here. You've built a life."

"*Nu*, so, Dina, when are you making *aliyah?*"

"I guess you'll ask me that until I move here. This may sound strange to you but part of me still needs to grow up in America."

Eric smiles, shaking his head like a disappointed yet loving parent.

Sara puts her arm around my shoulder and says, "I totally understand."

The next day we stroll through the town of modest buildings. Sara gathers flowers and weaves them into my hair. Eric points out where the Ethiopians live.

"You mean they don't live all over town?" I ask.

"No. They live at the end of the road, on the strip of beige, run-down apartment buildings." I understand suddenly why both Eric and a *Washington Post* writer referred to the area as a ghetto; the buildings are in the most depressed and remote area of town. We walk by Ethiopian teenagers playing in the street and listen to the rhythms of Amharic. Like other teens, they are content to play among themselves. Perhaps they feel most comfortable with their Ethiopian friends the way that I feel most at home around Eric and Sara, my North American friends.

In Petah Tikvah, as in other religious communities like Tzvat, Ma'alot and Jerusalem, you can feel the Sabbath going out. The quiet of the day is replaced by the murmurs of people rising from their afternoon siestas, songs pouring out of synagogues, the darkening sky. My friends and I sing a Sephardic melody of the prayer Dror Dri Qra, banging our fists against Eric's *marpeset* table. When the Sabbath finally leaves, Sara and I call out *shavuah tov* (good week) to the passersby beneath our window.

❦

On my own again, trying to find my way to Osnat's family home, the country opens for me. Transferring from bus to bus I speak Hebrew again after having reverted to English for days. I stay in conversation with a fellow passenger, an older woman who tells me that my destination, Ramat Eliyahu, is a "bad place." She wants to know why I'm going there. I tell her about Osnat, about my search for the truth about the lives of the Ethiopian Jews, and after much questioning on her part, I share with her some of the difficulties they're having.

"Well, do you think they'd be better off in America? Would America do a better job with them?" I tell her that that is not my subtext. She says, "Israel needs to give more to their soldiers. You expect them to give more to the Ethiopians, and they don't pay their soldiers enough. Besides, everyone in the country is having a difficult time." She tells me about her children and some of their financial struggles. "My thirty-three-year-old son runs a boutique. Do you want to meet him?" I laugh at the universal qualities of Jewish mothers as I exit the bus.

Ramat Eliyahu is in the middle of the country, forty minutes from Tel Aviv. The town center has a few stores and a fruit stand; it is smaller than any town I've ever visited in Israel except for the Arab village of Tarshiha. I ask a fruit vendor if he knows where Rehove Binyamin, Osnat's street is.

"Which family are you looking for?"

"I'm looking for the Melesa family."

"Melesa…I'm surprised but I don't know them."

"They are the new Ethiopian family that just moved to town."

He thinks for a moment and then escorts me to Rehove Binyamin.

Walking down Binyamin Street, my heart beats wildly; I wonder if Osnat received word from Reuven that I would visit today. I look for her address, watching the numbers on the buildings but they don't seem to follow an order. I am stopped, instead, by a pan of garlic drying in the sun. I stand outside the door for a moment, catch my breath, listen to their sharp voices in Amharic.

I am greeted by a girl who looks the age that Osnat was when I last saw her. This girl does not exactly recognize me.

"Shalom, I'm Dina," I say as she gestures for me to come inside.

"Of course! I'm Marta, Osnat's sister. I'll go and get her. She's visiting with our cousins down the street."

I am left in the living room of their new home with four men drinking beer and discussing something in Amharic. Some of the faces I recognize from Ma'alot.

Gaveret Melesa, Osnat's mother, greets me shyly in Hebrew, pours soda, and returns to the kitchen. I watch Osnat's younger sister who looks to be Batya's age, playing on the floor with her two sabra brothers and sisters who had both been born between my two visits. When the girl looks up and reminds me in Hebrew about the day that Jackie and I had taken her and Batya to the sea, I realize she is Liat.

Marble tile floors cool the house from the brutal August heat along with a revolving ceiling fan moving around what air there is. They have the same shelving system as the Ethiopian families in Ma'alot, but along with their woven crafts, they have more contemporary décor as well. Unlike the Ethiopian homes in Ma'alot, the Melesa family's new home has a spacious feel to it; two steps separate the kitchen from the dining area. On my way to the bathroom, just as my excitement about their new place begins to mount, I look into a bedroom to see that three children still share one small room.

Marta returns with the real Osnat, a pretty, stylish seventeen-year-old with long bushy black hair, leather sandals that lace up around her shins, a jean skirt that falls past her knees, and a red and blue flowered blouse. We hug with joy and shyness, as if we had not been exchanging adoring letters for the past four years.

"What do you want for lunch?" Osnat asks, barely inside the door.

"Don't worry about food; I'm not really hungry."

She goes to the kitchen anyway and returns with a platter of hummus, olives, Israeli salad, and a loaf of bread. "Here, eat," she says, placing the food on the coffee table in front of me. I savor my favorite Israeli meal while everyone watches except for her parents who spill large bags of teff flour into the bucket under the table in preparation for *injera*. Her father puts his arm around his wife's shoulder and laughing says in Hebrew, "Eshti: my wife." The other men remain in the corner, talking softly. I assume all of the men gathered here are out of work. Osnat's father, who had been a doctor in Ethiopia, now drives an ambulance.

Osnat gathers my dishes onto a tray, and in her perfect posture carries it to the kitchen, and I study the languages in their home. The youngest kids, who were born in Israel, speak Hebrew to each other with a few words of Amharic laced in when speaking to their mother who doesn't speak Hebrew. Osnat, Marta, and Liat are fluent in both languages like their father. When addressing family members they speak Amharic. Hebrew is used for outsiders.

Marta interrupts my reverie on language with a question. "Dina, is America a better place to live than Israel? Are the houses bigger? What do you do there?"

"I teach English in America. And there are big houses and small houses, just like here. But I think Israel is a better place to live, there is more of a sense of community, a sense of purpose."

"I think I know what you mean." I was grateful that she and Osnat were too polite to ask me the obvious question: then why have you made your home in America? I have no words in either language for what I want to say next, so I join Osnat in her silence.

The men's conversation grows louder again and dominates the room along with the TV; I ask Osnat to show me the town. We leave her home on the edge of Ramat Eliyahu, next to open and dry land, things waiting to be built.

"I'm so happy to see you," Osnat says softly.

"It is so good to see you, too."

I don't know how to tell her how amazed I am to be walking with her in this faraway corner in Israel, how pleased I am that she's grown from an adolescent girl with broken Hebrew to a young woman, more fluent in the language and culture of her new country.

I break a few moments of silence with a question that I've had been preparing in my head.

"Four years ago, in school, the Israeli children were not so nice to you. They would throw stones and call you names. Has this changed or is it still the same?"

"Of course it has changed. They did that because we couldn't speak the language. But now I can and I have a lot of friends." Later, when we return to her house, she shows me photos of a trip she'd taken with her class to Eilat, a resort town in the south of Israel. In most of the pictures, her arms were around the shoulders of other Ethiopian girls. In only one picture, there was a white girl. Osnat points to her and says, "They are very good to us. Everything is very good in school except that I have to work very hard."

On a bench in a small park Osnat unleashes her questions to me. "Are you married yet?"

"No." I answer apologetically as if I were talking to my great-aunt who is also anxious to see me married. Osnat looks disappointed.

"Do you have a boyfriend?" I ask, returning the question to her.

"No, I'm only seventeen. I study very hard. When I finish school I'll join Sherut Leumi (an army alternative for religious girls where they give their services to the country). After my service I want to go to university. Then to America to see you. I don't have time for boyfriends."

"Here, I brought you these gifts from America," handing her a Chicago t-shirt and two English books. "And this book is for Yael who I thought would also be home."

"Yael is living in Talpiot, you know in Jerusalem. She has an apartment; she loves living there."

"I wish I had known that when I was in Jerusalem!"

"Thank you, Dina. I'll give the book to Yael. But you didn't have to get us gifts."

Was this the same girl who asked for money? The girl who coveted my pearl earrings? I imagine that her politeness is another part of her maturity rather than something she picked up from Israelis.

Back at her house, we settle on the couch, her baby brother Baruch in her arms and Marta in a chair next to us peeling garlic into a pan. Osnat and I lean toward the breeze the fan brings in, serious in our conversation about her studies and my teaching. When she corrects my pronunciation or my Hebrew usage, I realize that she is now the teacher.

Returning to Ma'alot without Osnat deepens my sense of time passing, shattering the safe haven that Ma'alot had been for me. The more lonely and distant I am from the Eden that this place once was, the more I want to know the truth about their lives. Osnat wants me to believe that everything is good for her, and in many ways it is. She is involved in the same activities as other girls her age; she just has to work harder to get through school. But outside of Osnat's family that seems to be intact and nurturing, others have numerous complaints. Their longing for family still in Ethiopia overshadows the strides they are making. The social workers, absorption-center workers, and the average citizen agree that integration is moving very slowly for the Ethiopian community. I still haven't heard solutions, only more explanations of who is to blame.

I am growing tired of words: speaking mostly Hebrew, thinking mostly in English and listening as if across a desert to the rapid

sounds of Amharic. Yet I don't feel closer to the truth about their lives. I had felt this same wall when I was teaching refugees in Chicago. Back then, when I felt we had used up language as a tool for understanding each other's lives, I asked them to draw their countries. This time, I go in search of Ethiopian art. Dani, the Ethiopian man whom Prosper and I had visited weeks before, has an artist brother, Alemu, whose paintings are displayed at Hilai, the artist's colony of Ma'alot.

Hilai was founded in 1985, shortly after I left Ma'alot. It was run by a Tel Avivian woman named Corinne, who was in Paris for the summer. David Kesos, the poet who was one of the organizers of our bilingual poetry reading in 1985, is running Hilai for the summer. When I share with him my frustrations he says, "Dina, what do you expect? The Ethiopian Jews had to move one thousand, one hundred years into the future. Of course the absorption process is slow. And this is Israel. Don't expect to find consistent answers. But let me show you Alemu Eshtie's paintings. He was one of our first residents at Hilai. His work is primitive, and it is mostly of his birthplace, Gondar Province. We are so proud of him. His paintings and sculptures are now displayed throughout the country and abroad. He won an international sculpture contest and was flown to Paris to receive his prize. Here, see for yourself."

In the center of Alemu's painting that hangs on the office wall is a large yellow tent, a temporary dwelling. A man leans into the tent, his face and upper body could not be seen, only one of his legs that remains outside. Also outside of the tent are two suitcases, one large and one small. Next to the large tent is a smaller green one, perhaps a *bet nida* or menstrual hut. In the distance is a parked truck; in the greater distance is the landscape of Gondar-Province green, rolling, tranquil.

After looking at Alemu's images of leave-taking, I long to hear his voice. I go to the nearest phone booth with the number David Kesos has given me. I am amazed when Alemu answers the phone from his home in the Tel Aviv suburb of Ramat Ha Sharon. We begin our conversation in Hebrew, but within minutes Alemu tells me his history in fluent English.

"I came to Israel in 1981. I attended an ulpan in Pardes Hannah but didn't feel as though I was learning enough Hebrew. I was surrounded by Ethiopians and spoke Amharic most of the time. Six other students and I asked to be moved to a place where we could learn Hebrew. They moved us to Kibbutz Ben Shmuel where I was able to learn Hebrew fluently. After my ulpan on the kibbutz I attended a teacher's training school in Tel Aviv. This is when I also attended Hilai. I made some good contacts there and was able to work on my paintings."

"I saw your painting of Gondar; it's really lovely. Can you tell me about it?"

He tells me first about his work in general. Most of his art represents life and culture in Ethiopia; he has one collage of different images of Israeli life. His sculptures are more symbolic. The three pieces that won the international competition were of a horse, a man, a woman, dog, and an empty space filled in with a map of Ethiopia.

"This second sculpture," Alemu explains, "represents the culture of Ethiopia, how people help each other. I feel that this togetherness is truer of life in Ethiopia than it is of life in Israel. My third piece is of a man wrestling with a cow. I got this idea because I was an assistant vaccinator for cattle in Ethiopia; man has to cut cattle. Man has to have the energy to cut cattle. And that's all I can say about it right now."

Sensing he needs to get off the phone I begin to thank him.

"You caught me just in time. I just left my job as tour guide of the Diaspora Museum in order to begin the army. I'm leaving this afternoon."

"I better let you go, Alemu. I'm so glad I was able to see your painting and hear about your work."

His paintings are like brief glimpses of Ethiopia, a place that no one has been able to take me to with their words. I am surprised by his description of Ethiopia feeling more like a community.

Back in Israel after four years, I'm so aware of the lack of community in my American life and how sometimes this entire country feels like a huge community of people caring for each

other. Although Alemu is successful in many ways, I realize that because his is one of the only Ethiopian families in his neighborhood, he still feels isolated.

Alemu, like others, encouraged me to visit Tzvat. He said that many Ethiopian artists were displaying their work in the galleries there; in fact there was an Ethiopian section. At the same time, Hannah, an Israeli woman who had taught Ethiopian immigrants in 1987 and who now teaches in the Russian ulpan in Tzvat, invited me to join her.

Hannah lives a similar life to one I imagine living in Israel. She is a single, educated woman living with her boyfriend in a house on Rehove Iris overlooking the Galilee Mountains of Ma'alot. She teaches immigrants and is passionate about her work.

During the thirty-minute car ride from Ma'alot, along winding roads, Arab and Druze villages, Mount Harmon in the distance and so many shades of green, I'm struck by the contrast between Hannah's seemingly idyllic environment and the crowded, dirty, urban university where I teach in Chicago.

Hannah, casual in her cotton sundress, her thick dark hair blowing towards the breeze, is so familiar with these narrow roads that lead us through the mountains that she is able to keep her eyes on me as she speaks.

"Many of the difficulties are the same for all of the immigrants. The extra difficulty for the Ethiopians is that they have had to move further ahead in time. Language is the biggest barrier. The Americans in Israel aggressively hold on to their language because they can get by with it. American-Israelis expect others to bend to their way. For the Ethiopians, there is no bridge into Israeli culture unless they learn Hebrew. The younger Ethiopians very much want to be Israelis. They willingly give up their Amharic names and their old clothes. The problems are with the older people who have had to move 200 years into the future. They die in the desert. Have you heard that phrase? They are not free in their new country because they can't let go of their old customs."

I understand what Hannah is saying, yet her words make me uncomfortable. Was she blaming the elders for their inability to make Israel their home? Why do they have to let go of who they are in order to function in Israel? Wasn't there a way for them to contribute to their new country while holding onto their Ethiopian identity?

I accompany her to her classroom where Russian immigrants introduce themselves by announcing their professions. *In Russia I was a scientist. In Israel I study Hebrew. In the future, I hope to work at Weitzmann Institute in Rehovot.*

Soon I follow my eyes out the window.

I wander into the ancient city of Tzvat and discover that the Ethiopian section is closed, boarded up like Juderia, the old Jewish quarter in Cordoba, Spain, where once I searched for remnants of the Jewish community. That same summer, when I wandered through Morocco and asked everyone what happened to the Jews, I had received answers like *they went to Jerusalem* or *I don't know, we were very good to them.* I receive similar but modern-day answers when I ask those same questions about the Ethiopian Jews of Tzvat. Some shopkeepers say that everything is closed. When I ask why, they shrug their shoulders. Some shopkeepers insist that the Ethiopian artists are still there just as some Moroccans in Marrakech had said there were still many Jews in Morocco.

I ask one Israeli painter selling watercolors in deep reds and blues why he thinks the Ethiopian section is empty. "Because there isn't anyone to make art—one man moved to Netanya, near the sea. If I moved to Jerusalem, there would be no one here to make ceramics… but it was good for them here…. I don't know why they left."

A young sculptor says, "The Ethiopians moved from Tzvat in order to be near their families. We were very happy to have them here; it was good for them and good for us. They earned a lot of money and when we saw them we smiled and said hello…they didn't like being separated from other Ethiopians. They had beautiful sculptures."

A shopkeeper shrugs his shoulders and says, "They didn't make money, and so they left."

And, I too, prepare to leave Tzvat, without art or artifact, without a satisfying answer. I don't wait for Hannah to finish her workday; I board a bus for Nahariya where I will catch a bus for Ma'alot.

I sit on a bench at the Nahariya station, my head buried in Adrienne Rich's collection of poems *Your Native Land, Your Life*. So lost am I in her words, I barely feel the gentle tap on my shoulder. I look up to find Ofer standing over me, joined by Yosef who had been my student in 1985. They are dressed in identical outfits: light blue bell-bottom jeans and matching powder blue shirts.

"How are you? It is so good to see you guys...I have been thinking about you since moving day. How is everything in your new place?"

"Everything is good. I miss Ma'alot, though. We are coming to spend the Sabbath. Come share a *sheruit* with us," Ofer says.

We pile into the back seat of the taxi. Two other men from Ma'alot sit in front. Ofer pays my fare, ignoring my refusal. It is good to be returning home along the dense green mountains where a shepherd boy walks slowly with his flock as familiar Israeli music blares from the radio. As we approach Ma'alot, the driver asks which side of town he should stop at: the first or the second. Ofer immediately answers, "The first." The two Israeli men in front follow with "the second." The driver goes out of his way to the second entrance into Ma'alot, the opposite side of town from the absorption center. After he drops off the other men, he circles around although Ofer had given him directions.

Yosef says jokingly to the driver in Hebrew, "Don't you remember me? I've rode with you at least three times." Ignoring his question, the driver asks me if I live with them. The men say yes, laughing. He looks at all of us suspiciously and then lets us off at an inconvenient and unnecessary distance from the absorption center. Yosef and Ofer take it in stride. I am enraged. I have not witnessed such blatant discrimination in Israel. I don't know what

to say so I slam the taxi door. The driver calls me back, but I refuse to turn around. When Yosef finally returns to the car, the driver tells him that I had slammed the door too hard. The three of us walk silently into the harsh sunlight.

The last time I saw Yosef he was thirteen. I was there when he became a Bar Mitzvah with other students his age, including Osnat. Back then his head was always covered with a large kippah. We are gathered around the benches in front of the absorption center when I notice his bare head.

"Yosef, where is your *kippah*?" The others who are now surrounding him – Ofer, Batya, Orit and Amnon—laugh and shout out answers for him.

"It's in the house." "He lost it." "It became invisible."

"It's not a bad thing that it's not on your head. I'm just curious," I say smiling at Yosef's guilty expression. He shrugs his shoulders. The girls' skirts that cover their knees and their long sleeved shirts on this hot August Thursday, tell me that they are still observant.

My most relaxing hours are those spent sitting with the girls, on the bench outside our buildings. Batya, her older sister Orit, and their cousin Ora, home from boarding school for the summer, surround me. Sometimes Batya's mother, Gaveret Yamari, joins us as well as their older brother Amnon. Elad is always in the not-too-far distance. Today Ora is crocheting a *kippah* for her brother who is still away at boarding school. Batya takes turns with Elad, riding his bicycle around the absorption center. When it's Elad's turn, she sits next to me in a comfortable silence or asks me questions about America. Gaveret Yamari joins in with the few Hebrew words she knows.

"Is it more fun here or in America?" she asks me. Surprised by the slang Hebrew word she used for fun, *kef*, I say, "Israel—because there is a greater sense of community. It is a more beautiful place."

I am ashamed that in the days since I had tried to answer that question for Osnat and her sisters, I have not come up with a better response.

When sixteen-year-old Amnon repeats his mother's question, I tell them about America's poverty, ghettos on the outskirts of large cities, crime, anti-Semitism and the disparity between the lives of the rich and the poor. I do not want to paint a devastating picture of America, but I need to replace their images of streets paved in gold. When they ask so longingly about America, I fear they are giving up one dream, of finding a paradise in Israel, with another—America, land of the free.

Amnon is surprised by the darker side of America. He mentions rock groups, wrestlers, and basketball players I've never heard of. He can't believe that I'd never met Michael Jackson. When I tell him how large and crowded the cities are he says thoughtfully, "One probably feels alone there."

When I ask Batya and her mother if they prefer Ethiopia or Israel they both say Israel, refusing to explain why. The only thing that makes their contentment in Ma'alot incomplete is being separated from family. Gaveret Yamari still waits for the next airlift, which she hopes will bring her husband to Israel.

Elad shouts from his bicycle, "How was your trip?" As if he just noticed my return.

"*Kef*," I say as he speeds off in the other direction.

"He is so much more serious now," I observe.

Amnon agrees. "He is very quiet in school, but he does pretty well. He has a lot of Israeli friends."

"I have a lot of Israeli friends, too," Batya chimes in. Gaveret Yamari shakes her head, sadly, as if to say she does not have friends in the community.

In her house, where she makes her own food, she calls her children by their Amharic names. In the street she uses both names.

Amnon lives in two languages. "When I think about Ethiopia," he says, "I think in Amharic. When I think about Israel, I think in Hebrew. When I dream about Ethiopia, I dream in my first language."

On Friday evening, after Shabbat dinner with Elana Gabai, her husband Yehuda, and their three daughters, I return to my apartment early, looking forward to some time alone. My head still spins from Yehuda's question: When are you coming back to Israel to live? Out on the balcony I watch the lights in distant towns, the starlit sky until I'm interrupted by a knock on my door followed by whispers in Amharic. I recognize Ofer and Yosef's voices but do not answer the door. I want to be alone and my position with them isn't clear: A single American woman hanging out with Ethiopian boys/men late at night doesn't feel right. I don't know how they view me, so different from the women in their lives. The knocking finally stops.

Sabbath morning and a room filled with sun. I've come to appreciate my empty apartment that had seemed so barren to me when I first arrived. The mountains outside my window are like old friends who I feel inseparable from now that we are together again. Adrienne Rich's *Your Native Land, Your Life* is my most constant and welcome companion.

When the Sabbath leaves I finally open my door and walk to town. I find Batya waiting with Orit, Ora, and some of their friends for their buses back to their various boarding schools.

Ora announces, "Soon Batya will be the only one left. She'll be alone with Elad and her mother."

"*Miskena*," I say to Batya, "you poor thing."

"Don't worry about me. I have friends in school, and everyone else will come back to visit every two months."

"What about you Dina? Do you think you'll be getting married soon?"

"I don't have any plans. I hope some day."

"Did you know that the painter, Dave, is marrying a Moroccan woman who is five years older? I just can't believe it."

I wonder if this is the twelve-year-old Batya speaking or if this concept is just so foreign to her culturally. Often Ethiopian women

marry men who are considerably older, but I've never heard of the reverse.

"Batya, it's not that unusual." She looks at me with wide open eyes the way she had earlier in the month when I complained irreverently about the incompetence of the doctor I had seen for my "Ethiopian cough." I am no longer trying to give my friends a more polite image of me than what is true. For better or worse I am an American.

On the morning of my departure, Elad is nowhere to be found. I'm grateful that I've seen bits and pieces of how he is growing up. And I'm disappointed at how shy he sometimes is, how he spent more time spinning on his bicycle than sitting still with me. Yet I'm thankful that he no longer needs me the way I felt he had when he was a small boy. Now he shows others the way.

Batya comes with friends to my apartment to say goodbye. She seems suddenly shy as I hand her the food and dishes left over in my kitchen; I hug her and I let her go.

When I wave goodbye to Gaveret Yamari in the distance, I pray she will find a way to be more at home here while holding onto her beauty and her grace.

I came to Israel with a question this time; I'm not leaving with an answer but with many more questions. Teenagers still wear hand-me-down Israeli clothes and women wrap themselves in *shammas*. The families I helped welcome into this country four years ago are intact and thriving. They are studying, keeping house and moving forward. Others stand still as they wait for language, new homes, and family still in Ethiopia. I board the plane with heaviness. I don't know when I'll be back and if it will be a real return or simply another visit.

Has the dream come true? It is too early to know. The book is still being written.

September 8, 1989—Chicago

I don't know how to live my life anymore, what vegetables to put in my salad when nothing is fresh. During long breakfasts there is no Jerusalem wind pushing its way through my hair, no companion; my poetry books are closed. I don't want to wrap myself in nostalgia and wear her like a mourner's cloak. I have unraveled. My voice is blunt. It says I have no time for anything insignificant or unreal.

I don't know, spiritually, how to be a Jew or a poet in this country. In my dreams I live on borders between two worlds: Jerusalem and the territories, myself and the self I give to others, the Galil and Chicago. In the morning, the city noises are jarring. They insist on bringing me back or of holding me still in one world.

In Jerusalem, I walked by in my quick American pace while we were ordered to clear the area. I walked by as if I were above it, as if my tourist visa allowed me to turn my back.

In Chicago, I pick up the fallen red flower that lay on the sidewalk. It is red like pomegranate. I trust it will not explode in my hand, that someone picked it and dropped it because someone else was watching. It will bloom again in water. This is America. My flower will not explode.

April, 1990.

Thank G-d
Dear Dina,
How do you feel? How is it in Chicago and how is your work? How do your parents feel? Dina, everything is fine with me, thank G-d. Except for missing you. I am studying hard but doing well. Dina, my family feels good and they send their regards. I was very happy to receive your letter. Thank you very much and continue to stay in touch. [Or literally guard the connection] Dina, I hope that you will come and visit Israel again. Dina, have you gotten married yet or still not? And how are you getting along with your boyfriend? Dina, I miss you very much. I want to see you soon. Love you with all my heart (drawing of a heart) Osnat

And then in English she adds:

I hope that I see you soon. And I wish you a lot of success in your job.
Please tell me about your teaching and your students.

Osnat has come to understand the different parts of my life in America.

And as I unravel her sentences, she becomes more complex. I savor every word in her letters believing each one is a stepping stone to understanding her well-being. I consult dictionaries or copy down unfamiliar expressions and bring them to Ehran, across the courtyard, for translation. When I have trouble understanding large portions of her letters, I take a Hebrew class. I want to expand my language not only because of my love for it, but because it is my connection to Osnat and the rest of the Ethiopian community in Israel.

Operation Solomon
(1991)

The rebel forces in Ethiopia have captured major cities and are encroaching upon Addis Ababa. President Mengistu has fled. George Bush has paid billions of dollars to acting president of Ethiopia "bluntly insisting" that all remaining Jews are to leave. Over the next 48 hours 14,000 Ethiopian Jews will have landed in Israel via Operation Solomon.

—The New York Times, *May 1991*

In the beginning, the immigrants who arrived with Operation
Moses served as an important bridge for the newcomers,
between Ethiopian and Israeli culture. At best, they were there
to help translate for the newcomers and to make the transition
easier. The new immigrants, for example, did not care for the
food they had been given. One night some of the cooks in the
Diplomat tried to make injera. It took them only one hour (as
opposed to the twelve hours it generally takes) but it wasn't
authentic; the spices were Yemenite rather than Ethiopian. As
a result, family and friends from Operation Moses brought pure
Ethiopian spices and other Ethiopian foods. This made them
feel more comfortable and at home.

At worst, the immigrants from Operation Moses were
embarrassed at how barbaric their relatives suddenly seem to
them. For example, two Ethiopian men, one from Operation
Solomon and the other from Operation Moses, had gone to the
doctor because of the former one's illness. The gentleman from
Operation Moses was serving as his translator. When the Israeli
doctor asked what his symptoms were and the translator in turn
asked the sick gentleman, he replied that his stomach felt like
there were a bunch of oxen running around. The embarrassed
translator, who had now been in the country seven years,
translated it for the doctor simply as, "His stomach hurts."

—Yehuda
Jewish Agency Worker, June 1991

May 1991

At my friend Bernie's dining-room table in Los Angeles, I read the headlines of the *Los Angeles Times* about Operation Solomon. I've come for a reunion with part of the Katzenellenbogen family that has been cut off for decades. Now that we've found each other after a generation of feuding and silence, we can jump on a plane to be reunited. The Ethiopian families in Israel and Addis have been separated against their will. But now, after the miraculous airlift that took place over one Sabbath, Operation Moses has come full circle. When I ask my Ethiopian friends how they are, they will no longer say "Fine, except for my family still in Ethiopia." When I ask Osnat how she is, I imagine she will no longer say "Fine, except for missing you" the way she has in the letters she sent over past two years.

I've struggled with this question all winter. *Is it time to return?* During the Gulf War, while scuds fell on Tel Aviv, I was glued to the television, congregating toward groups of Jews and studying Hebrew in an *ulpan* in Chicago. Now, as I pour over the *Los Angeles Times*, returning is no longer a dream. The *aliyah* of 15,000 Ethiopian Jews to Israel in thirty-six hours gave me my answer. Only I wish I had been there for their arrival. I wish I could go back for more than six weeks. I want to witness the earliest stages of this group's absorption into Israel. I want to help them take their first steps onto Israeli soil, to be a part of their lives instead of an American woman who writes in a notebook, speaks Hebrew haltingly, and flits in and out of their lives. Part of me wants to resign from my teaching position at the university and stay in Israel now that the exodus has come full circle. I feel this desire in my body as I walk the manicured lawns of West LA, reunite with my father's family, the children of Saul's brother, Herman. All I can think about, now, is my larger family and the part that after centuries of longing, has finally come home to Israel.

Will this be the honeymoon period? Will the Ethiopian community finally be at home? Those of us who can choose, will we ever understand which is our true home?

In June, when I arrive in Israel, I think the presence of the new Ethiopian immigrants will be felt everywhere. I am wrong. One hundred and forty-five thousand Russians have also arrived in Israel over the past year. The country is recovering from a war. While scuds from Iraq were landing in their soil, Israelis had been forced to sit in sealed rooms with their hands folded in their laps.

In Jerusalem, more small groups of Ethiopian teenagers walk on Ben Yehuda Street. The newcomers, in two Jerusalem hotels, sit outside of the modern imitation limestone buildings. Tour groups from the United States are taken through the dim hallways of the Diplomat Hotel where the majority now live. In conversations with Israelis, their absorption is rarely mentioned. However, the miraculous nature of their arrival is what remains on people's minds when they think about their new neighbors from Ethiopia.

The Diplomat Hotel in Jerusalem has become synonymous with the words *Operation Solomon*. But with the influx of 15,000 immigrants into the country over one Sabbath, things are not as casual as they were two years ago. During my last visit, I wandered into any absorption center as either a visitor or a journalist. Now, I need permission from the Jewish Agency, an appointment, and a chaperone. As a result, I spend days making phone calls and explaining my intentions before I get an appointment.

Yehudah, a Jewish Agency worker who has been involved with Operation Solomon since it was in its earliest planning stages in 1989, finally makes appointments for me at absorption centers throughout the country and agrees to serve as my tour guide at the Diplomat Hotel.

I wait for Yehudah in front of the building in Talpiot, not too far from my own absorption center of 1984, Ramat Rachel. Men and women sit on the benches dressed in traditional garb: the women have green etchings on their necks, typical for the women of Gondar Province from where many of the newest immigrants originated. They nod at me politely, less shy than the women from Operation Moses. Many attended the schools in Addis Ababa that the Jewish Agency set up to teach the Jewish community some Hebrew and facts about Israeli life.

Yehudah tells me the story of Operation Solomon:

On May 24, 1991, when the Ethiopian government fell, the Jews were told to arrive at the Jewish Agency without any belongings. Some were told, for the first time, that they were going to Eretz Yisrael, the land of Israel. Others were told that they were going to get shots. When one man discovered the truth of why they were being gathered, he ran back to sell his house. As a result, he missed the last plane to Israel.

The others arrived in time, and three planes landed every hour to take the Ethiopians to Israel. There were forty-one flights all together, all El Al, except for one symbolic Ethiopian plane. Mattresses were laid out and the Ethiopians were loaded over capacity with numbers attached to their foreheads to identify them and to which group they belonged. Their names were checked off a list before they were loaded onto the plane. The military operation moved smoothly; 1,000 people fit into one jumbo jet. Besides moments of last-minute panic and converts begging to come along, the operation took place with extreme efficiency. Seven babies were born on the way. The Ethiopians behaved with dignity and patience until they arrived in stunned silence and elation at Ben Gurion Airport on Shabbat, May 25. Some bent down, wept, and kissed the earth. Some blinked into the sunlight in silence. Old men had trouble descending the steps of the jumbo jet and were escorted by excited Israelis who had come to help. Israelis had come from all over the country to witness the arrival of the people who overnight had changed from victims to heroes because of the miraculous nature of the airlift. People have said again and again that no other group of Jews could have helped the operation move so smoothly. Israeli men and women dropped their cynicism and wept at the sight of the mystical people who had come from what they suddenly saw as a mystical land.

From the airport, the new immigrants were taken to absorption centers throughout the country. At rest stops along the way, cookies and juice were available. At first, the Olim

(immigrants) did not approach the food although they had not eaten in a long time. When the workers finally handed the food to them, they ate it.

Many of the absorption center buildings were former hotels that the government rented in order to temporarily house the new immigrants. When they finally arrived at their absorption centers they were greeted by well-wisher Israelis who had come from all over the country to drop off clothes and food. Some family members were also waiting at the absorption centers. There was much confusion in trying to reunite families since many did not have family names. The reunions that did take place were dramatic and moving: fathers hugged sons and mothers wept at the sight of their now Israeli children. The distances that had grown between families would be felt on the morning after.

The doctor in the absorption center clinic notes the importance of a translator for immigrants dealing with medical issues because they do not locate particular parts of their bodies. They say headache when they really mean back or shoulder ache. They say heart when they mean stomach. Some of the newcomers have chronic illness, but mostly their problems stem from new germs, acclimating to a new environment. Because the Jewish Agency had also set up clinics in Addis Ababa, immigrants arrived in a healthier state than those of seven years ago. They did not have to walk through the deserts of Sudan or spend time in transit camps, as did the Operation Moses group.

When Yehudah stops speaking, I am still caught in the moment he described a few minutes ago, when men and women got off the plane and kissed the ground. Although this is a common response to landing in Israel, for this community and because of the nature of the airlift, I feel it so profoundly I can't speak. I also can't let go of certain Holocaust images like names on a list and stamps on foreheads rather than wrists. This time Jews were being rounded to go up to Israel rather than down to a hell of fire and ash.

I can see Yehudah tire from the telling. With wet eyes, we sip tea and then head to the clinic where we finally reach the children. We are welcomed into their *gan* with hugs and their paintings of cows and hands. On the walls are paintings of the huge planes that had brought them, just a month earlier, to Israel.

Among the children I feel the energy and hope of Operation Moses; the unabashed excitement of those who don't know of the long journey that still lay ahead for their families. The older children who months before gathered food in their villages in Gondar are now involved in computer games. This time, no child sits alone, longing for a parent who remains in Ethiopia.

"When do they get to leave the hotels and begin their lives?" I ask Yehudah as we walk the dim hallways where the adults sit in silence.

"The newcomers are not allowed to leave the center for six months to a year depending upon their absorption. Soon the adults will begin *ulpan*. They want to give them sufficient enrichment first," Yehudah explains. When I look at him curiously he says, "I couldn't go to Ethiopia and live without first learning how to make *injera* and speak Amharic."

"It just seems like such a long time."

The atmosphere on the streets of Jerusalem is even less cheery than two years ago. The Intifada has spread, no longer just stabbings on the border of Jerusalem but in Netanya, the center of the country, as well. In the overcrowded streets, the mood of people shopping and pushing onto buses is downright crabby. People spent their spring in sealed rooms hiding from the possibility of chemical weapons and the probability of scud attacks. Everyone, not just the new immigrants feels the lack of housing and jobs. My American friends who have lived in Israel for decades say the country is going down the tubes. While they had been urging me for years to make *aliyah*, they now muse about their own departures.

In my rented room on Rambam Street I'm awakened by what sounds like the city falling on itself, the echo of an enormous tumbling down. I imagine boulders being thrown down the Mount of Olives, stones being thrown on the borders of the country. When I become fully awake, I realize it is only the sounds of buses moving down the steep streets on their way to the center of town.

Each day I walk among those narrow streets that almost made me leave America for good in 1984. But I'm not longing for my Jerusalem of 1984. I'm longing for the Jerusalem of ancient dreams, the mystical Jerusalem that the Ethiopian Jews have longed for over centuries.

This time, I wonder what the dead poets would think if they heard the sounds of buses in Jerusalem, what Bialik and Tchernichovsky would think of their dreams of a peaceful Jerusalem, swallowed by the dark air the bus exhales. For the dead poets and the old Zionists—I imagine during my most romantic moments—poetry, dreams and ideals are all that mattered. They memorized the holy texts, even if they didn't live by their rules. They knew the words and the rhythms. They worshipped and worked the land. The air was still enough to hear the voices of the jackals. Their footfall was hard and steady on the yet-to-be-paved roads. As Bialik described it, the very dust came alive under their "bare and sacred feet."

From my porch on Rambam Street, I continue to wonder: What would the Zionists of 1905 think about the new immigrants from Ethiopia? What would they think about the immigrants who came from Morocco in the 1950s, the ones who still live in their own cultures in development towns like Ma'alot in the north of the country? What about the Gulf War when Israel sat with her hands folded in her lap? When I dream on my porch, or walk Jerusalem's sun-drenched streets, I want to write these questions on a piece of paper, but I am too exhausted. I want to write this in a poem, but I don't know which voice to speak in. I feel closer to the dead poets than to the living activists who surround me at the *Tikkun* conference I am attending. I am living in two Jerusalems, the Jerusalem of ancient dreams and the one of shattered illusions.

At night, I do not go to discos with the other Americans. I do not march with the Women in Black, an anti-war group. I walk the streets with my dear poet friend Robert and listen to stories about the lives of poets. I imagine Bialk, Buber, and Alterman rising from the dead into the cool Jerusalem evening. I escape into a past that I imagine to be more vibrant, more essential, more true; a people whom the writer Amos Elon describes as "secular rabbis of a new faith of redemption." Some nights I walk Rabbi Kook Street enticed by nearby cafés, bewildered by the sound of English rising from the tables. Like Ben Yehuda, the founder of modern Hebrew, who kept his child isolated so she wouldn't be polluted by other languages, I long to hear the holy tongue.

Only when I read the accounts of the miraculous airlift which brought 14,000 Ethiopians into Israel during one Sabbath, and forget about the dim hallways the *olim* now walk through and think instead about the dream of the ingathering of exiles, do I remember that there is still a purpose to all of the noise and music of this country. If my dreams of finding home on kibbutz had been dashed in 1985, and my dream of making Ma'alot the new shelter for dreams was shattered in 1989, in 1991 my dreams still connect to the lives of my Ethiopian friends, whom it is taking me so long to reach this visit. And even if the excitement of Operation Solomon has dissipated with the reality of daily life for most Israelis, I am still aglow in the aftermath of this miracle and excited to learn how this news will effect Osnat and Elad and their families.

❦

At the neighborhood market, buying flowers to fill my room for the Sabbath, I look up when I feel someone's eyes on me. It is the man I'd met on the bus seven years ago. He had given me his knit sweater and helped me translate the poet Dahlia Ravikovitch's poems on our way back to Jerusalem from Ashkelon. I thought I had fallen in love with him as we watched the full moon over Jerusalem. Although I learned quickly that I could not trust him,

he remained my ideal of the perfect Israeli lover: dark, sensitive, handsome, intellectual and strong.

This time we recognize each other the way we had even before we'd met and smile the shy and sly way we had on the seventh of December 1984 when we had taken the #7 bus to his home. We look at each other in amazement.

"So you're back in Jerusalem and you still love red anemone," he says with a laugh.

"Yeah, I'm here for a conference and other stuff." I say, still a bit shocked at the sight of him. In 1989, I barely thought of him.

"I'm still not married," he volunteers. "Dina, you look good, more mature, fuller, but really, really good."

"Do you still live in the neighborhood?" I ask.

"Yeah, I live on #7 Ibn Ezra. A few blocks down."

"This is getting too weird. I'm staying on #7 Rambam Street. What is the meaning of number seven again? Doesn't it have some mystical significance?" I ask.

"I don't know. I think it just represents the distance between us."

That evening in my apartment, we look at each other again. In this city where I'm trying to make reality into dreams of other generations, this man who through the years I had begun to believe was only a dream, is sitting on the floor of my room. In 1984, there had been so few words. This time I give him the story of the past seven years of my life.

He listens quietly and responds, "You've become too much of a feminist."

As the night wears on, my image of Boaz, like my image of the Jerusalem of 1991, and my Ethiopian friends' image of Jerusalem 1984, shifts. Jerusalem is not only a mystical city but a bustling metropolis and a hotbed of tension. Boaz, I realize, is not the ideal man but hard and cynical. He is disillusioned with women and with the safety of his Jerusalem life. Yet he is beginning to feel like a brother.

Days later, in his room on Ibn Ezra Street, after we listen to the news I say to Boaz, "I hope we don't have to give up the Golan."

"We? What do you mean we? You live safely in Chicago. When the scuds fell you were in America, next to windows, walking and breathing freely, going on with your life..."

"You're right, Boaz." But I was glued to the television for a month. In my classroom at the university when my students called out from their Walkmen about how far we had entered the desert (in Saudi Arabia), I cared, mostly about how many scuds had fallen on Israel. When I didn't speak to my Israeli friend Ehran for a week it felt like months had passed, and I said to him "we haven't spoken in three scuds." I had no words to tell him that I understood his pain as he worried about his family in Tel Aviv. I couldn't imagine his daily fear and so I felt I had no right to speak. Between my friend and I there were two languages, but we had reached the place where uncertainty and sadness had surpassed both.

Boaz maintains that Israel is not my country, that our commonality is that we are Jews. I say it is the Jewish country and so it is my home, too. He tells me that if there is a war I am invited to share his sealed room with him. He takes me into the kitchen which is also the hallway connecting the main room and the bathroom, places his mask over my head and tells me about the hours he spent like that. I can't breathe and there are no windows.

Free of masks, Boaz makes ice cream sundaes for the two of us. When I volunteer to make the coffee he says, "I know you will make it incorrectly like an American. You'll use too much coffee and won't leave enough room for milk."

"You'd really have trouble with Ethiopian coffee. It is brewed straight from the bean with no room for cream."

"Dina, I'm amazed that you're still involved with the Ethiopians. I remember when you first proposed to work with the new immigrants seven years ago. I thought you were crazy for moving to Ma'alot. What are you doing now?"

"I'm trying to update a lengthy article I've written called "Five Years after Operation Moses." And I'm trying to find out how the newest immigrants are doing after being in the country two months."

Boaz, a social worker in Jerusalem, listens for a while. "There is a beautiful Ethiopian woman who comes to my office. I'm trying to help her find a job."

"Really? What's her name?"

"I can't tell you. I have to respect the confidentiality of my client," Boaz says with uncharacteristic formality.

On my way out of his apartment that evening, I am still wondering who this woman might be. Boaz invites me to return any time.

〽

"You look a bit out of sorts," Robert says after greeting me at his door with two of his cats.

"Yeah, I'm sorry I'm late. I got lost today, in the Arab Quarter, I mean I went there by accident, unknowingly."

"You know I've been going to the Old City for what...more than forty years, and it is only now that I know my way around. But I don't go there much anymore, since the uprising. And Dina, you shouldn't go there alone right now. If you want to go to the shuk, I'll join you. The small amount of Arabic I know helps a lot."

"Good. Let's do that together."

Soon the fear and incomprehensibility of the day vanishes, and I'm lost instead in the lives of Auden, Eliot, and Buber and the present day Israeli poets. It is Wednesday and like every Wednesday evening for the past 30 years, Robert's friend Arthur is expected for dinner. When he arrives with a package of dates, we gather around the table and rave over Robert's grilled fish with wild rice.

As we lean into our wicker chairs digesting our meal, Robert reads us a stanza from a poem he had written from Puerto Rico in the fifties:

1. The Impossible Sea

Beyond these walls, the home I could not build,
The window open on the legendary sea,
You wander, not wound in coiling springs of time
Deep in a mirror world, in your own eyes drowned;

"That's lovely, Robert, different from your other work, less formal, more imagistic. I really like it."

"Well thank you, dear. It's funny but I've been writing a lot about the past. I forget things, like what I had for breakfast this morning, but I can remember my days in Europe, during the war, as if they were yesterday. In fact if you weren't here, Arthur and I would be talking about those days like a bunch of old men!"

"Speak for yourself Robert," Arthur says laughing. "I'll always be a decade younger than you," Arthur teases his former professor. "And Dina will always be more than four decades younger. And so, youngest poet, have you brought us some poems?"

"I've been working on this Pomegranate poem since I've been here," I say handing it over to the master critic. He reads my fifty-line poem quietly and then hands it back. "I think the poem really begins here."

> This is not a bed of Pomegranates
> But a grove of small bombs.

"You're probably right, but I'll have to think about that. You know how hard it is for me to let go of things." By the time I leave Robert's home, my fifty-line poem is only twenty-five-lines long.

When I finally reach Eric by phone in Petach Tikvah, I learn that Osnat left me a message on his answering machine with her current phone number. I am awakened from my Jerusalem slumber, running down Karen Hayesod Street to a quieter phone booth on Jabotinsky Street. When I hear Osnat's quiet voice my exhaustion vanishes. She asks me in perfect Hebrew how it feels to be back in the country. "It's wonderful." For the first time those words feel true.

❧

I had forgotten, or was too busy to notice, but entering Osnat's town of Ramat Eliyahu is like entering a desert, not a godly one like the Sinai but a desert with ugly, identical buildings, the emptiness

of a place where people are just beginning to build lives with bricks and mortar. And in this desert is the home of the Melesa family.

I do not have trouble finding Osnat's home this time; I go by memory. Osnat greets me at the door and after hugs, we look at each other for a moment taking in each other's changes. Osnat's braided hair is twirled around her head. She wears a blue-jean skirt, which falls to the middle of her calf, and a blue and white striped football jersey with red letters. In her ears are white pearl earrings, like the earrings she had asked me for seven years ago, the earrings I couldn't give her.

At Eric's apartment in Petah Tikvah, I had changed clothes many times the way I would when I was trying to decide what to wear to my various lives in Ma'alot. At first I put on shorts because the heat is unbearable, but I know that would be too immodest. Then I try on a summer dress but it feels too tight and revealing. I settle on a green khaki skirt that falls to my knees and a short-sleeved shirt and the earrings that Charleen had made in South Africa while she was pregnant with her daughter. They are stuffed chickens: cute but not elegant. African style, exotic, but not something that I thought would elicit envy.

Osnat ushers me over to the couch in the living room, points to the bowl of fruit and urges me to take some. She doesn't ask me if I want lunch this time but disappears into the kitchen to prepare my meal. Her mother replaces her, sitting in a chair across from me and smiling. She still doesn't speak Hebrew, but I feel from her gentle presence that I am welcome. She holds her baby son, the newest arrival, with wrinkles around his eyes that make him look like an old man. He is now one of three *sabras* in their family.

Osnat carries a silver tray with pita, hummus and Jerusalem salad. She remembers my favorite Israeli meal. Although I know it is their tradition for the guest to eat first and alone, I still feel uncomfortable. As I dip the pita into the hummus, the other children, Liat, fifteen, and Tovah, four, are glued to the television. The eldest, Shai, a soldier in his twenties, is home on leave from

the army. He had recently been in a car accident where he lost a tooth. He was in the other room taking a siesta.

Osnat pulls out the family photo album, and as we flip through the pages, I am struck by the photo of a very thin model-like woman with long Rastafarian braids.

"Who's that?" I ask.

"Yael." Osnat answers matter-of-fact.

"She's changed!"

Osnat agrees. The last time I saw Yael she was a chubby fifteen-year-old in loose and worn Israeli clothes and a short Afro. Osnat continues to turn the pages to pictures of her younger siblings but I ask to turn back to Yael.

"What is Yael doing in Jerusalem?"

Osnat pauses for a moment and says, "She's a *ganenet,* nursery school teacher," and continues to turn pages.

Tovah, her younger sister, says to Osnat in Hebrew, "Why did you say that Yael runs a *gan* when really she wipes tables?" She makes a swishing movement with her arm across the table.

Osnat, in a stern voice, says, "*Tafsiski*"—stop it.

I pretend that I don't understand their conversation and grow more concerned about Yael who I had not been able to see during my last visit. I decide to return to Jerusalem that week in order to visit with her. Osnat scribbles her phone number onto a piece of paper for me.

While I start wondering about Yael, and how she's really getting along in Jerusalem, I feel proud of Osnat who is working hard and doing well in school. This week she will take her *bagrut* exam that high school students are required to score well on in order to graduate and attend university. When she finishes high school she plans to begin *Sherut Leumi,* a national service for religious girls in lieu of army service. Now that the new *olim* have arrived, she wants to do her service in the Negev where many of them will be living. She will teach them Hebrew and help them make the transition into Israeli life. She will be the one to welcome them home.

A new member of the household who had been taking a nap joins us, a sister who Osnat had never spoken of before. Today,

Osnat refers to her as *Hadasha* – the new one. She arrived in Israel with Operation Solomon. She had been staying at the Diplomat Hotel until her family convinced the officials to allow her to go home with them. There is something in Ziona's face that reminds me of Yael. She is shy and sits some distance from Osnat, myself, and the other family members who've returned to the family room. Although she does not speak Hebrew, she smiles when I speak to her.

Osnat walks me back to the bus stop.

"Good luck on your *bagrut*. I'm sure you'll do fine." I say reassuringly.

"I'm really nervous—it's only a few days away but I've studied so hard."

"Let's try to see each other again—maybe in Jerusalem or Tel Aviv—before I leave the country."

"Okay. Where will you go next?"

"First I'm going back to Jerusalem for just a day or so. I really want to see Yael. Then I'll visit your cousins, the Yamari family. And after that I want to visit more absorption centers where the new *olim* are staying."

"*Kol hakavod* (All the honor)," Osnat says, smiling bashfully.

When my bus approaches I wrap my arms around her thin frame.

In Boaz's apartment, where I stay during this short return to Jerusalem, I pull out the crumpled piece of paper with Osnat's handwriting on it and try to call Yael. On the third try, unsure of the last number she had written down, I give up. When Boaz returns from work that evening I tell him I'm having trouble reaching Yael, and how frustrated I am.

"Did you say her name is Yael?"

"Yeah, why do you ask?"

"Well, I must confess that the woman who comes to see me is also called Yael, but it can't be the same person. That would be too much of a coincidence."

I tell Boaz as much as I can about her. I describe the woman who I had seen in the photographs rather than the chubby girl in hand-me-downs that I had known. Boaz listens in silence, goes to his phone book and then asks me to show him the number I had been trying to reach. He compares the two and then silently changes the "3" which had ended the number that Osnat had given me to a "2."

The kabbalists had taught me that spring that when you give up, having reached the highest rung on the ladder of your own ability, something else takes over, a higher power and you are then able to complete your task. I did not have the correct number to reach Yael; it had gotten lost in my translation of Osnat's handwriting, but fate had reunited me with her therapist.

Although Boaz remains secretive, there is too much I want to know.

"You know you can help me by telling me in advance how Yael is doing. I'm feeling so nervous about calling her."

"Yael is bitter and tired of being patronized. She lives in a building in Talpiot that is partially subsidized by the government. It generally houses new immigrants who are more established or who have been in the country for a long time. Yael has high expectations and wants to further her education. I'm helping her find a job. Her mother is still in Ethiopia because her grandmother wants to die there. Don't patronize her. Don't try too hard to help her."

"Her mother is still in Ethiopia? What do you mean?"

"I only know what she tells me."

"But Osnat's mother is here, and Yael is her sister. That's strange. I guess there are still a lot of things I don't know about their family."

I am relieved that Yael is okay—just struggling a bit financially like many of my friends. And I am beginning to see there are more mysteries to unravel. Mostly I am grateful that I have the right numbers to reach her.

Boaz continues, "I told her to get a job as a model or selling clothes. I also told her to go on interviews in person. On the phone

she has a strong Ethiopian accent. In person, they will be overcome by her looks," he adds with a sheepish grin.

The next morning the changed woman who I'd seen in Osnat's family album, the slender and striking twenty-two-year-old woman who is counseled by my friend, greets me in the lobby of her apartment. I recognize the enveloping smile of the chubby teenager I had known. She is stunning, with long braids and bright red lipstick. I admire her apartment along with the abstract and vibrant paintings on her wall. She tells me that the paintings were made by some artist friends from America and Europe and that her Israeli boyfriend gave her the furniture and the plants.

"I just broke up with him after three years," she adds.

"Really? Why did you break up?"

"Well he's thirty and Ashkenazi. He's nice but not always so good to me. I want someone younger. Someone new," she says looking away. "Dina, sit down, eat some fruit."

"It sounds like you have a lot of friends," I say reveling in the sweetness of an apricot while scoping out the rest of her apartment.

"Yeah. Most of my friends are Israeli because Ethiopians don't live in Jerusalem. But I still speak on the phone all the time with my Ethiopian friends who I went to school with in Ma'alot.

"And your family?" I ask.

"Yeah—we're still close. I visit them for every holiday and my sisters visit me in Jerusalem. It's like I have two different lives. In Jerusalem I go to pubs and discos and dress how I want. In my father's house I still live by his rules. I dress *dati*—you know, with my arms covered and long skirts. My father thinks that's how I dress in Jerusalem as well. When I told him I want to be a model, he said it isn't a proper line of work. When I told him I wanted to go to America with a friend, he said I couldn't go. What can I do? I accept his commands."

While Whitney Houston sings about love from the stereo, I flip through her album of provocative photos. There are occasional photos of family and friends but mostly just Yael, in tight revealing clothes.

On the wall is an old black and white photograph of a woman. Instinct tells me the woman in the photo is her mother, of whom Boaz had spoken, still in Ethiopia. When I ask about it, she says it is her sister. I'm not sure why she doesn't want me to know that she and Osnat have different mothers. But then I think about all of the information I leave out when I am describing my life to them.

"Yael, I understand that one of your sisters just arrived with Operation Solomon! I met her at your home when I was visiting Osnat."

"Yeah, she and my younger sister Marta will come and spend Shabbat with me. We are so excited she is finally out of the Diplomat Hotel. Last month, when we went to pick her up, they gave us a really hard time. The workers there kept saying that she needed to be enriched first and that they couldn't let her go on direct absorption (to a home rather than an absorption center.) We tried to politely convince them that we could take care of her at home in Ramat Eliyahu since the rest of us have been here seven years now. They refused. They do not allow Ethiopians to go on direct absorption—only the Russians. Finally, I returned with my father one evening and was rude to them. After that, they let me take her home. If you treat them with honor they refuse you. If you are rude they do what you say!"

"That's really amazing. I'm so glad she got to go home."

"In an old photo album I have a picture of Jackie," Yael changes the subject again. "Do you ever see her?"

"No, we lost touch years ago. No one knows where she is."

"I miss those days. We all lived close together, and you were my teacher," she says, wrapping her braids into a scarf. "Dina, when you left Ma'alot, Osnat cried for an entire day."

"She did?" I ask, surprised. I remember her sadness but she had been so good at holding back her feelings.

"She stayed in her room all day until she had no more tears. She didn't eat or sleep."

"Osnat is very shy now, isn't she?"

"Yeah. She is very quiet. She doesn't talk a lot."

"So Yael, are you working now?"

"Well I worked in the *gan* with children, but it was very hard and so I quit. Now I am looking for work and studying in order to take the *bagrut*. I never finished school. If you remember I wasn't a good student."

"No, I don't remember that." I do remember that she didn't have a Bat Mitzvah and begin to wonder if it is somehow connected to the fact that she had come to Israel without her mother but with her father and his second wife.

Boaz told me her unemployment was running out and they were going to be strict about ending it on time in order to force her to get a job and not remain dependent upon the government.

The Canadian absorption center where Yael lives is adjacent to the *tayelet*, a long and hilly walking path that overlooks the Old City. When we agree to go for a walk there, I imagine we will just fly out the door, but Yael prepares by changing into a pink sexy top, jeans, and long sparkly earrings. She freshens her red lipstick. I suddenly feel bland in my gray T-shirt and purple leggings.

Once outside, Yael gets quieter. Wherever we turn, men, especially construction workers, call out to her. Two Israeli men tell me in Hebrew to tell her that they think black women are beautiful. They assume I am the Israeli and she the American. When it's time for me to meet my poet friend Betsy and for Yael to do errands in the city, we get on the crowded bus and Yael walks straight to the back where there isn't room for both of us. The casual conversation we'd had all day has ceased; she barely makes eye contact with me. When we get to my stop, I kiss her on the cheek and we agree to stay in touch.

❧

"Tell me where you are and I'll come get you," Batya finally says, frustrated by my American Hebrew. As I wait next to a bus stop in Kfar Saba, the town of the Yamaris' new home, I flash back to all of the different Batyas I had known for such brief periods of time: the tiny eight-year-old with large frightened eyes who I carried into the sea in Nahariya for the first time; the plump

eleven-year-old with an Afro who had come up to me at the absorption center remembering me from four years before; the girl who always watched over Elad and helped her mother in the kitchen; my friend with whom I loved sitting in front of the absorption center just "being."

The fifteen-year-old Batya with long braids and a green jersey who has come to take me to her new home has the spunk and freshness of an Israeli teenager— only the toughness is replaced by gracefulness. We greet each other Ethiopian style, a kiss on each cheek.

"How are you? How is the family?"

"Great. A sister of mine arrived with Operation Solomon; also, my father arrived."

"Congratulations," I say, stunned by the news and surprised that neither Osnat nor Yael had mentioned it. "My G-d, Elad must have been three and you must have been eight the last time you saw him. When is he coming home?"

"I was very excited to see him, but there is a problem with my father. He has another wife now and three small children. He got tired of waiting." By now Batya is walking ahead of me, staring at the ground.

"I'm so sorry, Batya. How's your mother doing?"

"In a strange way my mother feels better now because she does not have to wonder about it, about if my father will come home. She knows now that he won't."

I feel so sad for them, I don't know what else to say.

"This is it!" Batya says, pointing to a four-story newer white cement-slab building surrounded by pink azalea bushes and a small lawn. Elad, who is outside waiting, walks up to me smiling. I rush over and take his hand, holding it for a moment. I want to hug him like I would when he was a child but his body language says a handshake will suffice.

"So Elad," I say, climbing the three stories to their apartment. "What's new?"

"Nothing," he answers quietly.

"Nothing?"

Batya turns to Elad. "Dina knows about our father."

"Mazel tov, Elad!"

"*Todah*, thank you," he says sadly.

When Elad enters the apartment before us, Batya whispers, "Elad is angry that out father will not be coming home."

Inside, Orit, home from boarding school for the summer, greets us in her tight jeans and gold chains.

"Mazel tov! What a wonderful new home," I say walking over to where Elad urges me to sit down on the checkered absorption center-like couch. Batya has already set out a pitcher of juice, glasses and a bowl of fruit. On the wall across from us, a set of shelves holds a large colored television and family photographs. As my eyes scan the walls where more family photos hang, Elad urges me to eat. When my glass becomes half-empty, he fills it to the top.

"Let me see your view," I say walking over to the white lacy curtains that cover a large window.

"It's a field of squash and then after that is a village." Elad explains. "Sometimes we go to pick vegetables but we run home because it's dangerous. There are Arabs there in that village. At night, when all the lights are on, it's very pretty. But I miss Ma'alot," he adds thoughtfully. "I miss the people, the weather, the mountains, my first home in Israel. I also remember your roommate with the long brown hair."

Outside of Amharic, the Yamaris only speak Hebrew. Unlike Yael, they never throw in English words. I understand Elad, who speaks slowly and without a strong accent, the best. When I make a mistake, he patiently corrects my Hebrew. Two years ago he barely spoke.

"Where is your mother?" I ask now that we are all gathered together in one room.

"Our mother went to the Diplomat Hotel," Orit answers. "She's visiting our older sister, who arrived with Operation Solomon."

"Mazel tov! I didn't know you had another sister who arrived."

Everyone grows quiet. Batya says to Orit, "I told her," meaning I was in on the fact that their father had arrived but would not be coming home.

I feel a sadness among this family that I had not witnessed before. The cycle of coming together and breaking apart continues. Their dream of coming to Israel was tarnished by the separation of their family. And now that those left behind were finally brought to Israel, there are new breakages, more changes and still more waiting. Ten-year-old Elad now misses his mother who is in Jerusalem caring for her eldest daughter from her first marriage, the newest arrival.

"Do you think getting used to life in Israel is easier for the newcomers from Operation Solomon or for your group?" I ask them.

"I think it's easier for the new ones because they already have family here," Batya says and Elad agrees.

Orit adds, "Earlier in the month I volunteered at the Diplomat for a few weeks. There were so many people helping. Excuse me, I better get that," she says running for the ringing phone and then disappearing for a long time.

On TV an Israeli sitcom is playing. I do not take the time to understand the Hebrew or read the English subtitles, so I'm confused when Batya suddenly bursts out laughing.

"What did they say?" I ask.

"One of the characters said something about Tiberias and that all of the Ethiopians live there. It's amazing the things people say. Like we all live in the same place." Batya says.

"Well the Israelis like us better than the Russians." Elad chimes in. "The Russians eat pig. Dina, do you remember the food that *we* eat?"

"Yes. *Injera.* Do you still make *injera?*"

"Of course," he says running off to the kitchen and then returning with a large plate of it that Batya had been preparing all morning.

"You don't have to eat all of it," Elad assures me. "Eat want you want and then stop when you want."

I dip the bread into the spicy sauce in the center and cautiously take my first bite. I'm amazed by how much I enjoy it this time, how for once, I don't have to pretend.

When I finish my meal, Elad brings out *Louis the Fish*, the book I gave him two years ago. I am touched to see he wrote his name in it, that it made it through their move from Ma'alot and that he held onto the memory of our last visit. This time, *he* tells *me* the story of Louis Fish—in Hebrew. He knows the story by heart. Orit returns from her phone call and sits with me during Elad's recitation. She asks me what I do in America.

"I'm a writer and a teacher." Batya who had also listened quietly to the story and to my conversation with Orit asks me if I wrote *Louis the Fish*.

"No. I didn't write *Louis the Fish*. I write poems, true life stories." Everyone gets very quiet.

An Israeli neighbor from upstairs comes down for Batya to French-braid her hair. This is a daily ritual. As she pulls up a stool next to us she gushes, "Batya is so wonderful. She makes the most beautiful braids."

We watch as Batya's nimble fingers create an exquisite design in this young woman's hair.

"Dina, let me do your hair now."

"That would be great. It's so wild from all of this humidity."

It is a relief as she pulls the long curly strands into tight controlled braids. Next to us, Elad listens to Michael Jackson on his boom box with head phones on so as not to disturb the rest of us.

Orit returns again in high fashion jeans, a tight white shirt and more gel on her stylishly short hair. She is going off to meet someone.

"Who is he?" Elad asks like a concerned father. "Who was on the phone before?" She doesn't answer him but quickly leaves the apartment.

When I get ready to leave for Eric's apartment in Petach Tikvah, my temporary home in the center of the country, Elad protests. "Won't you be coming with us to see my brother Tuvia?" I had learned earlier that their eldest brother from Gaveret Yamri's first marriage lives down the block with his family.

"Dina has friends in Petach Tikvah. She has to go back," Batya explains to him.

I want to stay with Elad for a long time but don't know how to. I wish, again, that I had been there when he changed from the wild child to the gallant boy who had been my host all afternoon. I wish I had been there for all of the moments in between or on the day when Hebrew first began to flow naturally from his lips.

"Why don't we have a reunion in Jerusalem before I leave the country? We can invite Osnat and Yael—we can all be together in one place again."

Although we all know the impossibility of this small dream we agree to meet at the end of the month. Once outside, Batya and Elad grow quiet. I kiss Batya on each cheek, and she asks Elad to walk me all the way to the bus. When we get to my stop I shake his hand.

"I'll be okay from here, you don't have to wait for the bus. Thanks so much for everything, Elad. I'll see you soon." He walks away and then turns back to wave again. I wish that he were the four-year-old who I could carry in my arms—who I knew how to help grow up.

※

The artist Alemu Eshtie now lives in Hod HaSharon, a fifteen-minute bus ride from the Yamari family, and on the way to Eric's home in Petach Tikvah. This short balding man with a gracious smile greets me at the bus stop in the center of another small town outside of Tel Aviv. Two years ago I interviewed him on the phone so although I feel I know him, I've never seen his face. When he sees me he reaches out his hand to shake mine and leads me past the cooing of roosters to his home.

"We are the only Ethiopian family who lives here," Alemu announces as we approach his three-story building.

We sit down in his pleasant and spacious living room, and I know I am comfortable because my Hebrew is fluid. On his wall is a poster that says, "Come to Ethiopia" with a photograph of

a beautiful light-skinned Ethiopian woman with straight black hair. Next to the poster hang Alemu's paintings, a study in contrasts depicting the stark reality of his Ethiopia. I think about his painting I saw two years ago at Hilai, of a man preparing to leave his home. These paintings spoke of the rest of his journey.

When Alemu returns from the kitchen with a large bowl of peaches, apricots and plums, he tells the stories behind his paintings. The first one is a large image of his father climbing a mountain.

"My father's image looms large over the mountain he is trying to climb. Behind him the other climbers, as well as the mountain, grow smaller and smaller. You see my father, who died on his walk from Ethiopia to Sudan, had grown larger than life, had become a martyr, a hero who died in the middle of the desert."

The painting evokes the pain of his loss, the courage of the older men who tried to take this journey and the tragedy of the older generation who "died in the desert," either literally during the brutal walk to Sudan or figuratively in Israel, where they have not been able to build a life. His paintings speak of this more profoundly than any words have been able to thus far.

In the far corner of his wall is a painting of Israel, the place where the men in the previous two paintings of Gondar and Sudan had been journeying. The painting is based on a photograph of a long road with a soldier, Alemu, crouching in the corner.

"Alemu, this is really amazing work. What are you painting now?"

"I don't have time to paint now. During the year I teach art in the high school, here in town. Now, during summer break, I give lectures about Israeli life for the new immigrants from Ethiopia. I teach about *Shoah*, the Holocaust. Sometimes I work as a translator at the Diaspora Museum in Tel Aviv. And my wife works in a pill factory in Hod HaSharon."

On the mantel is a photograph of Alemu's sabra son on a tricycle. Another boy stands next to him who Alemu describes as his son's best friend. "He is like a brother to him," Alemu says as we gaze at the photos of the young boys, one black Israeli and the

other white. Also on the mantel is a beautiful woven basket like the ones I had seen in many other Ethiopian households.

"Alemu—this basket is the largest and most intricately woven I've seen; the material feels different somehow."

"It was made in Ethiopia instead of Israel. In Israel they don't have the same quality of materials as they do in Ethiopia." He pauses for a moment and then his eyes light up as he continues. "My sister made the basket in Ethiopia. She just arrived with Operation Solomon and brought it as a gift!"

"Congratulations. What wonderful news!"

"Yes. I was so excited when I heard the news of her arrival and then discovered later that she was staying in an absorption center in Netanya not too far from here. It was so good to see her. We had been separated since 1983 when I came to Israel." He stops for a minute, rubs his hand over his short remaining hair and then continues more soberly.

"My sister doesn't understand that things are different now. In Ethiopia when we had been separated for a few weeks, we'd sit for hours and talk and nothing would get in the way of that. This time we had been separated for seven years and she thought we'd sit for days and talk, but time is different here. I had to leave her to go to work. I am always running."

"Besides getting used to time, what else has it been difficult for your sister and the other new arrivals to adjust to?"

"Honor," Alemu answers without stopping to think. "There are many cases where parents who arrived with Operation Solomon come to find that their children (who arrived with Operation Moses) have become very wild, very Israeli. In Ethiopia they had been well-behaved. Other Ethiopian children still act "Ethiopian" (reserved and well-behaved) at home and Israeli (wild) outside of the home."

Alemu opens a cabinet to find more pictures of his son. A child's gas mask tumbles out.

"What a horrible time you've had to live through this winter—especially here in the center of the country where all of the scuds were falling."

"Yeah, we were okay. My son is the only one who was afraid. Even now, when he hears a siren, he gets scared. It was really a *nes gadol,* a big miracle that no one was harmed."

The phone rings incessantly. Alemu answers call after call on his white cordless, a luxury in 1991. He leans back into his comfortable leather chair and talks, sometimes in Amharic, mostly in Hebrew.

It is late afternoon when we shake hands at the door. Alemu invites me to return.

 ❦

At the end of the week, just before Shabbat, I walk down the tree-lined Ha Levy Street in the center of Tel Aviv, to Sara's apartment. She has just arrived in Israel for the summer. At the door we hug quickly, both of us covered in sweat.

"Can you believe the humidity here? I already went back to Jerusalem yesterday just to breathe some cool night air. This apartment is suffocating. Excuse the mess."

"Oh my G-d," I say, jumping over a colony of ants on my way to the kitchen table.

"Well, Dina. I didn't promise it would be the King David Hotel."

Sara is unhappy in her new home. After graduating from Harvard she came to work in a women's shelter, mostly to help with fundraising. She resents having to be in Tel Aviv rather than Jerusalem and is confused why she chose, at this point in her life, Israel over America.

"So I've been wrestling with all of these thoughts and constantly running back to Jerusalem, and so I haven't cleaned or cooked. Sorry. I can make us some rice. And thanks for the *challah.* That will help make it feel like Shabbat."

"I think I'm going to take a shower." A sudden desire to escape overcomes me. "I've been sweating all day, and I just feel so dirty from all of the bus exhaust. It's worse than Jerusalem."

"Go on. I'll try to find a clean towel. But make it quick. Don't take your usual long showers—I don't know if you remember there's a water crisis in Israel."

Under the dribble of lukewarm water, I am disappointed by Sara's gloomy mood and unwelcoming attitude.

The next morning we walk along the sea, from Tel Aviv to Old Jaffa, trying to find our way back to each other. We walked this same shore in 1985, the day before she returned to America. Back then she had said, "Dina, you'll always come back to visit, you'll never live here…with all your dreams…"

And it was just as Sara had envisioned it. I have not yet committed to living in this country and am mostly struggling with the question of home from American shores. But as I try to explain to her all these years later, I am still committed to my relationship with Israel even if I haven't decided to live here. I am still walking her streets, probing her psyche, and married to the dream of the lives the Ethiopian immigrants could someday live here.

"You know, it is so different for Osnat and Yael and all of the others," I say, watching the prints our feet make in the sand. "When you and I feel bored or dissatisfied, or in my case frustrated that my dreams haven't come true, we pack our bags and pursue our American lives. My Ethiopian friends can't pack their bags when they feel disillusioned. Sometimes I envy them for that."

Sara is impatient with my disillusionment. "Dina, unlike you, I didn't come to Israel for idealistic reasons. I came because it is an interesting place to live and the language and difficulty of daily life, like standing in line at the bank for an hour, gives me a new challenge. It's a challenge I have not been able to find in America."

In Old Jaffa, we share a baguette at an Arab bakery, as we watch the waves from the top of a cliff. I am ready to return to places and people who still feel like home.

I pack a small suitcase of clothes for a trip to Jerusalem and call Osnat to hear how her exam went. The *bagrut* is even difficult for native-born Israelis whose first language is Hebrew. Although Osnat is a good student, this was a major challenge for her. I remember

back to when she was my student in Ma'alot and I was able to help her spell English words. I feel worthless knowing there's nothing I can do to help this time; the Hebrew on the exam has far surpassed my language skills.

When we parted we had spoken of perhaps meeting in Tel Aviv at the end of the month and I want to see if this is a possibility. Although it is difficult to communicate with her on the phone, I can't wait to hear her voice.

"Shalom Dina, *ma nishma?*"

"Everything is fine. How was your exam?" I ask anxiously.

"It was difficult, but I think I did okay. I'm relieved that the first half is over. What have you been doing?" I tell her about my visit to the absorption center, my visit with Yael and my plans to return to Jerusalem. "Maybe I'll see you at the end of the month, when the second half of your exam is over."

"That would be great." Even as we make these plans, I know it is just easier than saying, "Maybe I'll see you in another few years when I come back." On the phone we do not allow for the silences. I understand now, that the pauses we sometimes got lost in during our last visit, don't have to do with changing feelings about each other, only about changing circumstances. I am relieved that Osnat has done okay on her exam. Now I'm anxious about a challenge that I will face the next day, giving my first poetry reading in Jerusalem.

❧

My first poetry reading in Israel was in a bomb shelter in Ma'alot in the summer of 1985. The reading I am about to give will also be below ground, in Robert's basement apartment on Jabotinsky Street. In Israel, I am still an underground poet. The Tel Aviv Association of English writers in Israel, including Robert and his friend the poet Simon Lichman, sponsored this casual event. The apartment fills with English-speaking writers and artists, ranging from my age to Robert's; every face carries distinction and character.

So many times before a reading in America, especially those not associated with a Jewish event (which was the majority in the

eighties), I would be hesitant about reading my Israel poems. Are they too Jewish? Will my audience understand my references? What do I want to reveal about myself? Do my poems convey my Israel experience in images they can absorb? Tonight the questions are different. How will *this* group respond to my Israel poems? How will they feel about me, an American Jew, writing about their country? How will these Jerusalemites respond to my love affair with their city?

I preface my reading with how good it feels to read my Jewish poems without apologizing for them. I'm not sure if the audience, many of whom left the Diaspora decades ago, know what I mean. I am surprised by the heaviness of my own words. It is dark in the room, and so I can't see the expressions on most faces. Straight in front of me under a small light is the American poet Shirley Kaufman, who emigrated to Israel in 1977. Her smiling face and often-audible response is enough. When I finish reading she is the first to congratulate me. I am grateful to be able to speak back to this poet whose own words of Jerusalem have inspired me, to speak through my private language which I'm sure in some way was shaped by her poems.

Over wine and cheese, Shirley and I discuss American poets we both know and self-hating Jewish poets with whom we are both acquainted. I'm surprised and relieved by her outrage at one poet in particular who had once called my work too Jewish.

Later, Robert and I gather the dishes scattered around the apartment, buoyant about the successful evening. He goes to his room behind an Indian print bedspread. I fall asleep surrounded by three of his cats.

❧

I receive word from the director of Hilai, the artist's colony in Ma'alot, that I've been accepted for a ten-day residency. At last I will have my own home in Israel to absorb everything I've gathered during my month in the country. I will travel through the Jordan Valley to Tzvat and finally settle in Ma'alot.

On the bus, I put Gershom Scholem's memoir *From Berlin to Jerusalem* on my lap, but I can't take my eyes off the white Judean desert outside my window. I've been reading bits and pieces of this book all month and often feel he is speaking directly to me or my situation. Gershom Scholem had been a European intellectual, fascinated by Jewish history and literature, a Judaic scholar. While his Jewish countrymen (and his family) in 1920s Berlin fancied themselves first as true Germans, Scholem was already an ardent Zionist. After he completed his doctorate in Germany in 1923, he came to Israel on *aliyah*. At the then new Hebrew University of Jerusalem, Scholem was an archeologist of sorts, digging up Jewish texts, immersing himself in Kabbalah and transmitting his knowledge to his students and to others in ground-breaking texts like *Sabbatai Sevi the Mystical Messiah*. He was a fervent lover of the land of Israel. As far back as 1923 in letters to friends, he proposed a two-state solution. Even as he lived through the Arab riots of the 1930s, he never lost faith in his dreams of Israel's potential and lived both in the Jerusalem of unlocked doors and the Jerusalem of fallen sparks.

I read a few sentences of Scholem's memoir and return the book to my lap. I still can't concentrate. Next to me, an elderly man with a long white beard whose head is mostly buried in a prayer book, keeps falling asleep and leaning against me. As the bus shakes and rattles against stone, the man is thrown back to his own space. The Bedouin villages we drive through feel dryer and dryer, and my legs sweat profusely in my black tight slacks. The dust from the desert finds its way into my eyes. Sometimes, when I don't hold onto the bar in front of me, I fall over. I bury my head again in Scholem's book as if he can somehow protect me.

When I lift my head again to gaze back out the window, the valley stuns me: oceans of dull white sand, overwhelming in its monotony and simplicity. I've never taken this route before; I know only the white stone of Jerusalem, her hills and valleys, the way during some seasons, the north welcomes with a vast array of greens.

The man next to me awakens from his nap and looks at my
book. In a slow and melodious Hebrew he says, "You are reading
Gershom Scholem?"

I'm not sure if it's a question or a proclamation, but I answer
him, "Yes, this is his memoir."

He looks at me for a moment with blue-gray eyes and says,
"He was a wonderful man. I studied with him at Hebrew University
a long time ago. I can't believe his work has been translated into
English. He taught me *Zohar*."

I am more stunned by this exchange than I am by the Jordan
Valley. Where else would I run into a disciple of Scholem, whose
book sits on my lap from Jerusalem, the city where he studied, all
of the way to Tzvat, the birthplace of Lurian Kabbalah, the
inspiration for much of his writing?

And it is these texts that the scholar Scholem had studied
in Jerusalem, understanding them in a new way, so that the
ancient Jerusalem and the Jerusalem he walked through would
connect. I am comforted that scholars and philosophers before us
have grappled with reconciling the mystical and real Jerusalems,
that this age-old dilemma is one more link that ties together my
spiritual life with the lives of the Ethiopian community.

And I know it is only in Israel, especially in the holiest of places
like Jerusalem and Tzvat that the texts I relish and the life I live
could come face to face. This man who sits next to me on the bus,
this one time student of Scholem who speaks very little English
and with whom I exchange very few words, has visited me in the
most sacred room of my home.

🌿

At Hilai, the artist's colony in Ma'alot, Ludmilla, a Russian
immigrant and the acting director, shows me to my room in this
run-down empty building. I will have this apartment for ten days
of writing: a small couch and coffee table, a desk beneath a window,
a small kitchen with a hot plate and a bathroom where the toilet

overflows. I wonder if I will feel more at home once I fill the place with flowers, hummus, and sweet tomatoes.

In the busiest aisle of the market I'm greeted by Elana Gabai, my American friend who is now the mother of four children.

"I knew you'd be here soon but it is so funny to run into you in the market—it feels just like old times!"

"It's so good to see you, too, I just got here a few hours ago."

"Can you come for *Shabbos*? I can't really talk now; I've gotta get home and wash the floor—it's Thursday evening. But come for *Shabbos*. We can talk then."

After unloading groceries in my new abode, I sit outside on a bench, taking in the last moments of light before trying to discover what language I will find here.

What I love most about Ma'alot is the sky. My windows have always faced west and when the sun sets, the different shades of red, orange, pink then purple are spectacular. There is also a lot of wind here. Doors and windows are always slamming closed. This place also has the other meaning of wind in Hebrew: spirit. Everything moves slowly, but there is a softness and wonder in the air. Shaul at the stationary shop who remembers me from 1985 said that the Russians sit outside all of the time in the square and that it has brought a great liveliness to the town.

My light skin is not as shocking to the Moroccans who still dominate this town because now they are used to the new population of Russians and their light color. I've learned already from Bat Sheva at the post office that the natives resent the Russians because of their degrees and their chutzpah. The Ethiopians resent the Russians because, as Elad had also suggested, they think that they do not feel like Jews. The Russians resent the Ethiopians because, at least for this moment, the aftermath of Operation Solomon, they have been the country's miracle children. The Russians, with all of their demands, have become the black sheep.

At the end of a long week, I finish writing an article in a voice I've never heard before. It is the voice of the reporter, the composite voices of all of the different people I've spoken to about the

Ethiopian Jews: anthropologists, absorption center workers, sociologists. The sounds that ring in my ear during my days in Ma'alot—axe against stone, Arabic, Russian, Moroccan, Amharic and Hebrew—has quieted. The reporter is taking over so the poet can rest.

The Sabbath is coming and I feel alone. My longing, now, is not ancient like it had been in Jerusalem. I long for the life I lived in 1985. As the days pass and I walk around town, I feel more of what is missing than what has remained. I visit with Shimon's siblings Prosper and Rimonda. I pass where Shimon lived, the hills we climbed up and down to be with each other.

I look for the woman who wanted to live here, who had stopped seeing the world through a window, who felt the textures of the lives around her, who hiked through and melded with the landscape, wore braids on top of her head and spoke Hebrew unabashedly. Seven years after Operation Moses and my own attempted absorption, I still can't commit to living here, and yet the book remains open. I've not chosen America either. Without Osnat, Elad and their families, Ma'alot is no longer home.

July 31, 1990, Jerusalem

Can I take all of the pieces of my life in Jerusalem: the streets, temples, homes of friends, and build a complete life?

Even when I put the larger questions aside I have the same fears: coming here alone, finding a decent job. But I feel life here, the texture of daily life, Hebrew, Jewish culture and room after room of books. I could no longer live in Ma'alot because there is too much ignorance there, because the simplicity that once embraced me is no longer enough. I am not simple. The north is lovely but too far from the pulse of life.

Back in Petach Tikvah, I fill my bags with clothes and books on this, my last night in Israel. Eric and his friend, a former American, are in another room drinking green liquor and asking questions about my travels. I can't tell them what the exhaust from the buses in Jerusalem has come to mean to me or that the longing I

carry for a pure Jerusalem matches the longing of our Ethiopian friends. I can't tell them that Ma'alot exists for me only in the past and so the present is painful, and that it is only my search into the lives of the Ethiopian Jews that anchors me. I can't tell them that the question of home, that they assume I've already answered, refuses to let me sleep.

To them, I am just another Jew getting ready to step down from Israel. They aren't interested in my confusion. They condemn Americans who live in the Diaspora. They throw clichés at me that pull at my heartstrings. They say my work with the Ethiopians is nothing compared to the commitment of living and shopping for food and breathing and buying cars in The Land. When I zip up my last suitcase, I feel as though I'm betraying them, Israel, myself and the Ethiopians, in one fell swoop.

Early the next morning, hours before sunrise, Eric drives me to the airport. I thank him for his graciousness and hug him goodbye; I do not apologize for leaving.

🌿

A year later, at an artist's colony in the Midwest, I try to finish the poem I couldn't write in Jerusalem, but finally began in Ma'alot. It is now in three voices: an older man, a reporter, and a young woman. My friend Sandi visited Israel for the first time. She heard Prime Minister Shamir's stepping down speech on an egged bus and understood only two words *"ani ma'amin"*—I believe. Then he sang *"Hatikvah."* She looked around to see if anyone was mouthing the words. The bus was filled with silent still lips.

Now, Yitzhak Rabin has taken over. The Labor Party is back in power. I imagine the smell of hope emerging from the smell of exhaust in Jerusalem. Robert writes that his garden on Jabotinsky Street is the most beautiful it has ever been. He made a path in it after three winter floods. After months of silence, he has written vibrant poems.

I am looking out at acres of Midwest summer prairie, listening still, for my own voice. One evening, during a pause in the dinner

conversation, a painter from Uganda asks if Americans consider Jews to be white, if they look at them as being different. There is a resonant silence. A black writer says that the word Semitic means mulatto, so perhaps Jews are black. A Jewish writer who visits ashrams in New York says that now she'll embrace being black and Jewish. The black writer who I had befriended and felt a sisterhood with from the time of my arrival, looks at me across the table. Two people mention in passing that they have Jewish friends. Someone says he wasn't aware there was still such a thing as religious Jews. A young painter asks if I was, "like" raised in a very religious home. For the first time in years, I hear insensitive anti-Semitic remarks. I can't believe there is still so much ignorance among educated artists.

I know I have to say something after the painter from Uganda mentions that all the Jews that he knows wear little hats and braids and are thought of as different. I say that Jews in America see *themselves* as different. I try to take back the power and say that we are Jews before we are Americans. I do not know if I am telling the truth when Linda, the only other Jew at the table, looks at me. I add, "At least that is the way it is for me." The painter from Uganda had not known that I was a Jew. The writer says she is a New Yorker before she is an American.

We've spent days watching the Democratic convention. Everyone defines themselves as progressives. They don't like what I said about *American* not being the largest part of my identity. A veil has dropped across the room. Someone asks why Jews think they are different from others when people of other religions do not consider themselves different from other Americans. The black writer says because Jews have been oppressed. The Jewish writer says it is because Jews are prejudiced against others. I say nothing. It is as if we are in the Tower of Babel speaking different languages. If I open my mouth, torrents of words will rush out and the floodgate will never close. I can't begin to tell them what it means to be a Jew in this country or in any other. There are too many centuries to move through.

In the kitchen someone asks why I'm so quiet and says I have a look of Aries superiority on my face. I am afraid she really means Jewish superiority.

I've sat around this dinner table with different artists three summers in a row. This place was my respite. This night feels different. It is from this Midwestern prairie and the silence that comes between too many words, that I long again for Jerusalem, where the pain of exile is shared, where when language escapes me I have the right to remain silent.

I have a month to write with no one breathing down my neck, with no other languages drifting through the window. I return to my poem about Jerusalem and remove the extraneous neutral voice, the voice of the reporter. The old man and the young woman move back and forth across the page, trying to live simultaneously in the country of dreams and the country of waking, the country of poets and the country of politicians, the country of now and the country of then, the country of home and the country of exile, the country of language and the country of silence, the country of peace and the country of rage. The old man and the young woman move across the page, trying to tell the whole story.

Don't Lose the *Conecshun*
(1993)
—*Osnat Melesa*

You try to be free through writing.
How wrong. Every word unveils another tie.

—*Edmond Jabès, from* The Book of Questions

In the less frequent letters I receive from Osnat, she ends not with the same mushy, girlish salutations of "Bye, my sister" and "I love you so so much" but with the more sophisticated and layered "Don't lose the *Conecshun*" that she writes in both Hebrew and incorrectly spelled English. It is a natural Hebrew expression that oddly makes me feel more connected to her. Connection has also been my concern. During the two years since my last visit, I have written fewer letters and I sense my writing about the Ethiopians has turned into a book in need of the next chapter. Osnat is at Haifa University, and I can't seem to reach anyone in the Yamari family. I fear there will be no language in the prairie of Ragdale where I've spent the last few summers writing. I know instead I need to connect with my families in Israel. The distances seem greater with the passage of time. I listen to my dreams.

The backpack that I carried around Israel two summers ago becomes the sea. But the blue changes to deep black water and white snow. The lot in front of the buildings where we lived in Ma'alot has also become sea. My friends are no longer playing soccer or sitting in the shade knitting. They are walking out into water. There are no longer distinctions between generations. I do not know who arrived in 1980, who in '84 and who in '91. Their clothes are simple and do not distinguish them. I cannot swim out far enough to reach them. The view they walk towards is spectacular—black water changing to white snow

and then blue. Osnat's mother, who doesn't speak Hebrew, tells
me in flowing language that they are all leaving for Canada.
I want to tell them to stay where they are. I have no place to
live. The view is too beautiful to speak. This time I am the one
without language. I understand that I will have to find a new
way to know them. Not through their clothes, or their color, not
through the time they arrived.

When I am in Chicago thinking about Israel, I imagine seeing Osnat and Elad upon my arrival. I forget how long it takes to reach them by phone and make a plan. In Jerusalem, I find first the word on the street. I go for falafel in Robert's Jerusalem neighborhood, Rehavia, and immediately befriend the Yemenite proprietor. This sixty-something-year-old man serves me a glass of mint tea and asks if I'm a new immigrant or a tourist. When I tell him I'm a writer and that my subject is the Ethiopian Jews, he pulls up a chair to join me at my outside table.

"The Ethiopians," shifting from Hebrew to English, "are civilized people. There is much to learn from them. In the army they are good fighters and soldiers unlike the Israelis who cause problems. I can't understand why the Orthodox rabbis say they aren't Jews. Fifty percent of the Russians aren't Jews, and they don't say anything about that. Most of the Hungarian Jews converted 1,000 or 800 years ago, and the rabbis never question the American Jews regarding their Judaism even with all of the intermarriage that goes on over there." He gets up to refill my glass of tea and then continues.

"My family arrived in Israel 100 years ago and settled here, in Rehavia.

It was a simple neighborhood then with dirt roads. Now it is a fancy, elite neighborhood with cafes."

"I've often dreamed of that Jerusalem you describe—with dirt roads," I add.

"Yes, it was even before my time, but even in my lifetime I have seen huge changes." We are interrupted from our talk by the usual

lunch time crowd. When I pay and thank him for the meal and for his hospitality, he asks me to return with my discoveries.

At a phone booth, where a businessman eavesdrops on my conversations with friends and anthropologists, I hear another spiel. "The Oriental Jews are the most pleased with the arrival of the Ethiopians..." Before he could finish I say, "because they are no longer the black sheep."

He smiles and says, "You understand better than I do? No? Their racism is less hypocritical than the racism of the Ashkenazim because they express it directly. The Ashkenazim say one thing and act another way. They pretend. The Oriental Jews are more primitive so they don't mask their feelings." He lights a cigarette and continues, "In the army, the Ethiopian soldiers are treated like second class citizens. Others call them *cushim*—a terrible word. On the bus, people don't like to sit next to them." Before we are interrupted by his return call, he tells me he's from Morocco, a beautiful town on the water called Essaouria.

Over coffee, Boaz proves the man's words to be true.

"Send them back to Africa. They have a darkness in them. They aren't happy here and only cause problems," he says half-joking, trying to get a response from me.

"Boaz, how can you say that? I'm sure life wasn't any easier for your parents when they came from Iraq in the fifties."

"Dina, you can't compare Iraqis and Ethiopians. The cultures are totally different."

"You can tell me another time about how different you are from the Ethiopians, but right now I have to meet Sara back at my place," I say, eager to get away from Boaz's darkness.

Sara has been living in Israel for almost a year now, working for CNN. When she arrives at my hotel with heavy gray jeans and a matching briefcase, curls in a neat bun, I say, "So are you here for good this time?"

"Dina, I've only seen you for a few minutes. Before we get into the big questions I want you to see some of my life here. The pub that I am about to take you to is a regular part of my life here now."

On the edge of Jerusalem, beyond narrow winding roads that I had not known existed, this large pub, where mostly journalists hang out, is bustling with writers and animated conversation. Many of the regulars know Sara. We move to a patio table where it's quiet enough to hear each other. Sara pushes a mop of curls that have fallen from her bun out of her eyes, takes a sip of sparkling water and sighs. "Okay, I'm leaving Israel in a few weeks."

"You're kidding… why?"

"Well I'll get to that. It isn't because I'm not happy; I've had a great year. I wanted you to see this. But there are things I need to do in America now. Decisions about relationships and career. I don't want to talk about it right here. Tell me what you've been up to?"

"I'm here for an update on the Ethiopian community. I'm going to spend time with Yael, Osnat, and the Yamaris, if I can ever reach them on the phone, and this time I'm anxious to meet with Ethiopian leaders as well."

"Forgive me for saying this, Dina, but they are the worst spokespeople. They have protests in order to share their concerns and yet when you call someone and tell them you are CNN and want an interview they always say that the person you want to speak to is sleeping."

One day in Jerusalem and I'm trying to digest the attitudes toward the Ethiopians as expressed by a Yemenite café owner, a Moroccan businessman, a second generation Iraqi psychologist, and an American intellectual working as a journalist. There is sympathy, concern, criticism of the Israeli attitude and blame towards the Ethiopians for not taking more control of their lives. Have two years really passed since Operation Solomon?

❧

The absorption centers have been replaced by the mobile homes that Yossi Har El of the Jewish Agency had alluded to two years ago. These caravans are trailer-like homes "planted" on the outskirts of towns and cities. The immigrants who arrived with Operation Solomon are to become absorbed here before moving to more permanent housing.

The bus drives south towards hills, passing civilization, it seems, until we arrive at the top of the mountain where clusters of mobile homes are outlined in green or yellow. Against the permanence of Jerusalem stone are tin homes where Ethiopian Jews wear their own garb, make their own food, brew their own coffee and speak Amharic to each other.

Shai, the leader of the Ethiopian residents of the caravan, is not there at our scheduled meeting time. I stand outside his tin office and watch. There is something deeply confident about the people who pass by, unmoved by my presence. It is as if it is 1985 and I'm just beginning again to enter the lives of these African Jews. I know I'll have to cross barriers of language, culture and time to reach them. I write in my notebook: *At last, they are allowed to be themselves.*

I try to capture the view of mobile homes contrasted with Jerusalem stone in the distance and on ropes, laundry hanging out to dry against tin huts. As I spin circles with my camera, I bump into a man hanging his clothes on the line. After I introduce myself he tells me he is an engineer and that he lived abroad for a long time before coming to Israel. Originally from Gondar he is now unemployed, complaining that the government doesn't give him much money because he doesn't have a family. He jokes in fluid Hebrew about his wet laundry in his arms and what a shame it is that he's missing the sun. This is the first time I've seen an Ethiopian man doing "women's work." Not wanting him to miss out on optimal drying hours, I excuse myself, and he invites me to return sometime for Ethiopian coffee, brewed from the bean.

The air is filled with the warm and spicy scent of *injera* baking for the evening meal and Ethiopian coffee being brewed for this in-between time. Women drink it in small cups sitting on stools or on the floor, braiding each other's hair and catching up on the day's news.

A man with the blue *kippah,* who doesn't want to be photographed, sees me writing in my notebook and shouts, "Go inside. Why do you sit outside? You'll get dirty!"

"I don't live here." I reply, surprised by his concern. "I don't have a home to go inside of."

He points to the open door of his mobile home and says, "Go inside. Finish writing." I gratefully follow his command.

I am greeted by his mother, an elderly woman who doesn't speak Hebrew or understand my explanation for why I am there. She smiles at me kindly and then walks me to a caravan across the way where her granddaughter warmly welcomes me amidst the blare of Ethiopian rock music. The source of this music is a video of Ethiopian teenagers dressed in white, singing Amharic rock songs while moving their shoulders up and down in their traditional dance. The daughter doesn't speak much Hebrew, but we work side by side as she weaves baskets, and I write in my notebook.

When the man who sent me there returns, the room fills with family of different generations watching the video. The granddaughter rests her hands for a moment and looks at me closely for the first time since my arrival. "The caravans are much nicer in Petach Tikvah. They have much more room," she offers and then returns her gaze to the video. The woman of the caravan arrives, smiles at me and begins preparations for the next meal.

I do not want to bombard this family with questions and besides, we don't share a language. I don't know if I'm welcome; no one offered me a drink. It is difficult, too, for me to move into their time and pace in my hectic Jerusalem mode. I can't sit patiently and wait for what might happen once the video ends. So I tell my gracious host, the man with the blue *kippah,* that I am finished. I thank everyone and return to Shai's office, still hoping to find him.

The way to a person is through many narrow roads, and it is the curves that lead to the deepest and most unexpected places. Yet I am traveling fast on a straight road expecting to enter the secret rooms of the Ethiopians and to discover some great truth about their lives. Haven't I learned that the truth is in the details?

This time Shai, the leader of the Ethiopians in Givat HaMatos, is in his office, talking with a Swedish volunteer. He invites me in, looks at me suspiciously and says, "Tell me exactly what you want to know."

"I want to get a feel from you of conditions in the caravan, how they compare to absorption centers, and how you would compare the absorption process of the Solomon people with that of the Moses people."

After looking at me blankly for a while Shai says, "Go speak with my chairman. I can't speak for all Ethiopians, and I don't know what is happening in other places in the country. And I don't know who you are—why should I trust you?" I am startled by Shai's response.

"I am not an anthropologist or a sociologist —I'm a poet and I just want to know the truth about your lives. I have no agenda."

"Yes, but like the anthropologists you are from the outside. I wouldn't try to write about America. Each person should write about himself," he says.

"I care deeply about the Ethiopian community. There are children I've known for nine years now. I've watched them grow up from afar..."

"All I know is about myself," Shai says.

"Tell me about yourself."

"Ask me anything."

I learn that he arrived in 1984, worked in Jerusalem and the rest of his family arrived in '91. I smile at his short, terse answers and say, "You *really* don't want to talk."

"I am so tired of professors, anthropologists and people writing books about the Ethiopians. I want to write a book about the Ethiopian Jews and so I am saving my ideas for myself. If I knew you and what you are writing about I'd trust you more."

"I can give you copies of articles I've written and the names of other people I've met with from the Jewish Agency and the Ministry of Absorption."

He doesn't look satisfied.

"Shai, did something happen to you that caused your mistrust?" He thinks for a moment and looks directly at me.

"There is this professor who wrote a book about us, and it is all wrong and stupid. I wrote to him and told him this myself."

"What did he write?"

"Well he came to the caravan, and we were all like family, and then he wrote a book as others have about how blacks are not Jews and he turned around what I said like other writers." He stops speaking as if convincing himself not to trust me and dials his chairman in Tel Aviv. He tells him about me and then about the *mamzeret*, bastard.

He apologizes for not helping me and hands me an Ethiopian calendar and a cup of mint tea. He is very Israeli in the way he is up front about not being open. He explains again why he can't give me information and I appreciate his candor, his mysterious, handsome and tough presence.

"I am so sorry. But this is all I can say right now. But tell me about yourself. Are you religious? How do you like Israel? Again, Dina, I apologize for not giving you information. But if you return next week you can speak with someone who knows English." I thank him, aware that language is not the problem this time.

Although Shai kept apologizing for not giving me information, he revealed a lot about himself, his desire to protect his own truth and his disappointment in and lack of trust for "outsider" journalists and social scientists. He reminds me of the fragility of the Ethiopian psyche. Shmuel, an Ethiopian leader at the Israel Association for Ethiopian Jews (IAEJ), had given me hard facts, evidence of how far the Ethiopian community still was from being accepted and leading productive lives in Israel. He placed blame on the schools who did not give the community the help he felt they needed. And everyone I had spoken to had in some way placed blame on

The Organizations, whose job it was to make life easier for the Ethiopian community.

In the caravans the details of their lives return them to their own culture. They are called, again, by their Amharic names. They drink coffee brewed from Ethiopian beans. They make baskets with yarn from Ethiopia, *injera* with authentic spices. Isn't this what the absorption center workers and social workers I had spoken to after Operation Solomon had hoped for? But how far they still seem from Israeli life. Although the center of Jerusalem is a short ride away, when I step off the bus in the center of town, I feel as if I've returned from another country.

"I'm dying to see you," Yael says when I finally reach her by phone one evening. But when I call the next morning to confirm our plan for an early breakfast, there is no answer. Frustrated after several tries, I go to Hamashbir, the department store where she now works, and approach an older sales lady and ask if Yael is working. She thinks for a moment and then asks, *Ha shachoor?* The Black?"

I look at her and answer, "The Ethiopian woman, Yael."

"Is she your friend?"

"Yes she is my friend and a former student of mine."

"*Ha Ethiopit?*" she repeats.

"Yes," I say, growing more annoyed.

"She won't be in until 11:30 today."

When I return later with my heavy blue pack on my back on my way to the bus station, Yael comes out of a corner in the jeans department and says in Hebrew "There's Dina." We hug and look at each other for a moment, Yael with her black hair pinned back, red lipstick, a flowered conservative blouse with short culottes. I think about what Boaz said two years before about how her looks could secure her a job.

"Dina, I'm so sorry. I had to take a friend to the clinic this morning. Can we go and drink something now? I can take a break."

"Yael, you have to work, and I don't really have time right now. I have to catch a bus for Kfar Saba. Batya and Elad are waiting for me."

"Oh, I can't believe you'll get to see them. Well then, let me walk you to the bus stop."

We pass a beggar collecting coins. He holds up a poster with pills taped to it and pictures of his family in need of medicine and care. *I am not shy,* he mutters. *I ask the people of this country, my extended family, for some help.* A man with a black *kippah* hands him shekels, speaks of the messiah and with the help of G-d. We walk on past models in storefront windows displaying short shorts and sleeveless turtlenecks. Crowds of people cross into each other at the intersection.

When we're finally alone for a moment on the sidewalk, Yael grabs my arm. "So, are you married yet?"

"No. I would have told you. There is someone new in my life, we're pretty serious, but I haven't known him for that long."

"Either stay with him and marry or find someone else," she advises.

"What about you?" I ask.

"No, I'm still not married, that's why I still live in the same place. I don't know if I want to marry my new boyfriend or not. It is difficult to marry here without an apartment."

"Tell me about him. Is he Israeli?"

"Yes, he's an actor and a life guard who spends a lot of time in different cities."

We reach the bus stop and Yael looks at me for a long time. "You always look the same, Dina. You don't change at all."

"Yael, each time I see you, you are more beautiful."

"Thank you. You are so sweet."

The morning sun beats down on us; I reach in my pack for my sunglasses. Round stylish glasses already protect Yael's eyes.

"Yael, you can return to work now—I'm okay."

"No, nonsense. I'll wait with you."

"Are you sure it's okay with your boss?"

"Yes, it's fine. So tell me about your work in America. How old are your students?"

"They are mostly eighteen to twenty-year-olds."

"They're my age!"

"They are! But they seem much younger. They haven't been out in the world much."

"So when did you arrive in Israel?"

"Nine days ago."

"And you just called now?"

"I tried to call you many times."

"At night?"

"More during the day. I don't have a phone so it is difficult to call at night."

"Oh. Where are you staying?"

"With *haverim*, friends."

Not sure she heard me correctly she says, *Aravim*, Arabs (which rhymes with friends in Hebrew).

"No. I said I'm staying with friends, Americans. And now I'm in a hotel."

❧

After a long bus ride and two transfers, I wait on a corner in Kfar Saba but there is no sign of Batya. On the phone the night before, we had made plans to meet at this stop not far from their home. I begin to wonder if we had mis-communicated. I know it is proper Ethiopian etiquette to miss a few appointments before actually meeting, but I didn't think this applied to friends.

From a phone booth I call the Yamari home. Amnon, the eldest brother explains that Batya had forgotten to tell me that there are two stops in the neighborhood; Batya had waited for me at one stop while I waited for her at the other. Amnon says to stay where I am, that he will come to meet me.

I barely recognize the young man who soon arrives. His long curls have been cut at the root so that his hair stands straight on top and is razor short in back. His handshake is strong, assuring

me he's in control of this situation and has become the leader of
the family. He leads me to their home. We pass a post office and
Amnon says, "Once I wrote you a letter, but I never mailed it, or
I gave it to my mother and she never sent it, or it never arrived."

In front of their building we're greeted by his sisters: Batya
in a long skirt and shirt, her braided hair hanging past her
shoulders, in contrast to Orit with a low cut shirt, tight jeans and
lots of jewelry.

At home, Gaveret Yamari is seated on the couch in front of
the television. She gets up to greet me and serves drinks. Batya
joins her in the kitchen and Amnon settles into the living room
couch with me.

"Elad should be home soon. He'll be so excited to see you."

"I can't wait to see him." A black American sitcom is on and
Amnon laughs at something I miss in translation.

"I love the style of Black American men," he says. "I like the
way that they talk and move and say things like 'hey man' and
'move.' I think it's so cool."

I look at him more closely, the gold chain around his neck, his
striped jersey and designer jeans, and realize he resembles an American
black more than an Ethiopian man. If I had not been expecting
him on the street, I would not have recognized him.

"So Amnon, what have you been up to? What's going on with
you?"

"I work in a store in Kfar Saba now. It's good; I have a lot of
friends here, we all do, and there is always something to do. In a
month I will begin my army service." He smiles to himself for a
moment and then continues,

"Dina, I was very bad when I last saw you in Ma'alot. I ran
from your camera."

"That was four years ago. You were away at school last time I
was here. But don't worry. I still got a picture of you that summer
in Ma'alot. I have a photo of those long curls you used to have."

"Yeah, of course. They were just like your curls."

An elderly man follows a knock on the door. Gaverert Yamari greets him with kisses on both cheeks, and he kisses all the children gathered around him.

Gaveret Yamari now speaks a few Hebrew words, so with Amnon's help, she tries to explain who the visitor is. "He is the brother of my father and their grandfather. We all grow confused until it clicks and I say to Gaveret Yamari in Hebrew, "He is your uncle!" "Yes," she replies and we all laugh long and hard at how difficult it had been for all of us to communicate that fact.

Finally Elad enters the apartment and looks at me shyly with a sly smile. His mother says something to him in Amharic. We approach each other cautiously, and I give him Ethiopian style kisses on each cheek. I hand him a Bulls cap that he immediately puts on, and his smile gets so large that I notice for the first time his teeth have grown in crookedly.

"I can't believe how tall and thin he is," I say to everyone as I study Elad.

"I know. Can you believe it?" Batya exclaims. "And Amnon is almost six feet!"

Gaveret Yamari serves her brother and me a platter of *injera* with chicken in the center. The uncle blesses the bread in Hebrew and everyone insists that I begin to eat.

The apartment has the same lacy white curtains as it did two years ago, but the atmosphere feels different. In 1991 Gaveret Yamari had been at the caravan visiting a newly arrived daughter. Amnon had been away at school. Elad and Batya were mourning the fact that their newly arrived father would not be coming home to live with them. The joy of Operation Solomon that had been spreading through the Ethiopian community had brought sadness to their doorstep as well. This year the apartment is full of family and a joyous, casual mood. The next knock on the door brings another brother I've never heard of who has arrived with Operation Solomon.

After hugging each family member and shaking my hand, this brother sits on the couch next to Amnon and Elad, smiling ear to ear and watching me carefully. Shlomo had spent a year in an

absorption center and was now staying with the Yamaris in Kfar Saba and working in a factory. Shlomo listens for a while and then speaks to me in a combination of English and Hebrew.

"My group's *aliyah* was so difficult because it was at the same time as the big *aliyah* from Russia. And we waited in Addis Ababa for so long. That's where I picked up some English. It had been difficult being separated from my family for so long. I had not seen my brother Elad since he was a baby."

I flash back to the Elad he would have left behind in 1984 and pull out the photo of him that I've been carrying around with me and that I had meant to share with the family. In it, four-year-old Elad is sitting on the couch with Osnat and Yael. I hand the picture to Shlomo.

"Yes, that is the child I knew." Soon the others pass the picture back and forth, squealing with laughter that Elad was ever that little.

Our conversation turns to their cousins, the Melesa family who were only teenagers in the photo. Gaveret Yamari mentions the newest member of their family, and no one can agree on when he was born.

"He is a new baby!" she says.

"Well he can't be too much of a baby; I saw him last time I was here and that was already two years ago!" At first no one can remember the baby's name. Finally it comes to me because I had written it down in my journal and had typed it up months later.

"*Baruch,*" blessing, I shout out. Everyone laughs that I of all people, the only one who isn't a member of the family, know his name.

All of this time the uncle has been listening quietly, watching our faces as if he could follow the conversation. Outside of the blessing for the bread, he speaks only Amharic. Sometimes Amnon translates something for him. Now, the uncle looks at me intently and lectures me in Amharic. I don't understand but listen along with everyone else. Amnon translates for me.

"You are a very good person, very special, not like other people. You are a good person and you remember everyone. You are very beautiful."

I feel a twinge of guilt. I think but can't say to them that I remember everyone because I am a poet and poets never let anything go.

Elad hands me the Fish book I had brought for him four years ago when he didn't remember me so well. Two years ago he had shown me the book and told me the story. Now it is our ritual as we look at the pictures together and he tells me the English story in Hebrew. He knows it by heart. I wonder if it is his relic of me as my photo of him as a child is what I keep of him in the far corners of my American life.

My return to Jerusalem coincides with Yom Yerushalayim and Yom Ha Zikarah. For Jerusalem Day, people from all over Israel gather for parades, free museums and school children visit the Western Wall. The city is in a celebratory mood and the city is surrounded by soldiers. The day of memory, or *Yom Ha Zikarah*, was established in 1987 by the Ethiopian community, to memorialize the 4,000 to 5,000 Ethiopian Jews who died in 1984 on their way to Israel. I choose to join the Ethiopian community on their somber day, instead of the celebrations taking place in the rest of the city.

I have trouble finding my way to the memorial service. I ask people on the street and an elder Ethiopian man says to take Bus #21. He is on his way to the bank and he says to meet him in a few minutes on Ben Yehuda Street and he will show me to the bus. A half-hour passes and I decide to find my way alone. As I lean into another bus for directions, I see the Ethiopian man and he signals to me to get on board.

Soon I follow him off the bus, telling myself that if he was able to find his way from Sudan, he can find his way to this ceremony which turns out to be on Hebron Street, the edge of Jerusalem. I follow him up Mount Herzl, studying his brown suit and fancy

running shoes. I sweat in my light cotton pants and shirt, but he shows no signs of discomfort. Climbing higher and higher, I don't take my eyes off of his brown suit or the sand beneath our feet. I imagine we are walking through the desert on our way to Israel.

On top of Mount Herzl, on the edge of Jerusalem, buses have arrived from all over the country and streams of Ethiopian men and women walk toward the band shell where the ceremony will take place. There are tearful reunions of families who are now scattered throughout their promised land. There are young stylish girls, older women in traditional garb, men in dark suits, men in white *shammas*, women under blue umbrellas, men under black umbrellas. On the stage *kessim,* Ethiopian rabbis, stand under purple, pink, turquoise and green umbrellas laced in gold. The chanting in Ge'ez is mesmerizing.

On another hill beyond the ceremony, the younger generation watches. Their prayers, mostly in Amharic, is the only sound resonating as Israeli flags wave against hill and stone. Hebrew prayers are transmitted through speakers set on top of the rocks.

As we sing the *Shema* prayer, slowly a few stand up and then a few more and soon everyone but the elderly stand tall. It is a bit like their journey to Israel.

I was here eight years before when they lost loved ones and found a new country. I am seated among them still wondering what it has meant for them to have arrived, to have moved from the house of Israel to the land of Israel. I see their struggle in their posture, their eyes, their warm but restrained greetings. I observe the different ways they've managed through their dress: the young women gossiping in miniskirts in the shade of olive trees; their mothers in white *shammas*, sitting in the shade of taller trees in silence. The chanting in Amharic stops for a moment and one of the few white Israelis, a Jewish Agency worker, gets on stage. His Hebrew, distorted through cheap speakers, resonates off Jerusalem hills. What I pick up:

Jerusalem is the heart and soul of the Jewish people.
The Aliyah of the Ethiopians is not only physical but spiritual as well.
Olim from all over the world should come to build this country and make it like all others.

Why, I wonder, as I walk down the hill to the rhythms of the prayer *Oseh shalom bimromav.* This country is like no other.

On my way out people are still trickling in. I have taken seventy-four photographs but still cannot capture this day.

I go back to the city alone. The Ethiopian man who led me to the ceremony is now lost among his people. I go in search of mine.

🌿

I sit on a bench on top of Mount Carmel, in the center of campus at Haifa University, and wait for Osnat. The grass is still green from the winter rains. The air is clear and the landscape lush. A stylish young black woman approaches the station across from me: this can't be Osnat, I think to myself.

I watch this thin, radiant woman in blue jeans and thick hair held back in an elastic band, until she catches my eyes, and our gazes lock, and we approach each other and kiss, Ethiopian style, on both sides of the cheek.

"I didn't recognize you. You look like a college girl—I mean a young woman—really great!" I say and Osnat laughs shyly.

"I didn't recognize you, Dina, with your long hair and everything. It's really good to see you."

She leads me to her favorite sculpture garden. On the way we pass a group of Ethiopian students who call to Osnat in Amharic. She does not call them over, but turns toward me and exclaims about how much she loves this modern structure that looks like a silver dollar tree.

I look at Osnat through the lens of my camera, trying to capture her next to her favorite sculpture, and try to figure out

what is so different about her appearance. I had never seen her wear slacks before.

"Osnat, are you still religious?" I ask, looking at her faded jeans.

"I still keep the Sabbath but I am not religious like before. I wear pants. It happened as soon as I left home."

Osnat is in the *mechina*, the preparatory program that allows immigrant students to work on skills needed to succeed in their university studies. In the kitchen of her suite I smell a familiar Ethiopian spice. "Do I smell *injera*?" I ask.

"No," she answers bluntly. "I don't prepare *injera* in my dorm kitchen."

"So tell me about your suite mates and your roommate."

"Two Russians. Two Americans. And the one I share a room with is my cousin." Carrying a bowl of fruit to the main room, Osnat explains, "We didn't know that we were both attending Haifa University. When we saw each other at the entrance exam we were so surprised and so happy and we arranged to be roommates."

I am delighted to be in Osnat's room. It is the first time I've ever been in a place that belongs to her. In the past we've met in her family home where Osnat would often run the kitchen and where she did not have a room of her own. This small tidy space where we sit, is equally divided in half; each student has her own bed, desk, shelf of books and her own wall.

Osnat's wall: a poster with big white letters that spell Ethiopia in English. Below the letters are photos cut out of magazines of Ethiopian rock stars and Amharic song lyrics, two posters of Michael Jackson, a photo of her youngest brother Baruch and a picture of her sister Marta.

"Can you translate this for me?" I ask pointing at what looks like a Hebrew poem.

"Sure, one of my teachers in high school gave it to me. It says that it doesn't matter what color someone's skin is but what is inside of him or what kind of person he is."

"I like that very much," I say, trying to read it again on my own.

Osnat pulls out a large box of tapes and asks what I want to listen to.

"What are your favorites?" I ask.

"I love Whitney Houston and classical music and I still love and follow contemporary Ethiopian music. Sometimes people bring it from Ethiopia and sell it in Israel."

"Let's hear some. I don't think I've ever heard Ethiopian rock music."

Sitting across from each other on the thin mattress, listening to traditional African beats jazzed up a bit and high voices singing in Amharic, I give Osnat the silver bracelet I had bought for her with an assortment of charms, pearls and stones dangling from it. When I picked it out at an import store in Chicago, I imagined the shy and modest Osnat, the girlish teenager rather than the young woman I've found who has come into her own style influenced by Israelis, Ethiopians and American blacks. She accepts my gift gracefully, and I clasp it around her thin wrist.

My other gift is a photo of her as a thirteen-year-old immigrant girl in hand-me-down Israeli clothes. Osnat's face opens into a familiar smile when she sees the images of herself, her sister Yael, and Elad. I had brought the same photo to Yael one day when I visited her at work and she looked aghast and held the photo to her chest. When a co-worker asked to see it, she refused to hand it over. Unlike her sister, the images of 1985 rekindled fond memories for Osnat.

"How is Jackie?" Osnat asks after a long reminiscence of Ma'alot.

"We lost touch years ago," I answer apologetically and not for the first time.

"I can't believe that you live in the same country and don't see each other."

I cannot properly explain why I gave up trying to find Jackie, but I am grateful for her question; it assures me that the thirteen-year-old girl is still alive in her.

I study the books on her desk and ask about her studies.

"It is difficult. We have a lot to do. But now I am taking general studies. This is a basic program to prepare us for the real curriculum which will begin next year... if we succeed."

"I bet you'll do just fine."

"I'm doing okay. What about you? Are you still teaching in America?"

"Yes, I'm still teaching... a lot. Teaching is my job, what I do to make a living but I wish I had more time to write."

Osnat looks both surprised and pleased by this. "What do you write?"

"Mostly poetry and essays."

She looks serious for a moment, "I didn't know that you write poems. I thought you were just a teacher."

"No, mostly I am a poet," I confess.

"I write poetry, too" Osnat says with quiet excitement.

"Do you really?" I ask, stunned.

I feel like I have been given a gift, that by finally revealing the most important thing about my life to Osnat, I am rewarded by discovering that she, too, is a poet. Somehow I never bothered to tell her this before, assuming that somehow she knew or that it wasn't really important.

"Who are your favorite poets?" I ask, not wanting this conversation to end.

"I love Amharic poets, Bialik, Agnon, the other great Hebrew poets. I also love Amos Oz novels—I just finished reading Black Box."

"Really? That's one of my favorite novels by Oz," I say surprised by the depths of what Osnat must be able to understand about Israeli society, about love and about betrayal. When had she transformed into this woman who feels so strongly about the things I hold most dear? How could we have not known this about each other in any tangible way? The twenty-four-year-old American woman and the thirteen-year-old Ethiopian girl who once joined over the English alphabet, who were joined by their mistrust for language, who were often separated by the difficulty of language, are both poets, that had been the missing link.

Osnat writes poems in Amharic in her English notebook. When I ask to read them she says they are *stom*—no big deal. She adds how difficult it is to translate them from Amharic into English. When I persist in my desire to see them she searches everywhere for her English notebook, but can't find it. Nor can she find the words to tell me what the poems are about. She says they are about nature and many things.

"Have you been to the caravans yet?" she asks, changing the subject.

I tell her about my interview with Shai in the caravan and how angry he was about the professor's book about the Ethiopian Jews' alleged Christian origins. She was familiar with the professor's work and had just returned from a seminar where his name came up.

"My seminar was led by the anthropologist Shoshana Ben Dor. It was about Ethiopian culture for Ethiopians. Shoshana presented us with prayers in Ge'ez as well as Hebrew and English. She also helped us to talk about our feelings and difficulties."

"That sounds wonderful; tell me more."

"Shoshana is trying to hand us back our own culture. Many of the young Ethiopians become lost in the desert. They are not exactly Israeli and they don't know enough about their own heritage, and also Ethiopian women don't pray and there is often a *kes*, an Ethiopian priest who prays for the rest of the community."

Lost in the desert is how many are describing the older generation as well. When Osnat goes to the kitchen, I think about the meeting I'd had with Shoshana earlier that week in Jerusalem. She felt that Israelis do not value Ethiopian culture and that college kids are dealing with issues of identity more than any other group. She had described the good and bad stereotypes that people have made about the Ethiopians. The good stereotypes are that they are quiet and diligent. The bad stereotypes are that they are primitive and slow learners. People value the Ethiopians for making the Israelis more Zionistic, not for what they can contribute to Israeli society.

Osnat returns from the kitchen with a carefully orchestrated question. "Do you remember when you told me you had a boyfriend? Why didn't he come to Israel with you?"

"He didn't come because he works and besides... I wanted to come alone. I have a lot of work to do here."

"What does your boyfriend do...is he Jewish?"

"Steve is a mathematician. He has an amazing mind. He remembers everything. He can tell you what happened on this exact day a year ago or maybe even ten years ago."

"Is he Jewish?" she asks again in case I forgot her question.

"Yes, he's Jewish—in fact he studied in a Yeshiva."

"Tell him that I studied in a Yeshiva, too," she says with a jovial laugh.

"And you, do you have a boyfriend?" Osnat smiles shyly but doesn't answer right away, so I continue talking. "I remember when I asked you when you were thirteen if you thought about getting married. You said not for at least twenty years. Have you changed your mind?"

"I don't know about that but, yes, I have a boyfriend, Dani." After many short but probing questions I learn that he is a twenty-four-year-old Ethiopian who loves to paint. She describes his paintings as very beautiful and something in her voice, a certain lightness and music, tells me that she is in love.

"Dani sounds wonderful. Where did you meet?"

"We met in Ramat Eliyahu where his family lives, and now he studies architecture at Tel Aviv University. He is very nice."

"Do you want to marry him?"

"I don't think about marriage now, I study. But is it permissible for me to ask you if you want to marry your boyfriend?"

I am not sure how I would answer her in English, and trying to do so in Hebrew feels impossible. Yet it forces me to cut to the heart of the matter, allows me to avoid describing the complexities I find in knowing the answer to that question.

"I'm not sure if it is right or not. I've known him for less than a year. If a time comes when I feel certain, then I will marry him."

As the sun becomes less potent we venture out to the edge of Mount Carmel and look down at a vast and silent valley. Osnat points to a monument in the distance from the 1973 War. On Shabbat she and her friends had walked all of the way there. They had only meant to go for a short stroll, but they just kept going until they reached it. Her story reminds me of the trips my friends and I would take on the Sabbath in Ma'alot when we would hike until we ended up in faraway valleys, sunburned, exhausted and happy.

We walk on towards a watchtower that Osnat speaks of excitedly, and on the way pass another group of her friends. The Ethiopian women, like Osnat, exude style, confidence and grace. I feel like the outsider among them, the white-skinned girl, affected by the elements, my skin red from the heat. My thirty-three-year-old body is heavier than their delicate twenty-year-old bodies. Earlier, in the elevator of her dorm, I looked at our reflections in the mirror, startled by how much thinner and more graceful Osnat is than I and at the deeper and more even color of her skin. I envy, too, the way they carry their silence so gracefully blended with their posture, their delicate yet deep eyes. My American silence seems louder, like an unwanted guest.

On top of the watchtower, we take in the view, running from side to side to see each angle of mountains, hills and valleys stunning in their late spring green.

"*Maksim, maksim,*" Osnat repeats.

It isn't until I hear the word several times in different contexts that I realize it means *enchanting.*

In the student cafeteria Osnat grows quiet. When I pay for our coffee she insists that I'm the guest and so she should pay. I'm not good at being the guest. Visit after visit to Ramat Eliyahu, she would prepare meals for me. I no longer have my own home in Israel to invite her to, so I invite her for coffee even if we are meeting on her college campus. During moments like this, maybe I still feel uncomfortable about the letter she once wrote, asking me for something I couldn't give her. During moments like this, do I see her as the hungry-eyed girl in a *medinah* in Marrakech who

had tried to sell me baskets, the same summer Osnat had written asking me for money?

Osnat's eyes are different now: they are open, knowing and content. But I still don't let her pay for the black coffee we sip as we watch the people around us, mostly groups of Israeli and Arab students laughing and talking.

A group of American students speak English at the table next to us. It seems too public, suddenly, to speak of our own lives.

Placing the bitter coffee on the table next to me and gathering my hair in an elastic band on top of my head, I adopt the journalist's persona. I am aware of time ticking away, and I fear I'm losing Osnat in the crowd, that we are losing the connection.

"So Osnat, how do you think the *olim* who came with Operation Solomon are doing?"

"The caravans are very bad. The Ethiopians don't socialize with Israelis or learn the language. We learned Hebrew faster because we had to. There were no translators then. Hebrew is coming more slowly to the newcomers because they don't have to learn." She pauses for a moment and then adds with a new severity, "They live in a ghetto."

The word *ghetto* is the only English word Osnat utters in our conversation. I wonder if she knows its connotations and the uncomfortable response it would evoke in me.

She continues, "When I began my studies at the university I volunteered in the largest caravan in Israel, it's called San Jen and it's outside of Acre. This is how I know this. If you want to see the Ethiopians from Operation Solomon you should go there. It is much bigger than the Jerusalem Caravan."

"Have you seen my cousins?" Osnat asks back at her dorm room as we sip cold cola.

"Yeah, I saw them last week. Can you believe how tall Elad is! And Batya has become a teenager. I can't believe Amnon will be going to the army soon. He has become so… stylish." Osnat smiles tenderly, listening to my descriptions of her cousins whom she only sees once or twice a year.

"And what about you Dina, what is it that you teach in America?"

"I teach mostly writing, but this year I also taught a course on literature of the Holocaust."

"Cool," she says with renewed energy. "I also want to be a teacher. Ethiopians are quiet in school, and so the Israeli teachers will ignore them."

"I love thinking of you as a teacher. And you're right. Israel needs more teachers who can relate better to Ethiopian students."

Osnat fingers a message that she found in her mailbox and that she seems excited about receiving.

"Am I keeping you from anything? Do you need to get back to your studies?"

"No, I'm fine" she answers looking down at the paper in her hand.

"Well I better get back to my friend's house before it gets dark and I lose the way."

"Where does your friend live?"

"Yossi lives in Ahuza…"

"Ahhh, that's nice…they say the higher you are on the mountain, the more money you have," she says laughing.

As the bus approaches, we kiss twice on each cheek and call back to each other, "Don't lose the connection."

On the bus back to Ahuza, I think about Osnat's eyes: deeper and wiser; different from Yael's perplexed, sad eyes. Before my visit with Osnat I had dwelled on my fears of seeing her. It was only after our visit that I realized that she had concerns about me as well. Osnat had said, "*Dafka*, what do you know, you speak Hebrew well. I was afraid that you had forgotten the language."

And I was relieved to discover that Osnat walks with one foot in each world.

In some ways she's like other Israeli college students: wearing the same styles, listening to some of the same music, and participating in many of the same activities. Outside of her teenage world, she has come to appreciate the literature and culture of Israel. And as a poet, she is trying to find a language for her emotions.

She tells me about an Ethiopian student group she belongs to and how they wrote and performed in a play in order to explore some of the struggles that the Ethiopian families are dealing with. She had shown me a photograph of herself playing the part of a mother who had just given birth. She looked beautiful in the traditional white cape she wore in the picture. Her son in the play was in the army and had just returned home. This mother also had a child at the university who was confused because she didn't fit into the old culture and didn't really feel Israeli. The parents also felt funny because they didn't understand who their soldier son was becoming.

Osnat's family also spans generations, from her soldier brother Simha to her baby brother Baruch. She is the college student in the drama of her own life, a self-possessed confident beauty, in love, fluent in Israeli culture yet in her heart strongly and gracefully tied to her own culture. She returns to Ramat Eliyahu for every Jewish holiday. It is too difficult for her parents to visit her but her older brother Simha and her sister Marta, still in high school, sometimes visit her at school.

ᴟ

Osnat had given me directions to the San Jen caravan where I have an appointment to meet with Shula, the caravan social worker. San Jen is off the main road leading to Acre. Like Givat HaMatos, the Jerusalem caravan, it is a village of mobile homes surrounded by young trees. Unlike Givat HaMatos, there are no mountains or holy cities in the distance. But if you walk west to the end of the campground you will reach the Mediterranean Sea. San Jen is a much larger village as well. This is where Osnat works with the new immigrants who arrived with Operation Solomon. She teaches them Hebrew and speaks with them in Amharic about their daily struggles. I imagine she feels at home here and that many look up to her. I, on the other hand, feel all eyes on me as one of the few white people roaming around, seemingly lost.

As I try to decipher which mobile home belongs to Shula, I discover the Elie Wiesel Enrichment Center, a grocery store with Hebrew, Russian and Amharic lettering in front and a park with swings and slides facing west to the Mediterranean. In the center of this caravan is a cluster of official mobile homes, an administrative office, a clinic and, I finally discover, the office of Shula, the caravan social worker.

This sincere-looking woman in jeans and a T-shirt, no taller than five feet is open yet hurried. She is about to begin a meeting with the *shemagleoch* or wise-elders of the community who generally solve disputes and are called upon to help with marital problems between troubled couples. The social worker relies on the elders because they understand Ethiopian culture. Under most circumstances, the goal of the elders is to keep the couple together. This is the first time during her two-year tenure as social worker that a meeting of this nature was to take place and Shula is nervous, waiting for the elders to arrive.

"I'm sure they'd be fine without me. This is still their job. But I was asked to help the couple communicate with each other so I am." I am pleased to see that at least here, the generation that so many have described as "dying in the desert" is still an essential and respected part of the community.

She invites me to sit in on this meeting, but as the room fills up with the elders and other relatives, she decides it would be better if I listen from her office; a thin wall separates me from them. Again, like when I first entered this community, I am watching through a door, a window.

The young woman tells her story in Amharic and an Ethiopian leader translates it into Hebrew for the sociologist. She encourages each member of the conflict to tell their side and the elders will later advise them. A week earlier, Shula had succeeded in bringing a couple back together. I only understand the words—love, money, and caravan—and have no sense of what's going on once the negotiations begin. Men yell in Amharic. A woman cries.

After some time Shula apologizes for how long it's taking. She grabs some tissue and introduces me to her secretarial assistant in

an adjoining office. Malka is a young Ethiopian woman, dressed quite professionally by Israeli standards, in a yellow blouse and white skirt that falls just past her knees. She looks me in the eye and in fluid Hebrew explains the proceedings.

"When one party doesn't want a divorce and the other does, the negotiations take a long time. The negotiators are trying to find a way for them to live in peace until the divorce is finalized." (Even the elders had given up on trying to repair this union.)

We listen to the voices in the other room for a while and then she continues.

"The woman next door wants a divorce. She says that she doesn't love her husband and that he beats her. The husband says that he loves his wife, doesn't beat her and has no other family. Everyone is confused. No one knows if he beats her or not. Divorce takes a long time—sometimes ten or fifteen years. Meanwhile the wife is forced to live with her husband all that time. They are giving her permission to live with her parents instead. But she says there is not enough room in her parents' caravan. They have many children, and she has three of her own children. Next they tell her that she can split her caravan in half—half will go to her and her children and the other half will go to her husband. The woman doesn't accept this. She is afraid he'll kill her." Malka pauses for a moment, her voice tired as if she were carrying the woman's pain.

"It is all because of Israeli law," she continues with new energy. "It is so difficult for a woman to get a divorce if her husband doesn't want one. Her relatives are encouraging her to live in peace with him until the divorce. Marriage in Israel is especially difficult for people who come from the villages of Ethiopia. Men had more power because they earned and controlled the money. Now, in Israel, Ethiopian women want power over their own money, the money that they earn or that was given to them by their family. Men are very angry about this. Ten men have killed their wives in Israel because of money or because of the law that a woman has to stay with her husband until a divorce is granted."

The door is ajar and I can see Shula's arms around the woman's shoulder as she weeps.

Malka continues, "I am not from a village like the woman next door. In Addis Ababa, where I am from, things are more the way they are in Israel. Women work and control money like their husbands do. But I also have a problem. My husband's parents want me to have a child, but I am nineteen and I want to work first. My husband is unemployed. In Addis Ababa he drove a bus. I want to study and get a profession, become a nurse. My parents are still in Addis and want to stay there. My mother wants to come and see Jerusalem and then go back. She runs a store. My father is a doctor. So I am in Israel alone with my husband's family; they live near us in the Acre caravan. I want to have children later, after I get a career. They don't understand. But things are generally okay in the caravan. What good would it do me to say it's not okay in our caravan? When we get an apartment, we'll move."

At a few minutes before four o'clock, Malka cleans her desk and promptly at four she leaves; her workday is over. I am sad to lose her company and her occasional translations.

Shula collapses in the chair next to me, trying to recap what had taken place in the room next door. She does not speak of love and beatings, as Malka had, but of money matters. While Malka felt it would take years to settle this situation, Shula thinks it can be handled in months. In two weeks, Shula explains, the couple will return to the rabbinate and after a few more follow-up visits, the divorce will probably be given.

"The woman in this situation wants everything to be on her terms. The elders are trying to negotiate so that the husband will be satisfied as well. I tried to explain to the elders what I thought the problem was between the man and his wife, but I think they are fine without me. They do a wonderful job. No one knows for sure if the husband beats his wife... but anyway they finally came to a settlement. They will split the caravan in half but the husband must stay away from his wife. They will also split the money in half until the divorce is final. In two weeks they will go to the rabbinate, and he will divorce or invite them back. If he can't convince them to stay married, he will eventually divorce them."

"After two years in the country," Shula explains during our short ride to the Acre station, "many of the Ethiopians in the caravans still don't speak Hebrew. As I'm sure you've heard from others, the caravans are a very bad thing. If the Ethiopians lived in the cities among other Israelis, they wouldn't need all of these enrichment programs. They'd just acclimate naturally. Professionally, it's not good for you to know all of this—I mean the details of the troubled couple who I counseled today. So you just heard it somewhere —okay?"

"I just heard it somewhere," I repeat, having wondered all day about confidentiality.

Alone again on the bus from Acre to Haifa, I look at the sea and think about the olive trees that had recently been planted around the caravan, and how long it will take before they provide shade. I remember my first day at the Jerusalem caravan when I was awed by the sight of the new immigrants living again in their own culture rather than in absorption centers where it had seemed that everything had been stripped from them. But the point was driven home again, that while they function from day to day in their own culture, life in the larger Israel goes on without them. Except on a stage in Tel Aviv.

In the concert Hall on Ibn Givrol Street, in downtown Tel Aviv where I sit with my friend Yossi, the sadness of life in the caravans is replaced by the joy of rock musician Shlomo Gronich and his Ethiopian choir: two young boys and nine girls between the ages of nine and twenty-one. The girls are in white fitted outfits, a contrast to the loose capes of their mothers. Each has a bright green, pink or blue ribbon in her hair or around her waist. Two girls wear long silver Magen David pendants. Yossi and I sit among the hundreds of mostly white Israelis, mesmerized as Gronich and his chorus sing in Amharic, Hebrew and English while footage from Operation Solomon fills up two screens. There are images of the new immigrants stepping down from planes with blinking eyes, old men descending with canes, images from the absorption centers, a soldier hugging a father who has

just arrived with Operation Solomon, two older men reunited, sobbing and hugging, and children playing with new toys. These images flash on and off two large screens as the voices of these children bring back the joy and the hope.

The performers stand poised yet motionless, holding their feelings in their bodies. When there is a solo, I stare intently at their lips to see which are moving. Shlomo Gronich pours passion in his drums, his voice and in his body. He is the motion circling their stillness.

There are tears in Yossi's usually stoic eyes. The man next to me smiles the entire time. Their music, still bodies, and small strong voices that sing of Jerusalem, the difficulties of caravan life, the joy of reaching the land of Israel, rise in the air above them. The audience feels, again, the miracle of their arrival. When their performance ends after two encores, I know I can't leave the concert hall or the country without speaking with Shlomo Gronich.

I find him in a corner, surrounded by exuberant and exhausted children who are being congratulated by audience members. When the crowd clears out and Gronich sneaks away to have a cigarette, I approach him and tell him briefly about my project. He gives me his manager's number in Tel Aviv and agrees to have an interview with me later that week in Jerusalem.

🍃

Back in Jerusalem I set up a new room at my hotel on Bezalel Street, hang my hat and go to Ha Mashbir to meet Yael for a dinner date. I find her in the men's department folding jeans in her tight pink dress, red lipstick, and elegant pearl earrings. This refined look is a change from her appearance of two years before, which was more exotic, and sexy. I remember how Boaz had told her to use her looks to get a job, that if she applied at Ha Mashbir in person rather than over the phone, they would ignore her accent and be overtaken by her looks and hire her. I had found his advice sexist and exploitative, but now I had to acknowledge that it was probably also true.

"Thanks for waiting, *motek*," Yael says, folding the last pair of jeans.

"Give me one more minute to change clothes and we can go to dinner."

At Café Rimon in the mid Rehove, a paved area of stores, cafes and small shops where no cars could pass, we choose an outside table.

"Yael, what would you like to eat?" I ask, trying to establish that she will be my guest. She returns the question to me as if she were the host.

I quickly learn to ignore the many eyes that devour us as we savor our vegetarian schnitzel, chips and salad, which we agree are the healthiest items on the menu.

"This cola is really good," Yael says leaning into her chair. "Why do you only drink water?"

"Well it has a neutral taste, doesn't interfere with the meal and it doesn't have calories."

Yael laughs, places her hand on her flat belly and says, "I am so fat."

"I'm the one who has gotten fat," I insist.

"No, I am fat," she protests.

I never had conversations like this as a college student or as an adult. I've always been thin and unaware of the subtleties of other people's bodies. It is only in 1993 that I changed from thin to average. I didn't feel overweight until I started hanging out with Osnat and Yael.

"Dina, when I saw Osnat at our parent's house during the Shavuot holiday she said to me, 'Dina said you were skinny but you are fat,' Yael continues, laughing.

"Well, Yael, if Osnat thinks that you are fat then she must think I'm huge. Was she happy that I went to visit her?" I ask anxiously.

"Yes. She said you walked all over and did so much. But she felt bad that you paid for coffee. She said you came all the way to the university to see her and yet you also paid for the coffee." I thought back to how quiet Osnat had become that day in the cafeteria after I paid. I had attributed it mostly to being in public.

"Osnat has really grown up in the past two years."

"Yes, she wears a mini... well not a mini but she dresses differently at home. My father thinks we are still religious."

"Do you have a good relationship with your family?"

"Yes, of course! What a question!" Yael exclaims.

"I asked because sometimes when people leave home they change and don't get along with their families in the same way."

"Well, not Ethiopians. For us the family is very strong."

"And very large," I add.

"Yes. It was so funny when Osnat and I were at home last week, we told our parents to stop having children. 'Enough already,' we told them. But we had so much fun over the holiday playing with the children, especially Baruch," she says with an adoring smile.

Yael takes out a mirror from her purse and reapplies her red lipstick.

"Osnat also said that you have such a good memory, Dina. She said you remember when she was thirteen and she said that she didn't want to get married for at least twenty years!"

I laugh, flashing back to the conversation we'd had earlier that week in Osnat's dorm room. "I was surprised and happy to learn that Osnat has a boyfriend and writes poetry! Did you know that?"

"I knew about Osnat's boyfriend but I haven't met him. She doesn't talk about him that much. I didn't know that she writes poetry. She doesn't tell me things," Yael says sadly.

"I tell my friends more than I tell my sister," I confess, trying to cheer her up.

"I guess I do the same thing," Yael acknowledges. "You eat so slowly, and so little at a time, like a girl. Eat more," Yael commands in the motherly tone she also uses when she corrects my Hebrew. She often makes fun of my thick, American Chicago-accented Hebrew. She'll sternly correct a wrong conjugation or when I emphasize the incorrect syllable, and she'll put her arm around my shoulder and say, laughing, "It's okay. If only I could speak English the way you speak Hebrew."

When Yael does offer a few English words, she over-pronounces them as if the language itself is a joke.

"When Osnat told me you paid for coffee I asked her if she thanked you and she said to me in English, 'yes, I said to Dina, thank you very much,' and we both laughed really hard."

I'm amused that the language I tried to teach them during their first days in Israel has become something that is only used in college books for Osnat or as a way of imitating Americans. The language we had all struggled with in 1985 had become their second language, almost as natural to them as Amharic. Having lived in the Diaspora all these years, for me Hebrew is still a struggle and the only language I can use to speak to Osnat and Yael. Although I have always loved Hebrew and mastering it has been a lifelong goal, they have become the reason I've held onto to it as strongly as I have and why when in Israel, I conduct my life and many of my relationships in Hebrew.

Unlike in the past, Yael often compares things to Ethiopia. She says the waitresses are more polite there (ours disappeared for a long time after slamming down plates in front of us) and that drivers in Israel are crazier. In 1985, there had been two places: America and Israel. Osnat and Yael could not speak of Ethiopia. Now we acknowledge three countries as home. But during moments like these we connect as outsiders whose mother country is elsewhere. When we first met, we just wanted to be Israeli. I was discarding my American identity that I felt only got in the way of absorbing life in Israel. They were busy abandoning parts of their Ethiopian identities, at least in the public domain, because it was getting in the way of their absorption. But as our relationships with Israel and with each other have deepened over the years, the American and Ethiopian aspects of our personalities have been welcomed back in their entirety.

When the check comes we both reach for it. Yael wins our tug-of-war and holds the check to her chest. I think about what Yael had said about Osnat feeling bad that I paid for coffee so although I feel uncomfortable about it, I finally agree to let Yael pay.

"You are visiting me in my city," she argues.

"It is our city," I protest. But I know that it is Yael's home. And this moment makes clear that I don't have to patronize her or treat her differently than any of my other friends.

We are looking for shoes. Yael wants a pair with a high heel, and I'm looking for a pair of black Na'ot sandals for my boyfriend Steve. We move quickly from store to store, not liking the high prices or the merchandise. Wherever we turn eyes are on Yael: the eyes of men, women and children. There are sometimes gentle eyes, admiring her beauty, her dark skin contrasted with her white outfit: white jean shorts, a white short-sleeved sweater with a long V cut out against her back. Her French braid shows off silver dangling earrings. I feel more and more clumsy as I look at the repeated images of the two of us in the mirror: my short stature next to her tall slenderness, my light curly hair, wild from the wind next to her neatly braided black hair, my white skin, burnt from the sun next to her smooth, even black skin.

We pass another store where Yael points to some girlish silver and gold flat sandals and chuckles, "This is something Osnat would wear." We walk on until we get to my room on Bezalel Street where we stop for sweaters since day has changed to evening and the air has grown cool. Yael looks around shyly at my rented room. I wish that I had my own home in Jerusalem where I could serve her cake and coffee. Instead I invite her to walk with me to the Ethiopian Coptic Church.

The Ethiopian church, which can be found just off the Street of the Prophets on Ethiopia Street, is one of the most peaceful places I have known in Jerusalem. The houses along the street have long entrances surrounded by gardens and have not been altered in the hundred or so years that many have stood. Sara and I had visited this church together on a hot August afternoon. Its cool interior, salmon-colored ceiling, subtle but elegant ornamentation kept out the noise and tension of 1989.

Now, at the end of my 1993 journey, I have not yet found my way back. My days have been so full of appointments and I don't want to go alone. Although Yael is reluctant to enter this Ethiopian Christian neighborhood because of the immodest way she's dressed, she finally agrees to go. I know she is only doing it for me and I allow her to.

We walk through the Ben Yehuda pedestrian mall and eventually reach the Street of the Prophets. We both thought that we knew our way but suddenly realize we are lost. A group of Ethiopian men in long robes pass us. Yael grabs my shoulder and says, "Dina, go back and ask those people for directions—in English."

I call out the English words "Excuse me," and the men turn around and greet us with warm smiles. One elderly man explains in English where we need to turn to reach the church and then quickly changes to Amharic, directing the information at Yael.

As we turn again in another direction I ask Yael, "Are they Christians?"

"Yes," she answers emphatically.

"How do you know?"

"Because they live here," Yael says, turning her head away from my questions. Another Ethiopian priest, robe covering his head, passes by us. He mutters something at Yael which she translates to me as "Shalom."

We are quiet for a while, trying to find our way when Yael blurts out, "Dina, I'm feeling embarrassed because we may run into people I know."

"Do you want to continue on?" I ask.

"Yes. Let's get to the church."

I don't know how she would know some of these people, but I don't ask. I wonder how it feels for her to meet this group of Ethiopian Christians in Israel. It becomes clear that walking to Ethiopia Street is a bigger compromise than I had realized, but I'm not sure why.

When we reach Ethiopia Street I see the dome in the distance. We approach the gate that surrounds the church, but it is locked. We stand in front for a while, peering in through the bars. I'm

relieved that we at least had found the place and also relieved that we can't enter. This visit evokes feelings that I see in Yael's eyes and posture, feelings she doesn't want to discuss. We study the houses surrounding the church and I say longingly, "I'd love to live in Ethiopia Street. It is so peaceful here."

"Not me," Yael replies. "It's too quiet. I need people around." She looks down at her feet.

"Are you ready to leave, Yael?"

"Sure."

"Would you like to get some frozen yogurt?" I ask, trying to shift gears.

"No, I'm so fat."

Back on bustling Ben Yehuda Street, Yael finally agrees to some yogurt. We run into people she knows. Young women take her hand and say, "Shalom, *motek*, is everything okay?" And as always, men stare. We rest on a stone ledge with melting yogurt before heading to Yael's bus stop.

"What is your Amharic name... and Osnat's Amharic name? I can't believe that I don't know this."

"We only use those names at home. Mine is too difficult to pronounce. I'll write it down for you some other time. Osnat's name is Asmerlach," she says, smiling again for the first time since our walk to the church.

"*Asmerlach*," I repeat. "What a beautiful name. What would she do if I called her *Asmerlach*?"

"That would be so funny. Next time call her that and see what happens," she says laughing.

"And Elad's Amharic name—do you know what it is?"

"I can't remember," and then changing the subject she says, "Some day you, Osnat and I should go to Eilat together, just the three of us, when we have vacation time."

I am looking for a string for my hat that the Jerusalem wind blows off my head. On our way to her stop I describe the hat to Yael.

"Dina, don't get string. Only old people wear strings like that." After that, I point to whatever chic model I can find in a store window who wears a string with her hat.

As we near the bus, a foreign tourist stops Yael and says, "You look very nice."

I see she is annoyed so I shout at him in Hebrew "Go from here." He persists until Yael says to him in English "Fuck you!"

"You can fuck me if you want," he replies.

"If you don't go from here I'll call the police," Yael screams.

When he finally walks away he turns back and says in Hebrew, "The funny thing is I am the police."

Frustrated and angry Yael says, "He is crazy like so many others." We wait quietly together for the bus, looking around to make sure the man is gone. When the bus arrives we kiss once, Israeli style and promise to call each other.

The next morning, tired suddenly of looking like a shlumpy traveler, I go to a fine dress shop on King Solomon Square where there's a sign in the window that says "Summer Dresses on Sale." The second dress I try on, with small red and green flowers, transforms me back into a woman.

I'm uncomfortable, however, at how low the dress is cut. When I point this out to the sales lady she asks, "What is it you have to hide?" I buy the dress, relieved that I'll have something to wear for my interview with Shlomo Gronich and for moments when the image of Yael's reflection next to mine makes me want to envelope myself in grace.

I carry my new dress down the narrow Jerusalem streets, and think about beautification. I remember what Robert had said at dinner the night before about Jerusalem—how he loved the new parks and the newly finished streets and corners. "Wherever you turn," he said, "I can see the beautiful, personal careful improvements. I can feel the touch of Mayor Teddy Kollek's hands." Both Jerusalem and I were under construction.

❦

A phone booth on a crowded corner of King George Street becomes my office. This is where I spend my mornings among impatient Israelis who wait for me to finish my calls or where I wait for them in what shade I can find. I lean against the pay phone telling Kevin, a young journalist who had been described to me as an "all around expert" by a mutual friend in Chicago, the truths I've found about the Ethiopian community's absorption into Israel; he responds in generalities.

"The Ethiopians are lovely and impossible. When they don't want to talk, they have nothing to say. They don't speak at all. It is part of their etiquette to break three appointments before they actually meet with you. There are some success stories but overall it has been very difficult for them here. It has been difficult for them to break the gap within the family. There is a big contrast between the children and the adults over thirty."

I tell Kevin the story of Shai, the Ethiopian leader of the Jerusalem caravan, and what he had said about the professor who had written a book about the Christian origins of Ethiopian Jews and how they see him as a betrayer. Kevin says it is a distortion and that it would be worth my while to speak with him directly. I had been trying to reach the professor since I had first arrived in Israel almost a month earlier but had just about given up. Kevin gives me a new phone number to try where he thinks the professor could easily be reached. I try the number and five minutes later have an appointment at Mount Scopus with the infamous professor.

I had not been to Hebrew University on Mount Scopus since 1984, when Boaz was a student there. Now I've come to meet with the de-mythologizer. I meet this tall, pleasant-looking American man in the faculty cafeteria. We find a table in the corner and over coffee talk flows freely between us.

"I was surprised by the suspicious way one of the Ethiopian leaders in the caravan responded to me," I tell him after describing

my project. He listens with concentrated attention and then leans over the table in order to be heard amidst all of the other voices.

"They have a certain idea about the role of the researcher. During Operation Moses, the 'researcher' served as a public relations person for the Ethiopians and taught others about Ethiopian culture. Now that people know a bit more about it, the role of the researcher is becoming more complex. They are looking more deeply into things and sometimes their findings are critical. The Ethiopians don't accept this and as a result have become suspicious." He pauses, wraps two hands around his half empty cup and continues.

"My view of the Ethiopians in Israel is growing more and more pessimistic, much more than before. Two major reasons are housing and the passivity of Ethiopian leaders. First housing: the Ethiopians, as you know, are now in caravans where their role models are Russians and homeless Israelis. They aren't integrating. The other problem is that they have been offered a mortgage, which would pay 85% of their apartment, and many aren't accepting it. They seem to be waiting for the apartments to be given to them for free. They are afraid of the responsibility. One woman was afraid that if her mother took the mortgage and died, she would be left with it. She couldn't figure out the value, and she is a banker. I think they should be given three opportunities to buy a house, and if they refuse all of them—that's it."

I cringe at his recommendation. I think of a story I was working on some years before about the Chicago Housing Authority moving a black family from the projects to the suburbs. Each family was shown three homes and if none suited them, their opportunity to leave the projects was over.

The professor continues, "It is unrealistic of them to be so demanding about where they live. They are practically being given free housing, so they have to realize that it can't be exactly where they want it to be. People are always comparing the Ethiopians to the Russians and saying that the Russians are getting more and therefore the Israelis are racist. Then the Ethiopians are suspicious because they are the only group being offered this housing deal.

"The second problem is the passivity of the Ethiopian leaders. They are focusing on essential secondary issues such as the *Falash Mura* and complaining about what isn't being given to them instead of farsighted issues like education and empowering themselves to be better leaders and training others to lead them. Let me give you an example. An Ethiopian leader went on TV and complained about not getting enough blankets or food in the caravan. He returned to the same station months later saying that nothing had been done. Meanwhile this man who had plenty of resources to do so, didn't take it upon himself all of this time to get blankets.

"I gave a lecture on this in the States, and a friend of mine said that I better not call the Ethiopians passive or else I will be called a racist. I think that the Ethiopians have been given too much help so they are not taking the initiative to better their lives. When I look back on the problems of Operation Moses they seem like nothing compared to what is happening now. There are 350 cases of AIDS among the Ethiopian population. There is one story circulating that Shamir said not to test them because we'll take them anyway. There is another story that Shamir said to test them, but the Jewish Agency said not to. They are now trying to control this problem. Everyone between the ages of twelve and fifty was tested. The general public doesn't seem to care because they assume that they won't be having sex with the Ethiopians. It's hard to convince the Ethiopians to use condoms. If the disease spreads, it could stigmatize the entire group.

"Bringing the Falash Mura could also strongly affect the public's view of the Ethiopians. There is no end to how many people will come. Many of these people converted to Judaism because it became convenient to be Jewish. Ethiopians with families still in Ethiopia are fighting for the Falash Mura. Those who don't have family among them are very quiet about this issue. Twelve *kessim* out of 350 are in favor of it. As I said, this large number of conveniently converted Jews will change the public attitude towards all of the Ethiopians for the worse."

The professor pauses for a moment and then looks me squarely in the eye.

"Dina, you've probably heard about the issue surrounding my research about the Christian origins of the Ethiopians." I nod and wait for him to continue. "Well this doesn't affect my feelings about them being here. They converted 500 years ago. Now they are Jews. I only have a problem with the people who are now converting to Judaism because it is convenient—six months before their anticipated *aliyah* to Israel. But it's up to the Rabbinate to decide. My book was written for scholars—not the general public. I did not attempt to change the Ethiopians' status as Jews—I attempted to get at the truth. I was on TV, and that's how the Ethiopians know of me. They did not read my book. And yes, there has been a lot of backlash. I have basically been *disowned* by the Ethiopian Jewish community. When my name comes up they say I am *lo beseder*—not okay—and they won't allow me to come to events. I, as the chairman of African studies, wasn't invited to a major Ethiopian cultural event. I understood that this would not have been an appropriate place for me to present, but it was a loud statement for me not to have been invited. I am also cut off from grants… so I'm going back to my work on Christianity."

"Regardless of how much you do for them, once you become an enemy, it's difficult to outlive that. Another researcher, for example, has been ostracized for refusing to bring the Falash Mura —the converts. People are afraid of making waves and making difficult decisions like forcing the Ethiopians to take control of their own lives and making decisions about housing, taking apartments, etc., in order not to be the bad guy. People are quick to say, 'Poor Ethiopians – look what evil people are doing to them.' People are quick to yell racism. During Operation Moses everyone defined the big problem as waiting for family still in Ethiopia and that once families were together, everything would be fine. No one wants to blame the other."

I absorb his words, along with his sadness, anger and disillusionment. It is time for him to teach his next class. I'm thankful that I got to hear the other side of the story and see that this man whom so many had spoken of was not a villain but a scholar, trying to get at his own truth.

I move to an outside table overlooking Jerusalem hills and slowly transform into a Jerusalemite. The nagging voice inside of me returns. This is my home—why don't I live here? My writing is about Israel. The Hebrew poets are the voices that speak to me most deeply. My greatest concerns and loyalties lie with this country, the country I visit every other year. In my long marriage with Israel, I am re-entering the honeymoon period a day before I am to leave again. During moments like this I forget that it isn't only that sometimes my view of living in Israel is idealistic and other times practical. In many ways this is not the same country I fell in love with in 1984. Values have changed and tensions, heightened. And as I had felt most dramatically in 1991, sometimes it is difficult to feel a profound difference between the concerns of Americans and Israelis—making a good living and getting ahead. Malls crop up in every major city.

But when I look at Jerusalem hills, which have remained intact and unchanged for centuries, I can still dream.

Every man or woman who walks by in the cafeteria looks like a potential friend. They are speaking about books I've read, arguing with conviction and animation about ideas; their faces open and alive. They are wearing Na'ot sandals and long or short curls hang down backs or crown heads. I relish every view around me and think about the cement jungle where I teach in America and how there are more complaint sessions than fulfilling conversations among my colleagues. Back at my Chicago university I don't feel deeply connected to many of my colleagues besides a poet here and there or a grad student who lived eight years in Israel. As I sit here, lost in Jerusalem hills, I can't remember why I had decided to live in America—or perhaps I never really did decide. I let gravity decide for me.

۱۶

The next morning I put on my new Israeli dress and prepare for my interview with Shlomo Gronich. Inspired by Yael's style and Osnat's grace I've become elegant. I walk downtown, stroll through

a stone courtyard and arrive at the Voice of Israel radio station to meet Shlomo Gronich. When I get to the main office I assume I'll have a lot of explaining to do about who I am but the receptionist has been expecting me; she assures me Shlomo will be finished with his radio interview shortly. I walk out into the garden where I had sat with my *ulpan* class in 1984. Now I am alone, no longer a visitor but a writer who is about to meet with a rock star.

A few minutes later Shlomo comes into the lobby in a T-shirt, jeans and his long gray ponytail falls down his back. We exchange pleasantries and walk along the narrow road outside the compound, acknowledging the charms of Jerusalem. As we awkwardly decide where to go, some guys from inside the pub call out to Shlomo, "Hey, come in, have a beer on us."

"I don't drink beer," Shlomo calls back laughing.

"Then come drink whatever you want." We sit down in the dark pub where they bring us mineral water and disappear into the woodwork.

I tell Shlomo how the Sheba Choir's music brought back the joy I had felt in the aftermath of Operation Solomon, the joy I don't see much of anymore.

"I'm pleased to hear that," he says, loosening his posture, "That is what I want to express in my music—it would be too easy to draw upon their pain."

"How did you get involved with this group of children?"

"Two years ago, two months after the big Solomon operation, the Israeli television program for youth wanted to produce a day of broadcasting for the Ethiopian immigrants. They contacted me and asked me to establish a choir for this occasion. I went to a station and met a group of forty Ethiopian kids from Hadera, which is an amazing point because I was born in Hadera. I chose six out of them, and it was the root of the choir."

"How did they feel performing in public?" I ask, wondering about their shyness and strong sense of privacy.

"It is constant work and effort to make them move and make them feel free and bouncy and loose on stage. When they go on stage they close up. It embarrasses them to sing in front of so many people."

"But they are very professional. It looked like it was very hot. They were probably very tired but they never showed it."

"Yes, yes. I'm not sure it's only because they're professional; it's just like that; they won't show it. I think they've made amazing progress since I've worked with them, amazing. They are getting better all of the time and each performance is a bit looser than the previous one. When they are old, they'll be all right," Shlomo says with a laugh.

"I wasn't able to understand all of the words in your songs," I confess. "So what is the caravan song about?"

"The caravan song is the only song that expresses protest. In continuation of what we spoke about before...I'm not trying to show any bitterness in this project. The opposite. And the only song that is expressing bitterness is the caravan song that says:

we don't have anything much to eat
we don't have many clothes
daddy doesn't have a job
mommy is silent and weeping at home.
Here they call me Elidor, sings Daniel,
at school they call me Nigger and they mean that I am black.

"There is another interesting point," Shlomo continues. "The Ethiopian people don't like to make a comparison between them and black Americans. But I think there are similarities. They are a minority and there is (my English)... A lot of ehhh, racism. They've originated from Africa. Also, they love Michael Jackson. They relate to black music easier maybe than other music. One of the songs we are doing is called Motherless Child. It's a black American spiritual which I took into their heritage." Shlomo begins singing,

"Long way from home, long way from Ethiopia...They are just wonderful kids. It is difficult to work with them but on the other hand it is so easy, so full of love and appreciation. They listen so well. It's so wonderful that all of the difficulties become only stones on the way; it's a long way..."

"Shlomo, how do you get at...I'm not sure if there is an answer to this, but how do you bring out the joy in them?"

"There are no secret methods or I don't think about how to do it. We are like family, so we feel we are together and when we go on stage warmth is already there; warmth brings joy. We meet and music is secondary almost, not always, but we meet in order to meet and then we also sing, we speak, we watch TV, we go to Luna Park. I listen to their music quite a lot, to the music they brought from Ethiopia, and I try to get it into my blood. What I have taken inside has come out in my music as well."

He continues, "They are very soulful people. They are still innocent, and they've kept their real belief in G-d or whatever. I say real because they had to have a true belief in G-d for so many years, so far away, in order to sustain their identity. And they came here after thousands of years as Jews. It is amazing to think they've kept their Judaism for so long. They don't like to talk about their problems in school or the racism they experience, but when you enter their souls you find out that they are very sad and uh... depressed. It's a very sad story, the whole *aliyah* from Ethiopia... the way we brought them here so gloriously and then they are stuck in caravans in the middle of nowhere, and they have no work and nothing to eat."

"Nothing to eat?" I repeat.

"Not nothing to eat, but they are very poor. A cynical person might say—what did they have there? But the truth is they lived quite well in Ethiopia. They had their life."

"And agriculture, the land," I add.

"Yes, of course, the land."

Shlomo leaves first, anxious to return to Tel Aviv, his home. There is no limo waiting for him, as there would be for an American rock star of his stature. I sit for a moment, motionless, wondering how our talk had taken such a sad turn. I had come to talk to him about joy. I pour his remaining mineral water and mine into one plastic container and saunter into the hot sun. I go straight to the record store where the tape of Shlomo and his chorus that I've been waiting for has just been released.

At Sara's apartment on Shebazi Street, in the Old Iraqi neighborhood in Jerusalem where I've come for Shabbat, I unwrap the tape and hand it to her. She places it in the tape deck and we stand there together as the voice of a young Ethiopian boy blares from the speaker, "My mother and father still dream of the land of Israel in the caravan...my mother and father still love the land of Israel..." Sara and I look at each other with huge smiles as both the joy and the sadness reverberate off of the ancient Jerusalem tile.

A Garden; A Country
(1995)

Out of a handful of sand
We will make the beginning
Of a garden just as, since the exodus
We have made our sky out of all
the grains of silence.

—*Edmond Jabès*
from The Book of Questions

Most of us work. We work in factories and we work for Karen Kayemet planting trees. Whatever work we get we are satisfied with. The Russians came with degrees in medicine and engineering. When people give them a mop and ask them to wash the floor they refuse and say 'I'm a doctor.' It is very difficult for Russians to pass the medical exam here and so they suffer. We, on the other hand, will take whatever job we can get. We want to work.

—*Shai from Givat HaMatos Caravan*

When I left Israel in 1993, the voices of Shlomo Gronich and the Sheba Choir followed me back to America. I moved to their rhythms in the new home I now shared with Steve. As he and I danced in circles, I would look out the window to the east, Lake Michigan, where on still days, I could hear the waves. Sometimes they lulled me to sleep. In my dreams I would still be leaning further east, toward Jerusalem.

When I board the plane for this next return, Steve is by my side, cameras in tow. My mathematician lover points out that since I left Israel in 1985, I always return during the odd years: 1989, 1991, 1993 and now it is 1995. I sense that during this trip patterns will shift. I am not a lone traveler and my own question of home has grown more complex since it now includes Steve. Can Steve and I be for one another a permanent home? And on which soil would we plant our tree?

And what about the Ethiopian community? How far do they still have to journey until they are finally at home? I know that my friends' lives are moving forward. Osnat is studying hard at university, part of a community of friends and maintaining her Ethiopian identity, replenishing it with what she is learning as a student. Batya is close to graduating from high school, Amnon will soon finish the army, and other family members work hard and live in a large and integrated town. But many of the Jews who arrived with Operation Solomon are moving slowly or staying still. If being at home means being allowed to be oneself and at the

same time contribute to one's community, then they are still falling short. At least that was the truth of 1993. How far had things moved in two years?

The Ethiopian community still speaks in whispers, protests in silence, but more and more voices could now be heard in song and in other forms of expression. Over time, the singers, dancers, artists and artisans have found ways to express their struggles, their history and their identities through their art. In the Jerusalem of 1995, Ethiopian culture is not only found in the hills of Givat HaMatos among caravan sites but in fancy shops and galleries as well.

In the Exodus Gallery in Jerusalem, I run my hands through the woven baskets that Ethiopian women now make with the lesser quality materials they find in Israel and sometimes with materials sent from Ethiopia. These baskets which I've admired in the homes of many Ethiopian families sell for hundreds of dollars. I get lost in their raw textures, clay sculptures, knitted pillowcases and Matzoth covers. The most popular item, the friendly Australian proprietor informs us, is a clay fertility box. The two halves of this ceramic egg-shaped sculpture are held together at one end by a small piece of rope. Inside the egg are the figures of a man and a woman embracing. A couple is supposed to leave this object next to their bed. If the egg is closed, it means the woman does not want to make love. If it is open, it means she is in the mood. True to Ethiopian etiquette, there need not be any additional discussion on this delicate issue. The proprietor, a handsome man in his mid-fifties explains this to us, laughing, "At my age I'm the one who needs this at my side; I'm the one who is not in the mood. I think this is a sexist object. Or, every couple should have two of these." Steve and I buy one for some friends of ours who are getting married on our return from Israel, and one for ourselves.

Ethiopian art is also the main attraction at Colors of Israel, a small shop in the Old City. The reds, greens and deep purples of the baskets, scarves and tapestries call out to us from the narrow alley that surrounds the shop. Colors of Israel is much smaller and focuses mostly on Ethiopian art: what the new immigrants create in Israel as well as exports from the Jews who remain in Addis

Ababa. Most popular are the canvas wall hangings, which in drawings tell the biblical story of King Solomon and the Queen of Sheba.

Colors of Israel, like Exodus Gallery, carries the work of Mulu Geta, Israel's most prominent Ethiopian artist, known for his intricately sculpted pieces of Ethiopia. In the store window sits his sculpture of a woman in a *shamma* making *injera* with her baby on her back. The mother image, always beautiful and proud, is prominent in his work. Another sculpture shows two Ethiopian families—one happy and one on mourning. In the latter sculpture the mother is missing.

In an interview in the *Jerusalem Post*, Geta described his work as dealing with "the yearning for another world and for the ability to speak in another language—as a person who resides in one place but whose whole being yearns for many other places and times." Geta has been sculpting since he was a young boy in Ethiopia. He would help his mother make dolls for the local tourist trade and cooking utensils for the family. He later worked in a ceramics factory making dishes and teaching ceramics at the factory's in-house school.

Geta arrived in Israel in 1984 with Operation Moses along with his wife and two children. In Israel, he started making his own sculptures at a program initiated by joint distribution committee to help talented Ethiopian artists develop their craft and gain exposure. Ten years later Geta has his own studio in Jerusalem where his work sells for thousands of dollars. His work has also been exhibited in museums throughout America and Europe. He is the only Ethiopian artist who earns a living—a good one at that— solely through his artwork.

❧

"What a day," Steve sighs over Yemenite soup. "I really envy the lives of those proprietors, especially the guy in Colors of Israel. I'd love to hang out in the Old City all day selling art and watching people walk by."

"Well not all of the tourists are as pleasant to deal with as we are," I remind him. We are at a small Yemenite café on King Solomon, a narrow stone street just off the bustling Ben Yehuda Street. While Steve romanticizes the lives of the art dealers, I'm feeling hopeful about the burgeoning number of Ethiopian artists whose work is being displayed.

I dip a piece of *malaweh,* fried bread, into my hummus and try to articulate for Steve what the afternoon has meant to me.

"You know in Ethiopia ceramics was not an art form. The Beta Israel were actually looked down upon for doing handiwork. It is so wonderful that their crafts are finally recognized as art and they are valued for their skills. The best part is that these artists are both expressing their Ethiopian identities and contributing to the larger Israeli community. That's a really hard balance for new immigrants to achieve."

Earlier in the evening we had spotted a poster on Ben Yehuda Street that said *Ethiopian Singing.* With full stomachs we return to the sign and try to decipher the Hebrew directions that would lead us there. After many wrong turns and poorly labeled maps, we find ourselves in a sparsely populated club.

A young Ethiopian woman collects tickets at the door. Steve and I are the only white-skinned customers besides two European tourists. On a wooden platform that is the stage, an Ethiopian man sings in Amharic while two European musicians support him with a drum and French horn. Amharic letters on fabric the color of Ethiopia—red, yellow and green—announce the name of the group: Rainbow.

Ethiopian men sitting at tables drinking Maccabee Beer populate the club. I am consumed by the African rhythms of the drum, the singer's passionate voice. After about an hour Steve is ready to leave, and after I talk him out of it, the scene begins to change. Two young Ethiopian women stroll in.

At first they stand in the doorway mouthing the words to the song and then join a table of young men. A white couple looks in and then leaves. Soon two men get up to dance, joined by others

until there is a large group dancing Ethiopian style, moving their shoulders and their necks.

"What a strange scene," Steve says on our way out.

"It's nice to see them dancing to their own rhythms, forming their own bands, but I wish they performed for a larger and more integrated audience." I say.

"They need to advertise better as well. It's pure coincidence that we found out about this," Steve adds.

"Yeah, maybe I'm reading the wrong newspapers."

It is inspiring, though, to hear Ethiopian music in Jerusalem, to purchase Ethiopian art in galleries and pass the teenagers on the street, proud in their African Israeli beauty. But as the days pass I see how so many are also dressed in the uniforms of janitors, scrubbing floors or taking trash away from tables at Burger King. And too many still live in caravans.

The next morning Steve and I take the bus to Givat HaMatos, the Jerusalem caravan. We board along with many Ethiopian families who are returning from the city to their caravan homes. I study one man's familiar face and realize it is the engineer who I had met two years earlier; he had been hanging his laundry to dry. A young wife and a baby now accompany him. Two years ago he complained about the lack of support he received from the government as a single man. He was considering leaving the country. He planted his seed instead.

Givat HaMatos is still the last stop, the top of a hill. Steve looks around, amazed. "This is one of the most incredible views of Jerusalem I've seen. The pictures you've taken of this place really don't do it justice. I had no idea." He photographs the shapes of Jerusalem stone in the distance.

At the central caravan the Ethiopian leader Shai smiles warmly as if he knows me and signals for me to wait. He's on the phone and someone else is waiting in his office so I get comfortable outside on the stoop.

When he finally steps out of his cramped office I ask him in Hebrew, "Do you remember me?"

"Your face looks familiar. What can I do for you?" he says smiling. I am careful with my words this time, remembering how he feels about foreign writers who think they know about Ethiopian Jews.

"I'm writing about my experiences with Ethiopian *olim* who I worked with in Ma'alot..."

"Yes, yes, of course I remember," Shai answers reassuringly. "Has it really been two years? When I saw your face earlier I thought that I had just seen you a year ago." Shai is not the first person to say this to me. Many of my friends as well as shopkeepers in Jerusalem and Ma'alot would say the same thing. When I insist that it has in fact been two years, Shai just looks at me and mutters, "How time passes."

Shai answers all my questions with numbers. Forty families have moved out of the caravan. Thirty-one bought apartments through the mortgage program. Nine are living in Amidar (government housing). Twenty-seven of the families who left the caravan live in Jerusalem and four live outside of the city. Sixteen families and forty single people remain in the caravan. Most of the people who remain are those who don't have family or who lack the skills and or confidence to get jobs and enter the Israeli world. Many who left the caravan moved to remote towns like Petach Tikvah, Hadera, and Ashkelon. The fortunate moved to Jerusalem.

When Shai speaks about Ethiopian Jews he uses the pronoun *we* whether he is describing his group who arrived with Operation Moses, the next group who came with Operation Solomon or even the *Falash Mura* who are still trickling in. Many other immigrants make distinctions between the different groups, the different airlifts to Israel or the varying parts of Ethiopia that people came from. Shai carries everyone's burden, worries about all of his people's livelihoods equally.

As the bus drives down the mountain, I try to understand why Shai's last words, *maybe next time you come back, the caravan will be gone,* make me so sad. I am relieved to think that someday the Ethiopian *olim* will be out of temporary homes tending their own gardens and leading more productive lives. But I will miss this small world on top of Jerusalem mountains where Ethiopian culture is

preserved, where so many live next to their beloved city, where I am always intrigued and at home among the smells and sounds that first introduced me to this culture. I am afraid that all of this will dissipate with the winds of assimilation.

§

Although for days now I have been trotting along my familiar paths in Jerusalem and floating in the Dead Sea, I am not completely settled in yet because I have not spoken to Osnat. I called her dorm upon my arrival in Tel Aviv the week before, and she left me a message on our friends Duki and Galai's machine in Tel Aviv where we spent our first days in Israel, but we keep missing each other. So the night we return from the sea I am thrilled to hear her voice on the other end of the line from the Hotel on Bezalel Street in Jerusalem where Steve and I are now staying.

A nasal yet cheerful Osnat greets me, not with her usual "everything is okay" but with news of her bad cold and exhaustion.

"Can it be from the stress of studying so much for exams? Do you get enough sleep?" I ask anxiously.

"No, very little," she answers with an embarrassed laugh. "When did you arrive in Israel?"

"I arrived on June 8th."

"You've been here a long time."

"It feels that way. We spent a few days in Tel Aviv with our Israeli friends Duki and Galia who we know from Chicago where they lived for almost ten years. Since then we've been in Jerusalem."

"Dina, you love Jerusalem," Osnat says, affectionately.

"I do, and Steve loves it too."

"Your boyfriend is with you." She asks rhetorically. "How does he like Israel? What have the two of you been doing?"

"Well, we went to the Dead Sea. It was 100 degrees or more in the desert but it was really fun."

"Great! Did you get burned?"

"No, not so bad."

I do not tell Osnat that my skin had been protected by black
mud or how it felt to rub it all over my sensitive and imperfect
white skin, so easily colored by the Mediterranean sun. I don't tell
her that I walked around for over an hour as a black woman, and
I felt protected, for once, from the harsh sun. I do not tell her that
when I looked at myself, concealed yet radiant, in the small mirror
that hung above the vat of mud, I longed to keep this color.

Bringing me back from my mud daydream Osnat says,

"You know that Yael is still in Jerusalem."

"Yeah. I left her a message on her machine, but I haven't heard
back yet. Does she still work at the store?"

"No, she's not there anymore," followed by a long silence.

In the last letter I had written to Osnat, I asked her if she would
want to visit Ma'alot with me. I still believed that our memories
were on the surface of the fertile soil, that by retracing our steps
we could become the girls we once were together. Or, failing that,
perhaps the memories of those days would come back more clearly.
I ask her again on the phone.

"Sure, why not? I love Ma'alot and I haven't been there in six
years."

"I just can't believe that, Osnat. You're only an hour or so away,
and you haven't been back since your family moved. We really
must go back."

"It was good to hear your voice," Osnat says sweetly.

"Yours, too," I answer.

"I can't wait to see you."

"*L'hitraot.*"

*

Peace spreads out its hands and caresses the entire city as the
Sabbath arrives. Steve and I walk to the Great Synagogue and
separate as he goes to the men's section and I to the women's
quarter. It is awkward, at first, to sit alone without a book, but I
am soon taken in by the way the falling light changes the colors
of the stained glass windows, the rabbis resonating voice, the

swaying bodies of men and the stylish hats of the Modern Orthodox women who sing quietly, never quite sure when to stand and when to sit down.

Strolling back to our room in our new and nicer hotel on Karen Hayesod Street, a computer-generated note from Yael sits on the bed. She apologizes for not having returned my calls: she had not been home for three days. How strange it is to read her words, translated by the receptionist from her Hebrew to their English and then typed on computer paper. I call her back, thrilled to hear her voice rather than a taped recording of it.

"Shalom, Dina, it is so good to hear from you. What are doing? I'll come over right now!"

"Now? But it's Shabbat and it's evening already. How will you get here?"

"Don't worry, Dina. I'll take a taxi or have some friends drive me."

"Really?" In my mind everything still stopped on the Sabbath in Jerusalem. And I assume that Yael still keeps the Sabbath.

Hearing the tiredness in my voice Yael says, "Maybe tomorrow will be a better day to meet." Hearing the same tiredness in her voice, I agree.

"By the way, I stopped by Ha Mashbir to see you the other day but you weren't there."

"Yeah, I haven't been there in a long time. Did you ask for me? What did they say?"

"They didn't seem to know you." There is a long silence. If it had been one of my American friends, she would have told me every detail leading up to her departure, every feeling involved. Yael says nothing, and I don't want to intrude upon her silence, a silence that sometimes perplexes me, but a silence that I understand and respect.

"Why didn't you tell me you were coming to Israel?" Yael asks as we prepare to hang-up.

"I don't have your address. I wrote to Osnat and told her...I thought that she would have told you."

"No, she doesn't tell me anything."

Yael's long braids dance across her back as she approaches the receptionist in our hotel lobby the next day. I call her name, and we quickly walk toward each other, taking in one another's latest appearance. Yael is on the cutting edge of fashion with tight white jeans, and a denim vest with a sleeveless white T-shirt. I feel older and heavier in my cotton summer dress than I had five minutes before.

"How are you?" we ask simultaneously, Yael in English and me in Hebrew, as we kiss on each side of the cheek.

Yael introduces me to her two friends, Liora and Shlomo. I am so surprised by their presence and by the cigarettes they are smoking on the Sabbath in a hotel in Jerusalem where many of the clientele are religious, that I am unable to tell if they are Israeli or not.

"Do you speak Hebrew or English?" I ask, trying to make some conversation. The young woman, Liora, who is about Yael's age laughs and says, "We speak Moroccan." We settle into some couches and wait.

"Where is Steve?" Yael asks anxiously.

"He'll be down in a minute," I assure her.

"Does he speak Hebrew?"

"Very little, but I'll be his translator."

She laughs nervously.

"Oh, there he is now," I say pointing at Steve who has just gotten off of the elevator. Yael runs up to him, takes both of his hands and looking into his face with an open smile says in English, "It is so good to meet you."

"How did you guys meet Yael?" Liora asks us as we gather again. I look at her for a moment and then remember with sudden disbelief.

"Dina was my teacher in Ma'alot. She taught Osnat, and my friend Ora, too," Yael answers.

"You're kidding," her friend says with an amused smile.

"Yes, it's true. And the girls were great students," I say proudly.

"No, not me," Yael says apologetically.

Suddenly we are seated around a table in the garden of the King David Hotel overlooking the Old City. I've often peered

out at this terrace with longing but never considered having a cup of coffee here because it is too expensive. But Yael and her friends insist that this would be the perfect place for us to gather. So there we sit among the privileged, Yael on my left side and Steve on my right.

The two friends order strawberry cheesecake. Steve and Yael drink cola, and I order a cup of Nescafé. Wild peonies in deep purples and reds along with beds of roses in orange pink and white next to lush green grass surround us. Everywhere else in Jerusalem the green has turned to brown since the winter rains have long passed. Yael and Shlomo watch the attractive men and women who pass and make comments like "What a piece." After one of these commentaries they argue in loud Hebrew whispers. The only words that make their way to me are Yael's: "I am a serious woman!"

Turning back to me Yael asks, "So are you and Steve getting married?"

"I don't know," I say, a bit tired of the question. Steve is deep in conversation with Shlomo.

"And you?" I ask Yael.

"I don't have a boyfriend right now," she says sadly.

"How much does a room cost here?" Shlomo asks interrupting our girl talk.

"Probably about $700.00 a day for a suite," Steve surmises. As the men share their amazement about room prices, Yael falls silent.

"Tell me something," I say to her.

"That's all," she says.

We walk hand in hand to the lady's room and while washing our hands in front of a huge mirror Yael asks again, "So, will you get married?"

Before I say anything she continues, "When you get married, that is when I'll come to America." She places her hands on her face and laments, "Look how fat I am."

"Yael, you are not fat."

"Yes I am. Do you remember how fat I was in Ma'alot. Well I've gained back all the weight I lost since then."

"You don't look fat to me."

"Well I am," she insists.

Back at the table Yael asks the waiter for the check and announces that we are all her guests. Steve pulls out his wallet and says, "No, this is our treat." Her other friends accept her gesture immediately and eventually, when she adamantly insists, we acquiesce as well.

Yael and her friends prepare for a night on the town. Steve and I will stroll through the city, hand in hand, waiting for the Sabbath to go out.

<center>❧</center>

Down a sand hill from our hotel is Robert's home on Jabotinsky Street. I had brought Sara with me to his home during other years, but usually I arrive alone to his basement apartment. This time Steve joins me through the wild garden that Robert spends hours tending, and past his mulberry tree which is already dropping fruit and finally down three stone steps to the green door that says FRIEND in Hebrew and in English.

Robert greets us with his characteristic warmth. As we settle into the sitting room, the men make small-talk about Steve's reaction to the minerals in Jerusalem water and the hot weather.

I've brought Robert the late poet James Merrill's last collection of poems, *Sea Salts*. During the winter Robert had written to me about how much he was enjoying Merrill's memoir. In the spring Merrill died of cancer. At a bookstore in Chicago, Merrill's last collection of poems seemed like the perfect gift for Robert. But in his simple and honest home in Jerusalem, we dissect them, agreeing that we are perplexed by them and in Robert's words "put off by their needless complexity" which gets in the way of their meaning. For Robert and me poetry is how we find the deeper truth; we have no patience for disguises. "But don't get me wrong. I appreciate the book greatly," Robert adds to our analysis.

The baby kittens that have become cats during the two years I've been away are chasing flies near the lamp, on top of which they will land and die instant deaths.

"This is the best fly swatter ever made," Robert announces as he comes back from the shelf with his new translation of the Israeli poet Rachel's poems. Robert rendered them so perfectly in English that for the first time, a non-Israeli audience could get a real feel for this poet and pioneer who became a legend after her early death. She wrote love songs to the country that became national anthems and she wrote laments about lost love. Robert inscribes the book to both Steve and me with "old friendship—new friendship," and I know that Steve has arrived.

<center>❦</center>

The phone number I've used since the Yamari family moved to Kfar Saba in 1991 suddenly doesn't work. I add the new area code but I still can't get through. I ask the operator for the Yamari family on Masada Street.

"The what family?" The operator asks.

"The Yamari family. *Y-A-M-A-R-I,*" I say a bit louder.

"You must have made a mistake," the operator informs me. "That's not a Hebrew name."

"No, it isn't a mistake. Can you please look it up for me?"

"I'm sorry. I'm not finding anything under that spelling."

The only way to get to Kfar Saba this time is unannounced. In some ways it's a relief; I don't have to make plans with Batya on the phone or decipher her often vague directions in Hebrew. The more I think about it, the more exciting the prospect seems; Batya has no idea that I am in the country. Instead of transferring from bus to bus as in years past, this time I have a rented car and a traveling companion who reads maps.

As we wind our way out of Jerusalem and her surrounding hills, and forty minutes later find ourselves on the outskirts of Kfar Saba, the maps no longer help. Hebrew and generous citizens are

our only hope. If maps and numbers are Steve's terrain, language is mine. Although I had brushed up on my vocabulary in the spring with the Israeli wife of one of my students, I still panic, sometimes, when I have to get essential information in Hebrew. After much circling, long Hebrew explanations and a lot of luck, we find our way to Masada Street.

I don't recognize anything from our last visit. Another block of apartments has been built along with a neighborhood park. I'm not completely sure that we are in the right place. I ask two women pushing their children in strollers if they know where building number twelve is located.

"I'm looking for the Yamari family."

An elderly woman who had been walking by and joined our conversation says, "No, I'm sorry, you have made a mistake. There is no Yamari family in Kfar Saba." As I walk away from my unreliable sources, the elderly woman calls after me.

"Wait a minute, Miss. Are they Ethiopian? They live in that building, over there," she says pointing to a four-story apartment across from the park.

We climb the steps to their alleged building and peer into the open door of a Russian immigrant family's apartment. A young Russian boy calls after us,

"Who are you looking for?"

"The Yamari family," I pant, a bit out of breath.

"Oh, they live on the top floor. But you know, they are Ethiopian," he informs us.

Steve gets to the top landing first. I look up at him through the stairwell and he points to an Ethiopian stamp pasted to the door and a huge smile spreads across his face. "This is it!"

We knock and then wait, my heart pounding, wildly. A tall, elegant young woman opens the door, looks at me without saying anything and then throws her arms around me, recognizing me before I do her, a thin and more sophisticated Batya.

"What a wonderful surprise! It's so good to see you!"

"I'm so glad we finally reached you."

"Come in, come in," Batya says after greeting Steve. She leads us over to the couch, disappears into the kitchen and returns with a bowl of fruit and two tall glasses of soda. We look around the sparkling clean apartment, wondering why it's so quiet.

"Where's Elad?"

"Elad is on a field trip with his school. He'll be so sad that he missed you." The disappointment sinks into my stomach.

"And what about everyone else?"

"Well, Amnon is in the army. He's not stationed too far away so he comes home for Shabbat sometimes. It's a lot of work and he's very tired all of the time. And Orit lives in Tel Aviv, now, with her boyfriend."

"And your mother?"

"She's in Beersheba today visiting her sister. She should be back this afternoon, Maybe you'll get to see her!"

Batya listens eagerly to stories about our travels through Israel; I hold her long braids in my hands.

"I want braids like this."

"No you don't, you have beautiful hair...and besides, these braids aren't completely mine. My hair stops about half-way, and then I braid the other hair into my own."

"Well then whose hair is it?"

"I'm not sure. There is a store in Tel Aviv where they sell braids, and you can stitch them into your own hair."

Steve tries to tell Batya that *Marcus Welby M.D.,* one of his favorite shows from when he was a child, is on the TV and how excited he is to see it on the screen in their living room. When he finishes talking, Batya looks at me laughing,

"You must tell me what he said." After I translate, she smiles, nodding her head approvingly toward Steve.

"So how is school in Kfar Saba going?"

"It's hard for me. I'm preparing for the *bagrut* exam right now."

"Do you want to continue on to the university?"

"No, that's not the exam that I'm taking. I'm taking the other one that will allow me to graduate from high school on a vocational track."

"Do you like your teachers?"

"Yeah, my teachers are good. My school is great."

"Batya, what will you do when you finish school?"

"I don't know. Stay home. Work. Maybe college." A shy smile blossoms on her face. Reading it correctly I ask, "Do you have a boyfriend?"

Her smile grows in acknowledgement. "You can say that." She tells me about this young Ethiopian college student that she met at a wedding. He studies at Haifa University and knows of Osnat. I can see in Batya's eyes that she is in love.

"Does your mother know about him?"

"*Pashoot o yoter*—more or less, she says. I soon realize that "more or less" and "it is possible to say so" are Batya's favorite expressions of 1995.

An hour or so into our visit I accept the sad truth, Elad will not be coming home. With this acceptance, I hand Batya the gifts I brought for both her and her brother.

"These are beautiful!" Batya exclaims holding up the earrings with pastel gems and the gold bracelet. "And Elad is just going to love this," she says skimming through the Michael Jordan book which contains his philosophy of success, working hard, and large photos of Elad's hero.

Steve and I admire the woven baskets in the bookcase. "I think Gaveret Yamari made these," I proudly tell him.

"You're kidding. These are the most beautiful baskets I've seen." Batya assures us that they were made solely by her mother's hands.

"Does she have all of the materials she needs in Israel?"

"Yes, she just uses yarn mostly." Remembering an earlier conversation where Batya explained that her mother could not work because of her asthma, I tell Batya that her mother could

sell these baskets and that in shops in Jerusalem they sell for hundreds of dollars.

"Really? Thank you," Batya says shyly. We write down the names of some shops in Jerusalem for her to give to her mother.

Batya disappears into the kitchen and returns with two huge plates of *injera* with beef that had been marinating on the stove—as if she'd been waiting for guests to arrive. Batya watches as Steve and I hungrily and happily savor it.

After lunch Steve moves through the apartment as the lens of his camera swallows the kitchen where *injera* sits on the stove, and a photograph of Elad from a few years back shows a huge *kippah* on his head and a familiar mischievous smile. On the same wall is Orit's certificate for having completed *pnemia* and her class picture. On the opposite wall, in a space all its own, hangs a black and white photo of an uncle who remains in Ethiopia.

Next Steve's camera devours the two bedrooms. One belongs to Gaveret Yamari; spare and simple. Her traditional cape drapes a small closet door. The second room, shared by Batya and Elad, is also sparse and neat, especially for an adolescent boy and a teenage girl. On Batya's table are many Johnson's baby products: lotion, powder, cream. Elad's side is empty. Even the walls are bare. The rooms look out onto the large field beyond which one can see the West Bank and Arab town of Kakillyah. Steve and I had just read an article in the *Jerusalem Report* about a wall that was being built to separate Kfar Saba from the territories, but Batya had not been aware of it.

There is a knock on the door followed by Gaveret Yamari. She greets both Batya and me with hugs. We gather around the living room again and she and Batya embroider with the colorful threads she brought back with her from Beersheba. Batya explains that they would encase their embroidery in plastic to make *mezuzot* and sell them in a shop in Kfar Saba.

Steve focuses his camera on their hands moving in and out of the cloth. As if to explain the strange phenomenon of Steve's camera to her mother Batya says,

"They are filming their whole trip!"

"How wonderful," she replies in Hebrew.

Batya continues talking to her mother in Amharic which she later translates into Hebrew for me: "Dina is going to see Osnat next week. She is studying at Haifa University."

"Really?" Gaveret Yamari asks.

I am struck by her surprise. After all, Osnat is her niece. When they lived in Ma'alot they saw each other every day and knew all of the details about each other's lives. And in Ethiopia, although the Yamaris lived in a rural village and Osnat's family lived in the city of Gondar, their lives were intertwined.

"You don't see each other much," I say to Gaveret Yamari.

"No, they live in Ramat Eliyahu (about an hour away by bus) we haven't seen them in about a year... since the last family wedding," Gaveret Yamari explains in a much improved Hebrew. Batya places her hand over mine and says,

"You're okay... you never lose touch."

I promise Gaveret Yamari that I'll be back the next week to see Elad. Steve, who without language has developed a nice rapport with the two women, runs ahead to the car to study the maps that will lead us to the Galil.

Batya and I stand in front of her building, and I photograph her next to red and pink azalea bushes. A light-skinned, blond-haired Russian girl approaches us.

"Why is she taking your picture?" the girl asks Batya.

"Because I'm special," Batya answers, eyes sparkling.

"Who are you, and why are you here?" she asks me.

"I'm Batya's cousin," I say, as Batya and I walk away laughing, all of the way to the car.

Steve does not share my passion for the Galil. He is worried about how to find his way on mountainous roads; frustrated by the inexactness of maps, the deceiving landscape that fails to announce the sudden turns over valleys. Although the views of majestic mountains and deep valleys are spectacular, Steve is focused on not driving over cliffs, and my memory is occupied by a life I once lived here.

June 1995

I bring the person with whom I am trying to build a life to the home I left ten years ago.

The road there from Tzvat is narrow and winding. It is both treacherous and exquisite, but he can't see the beauty. He cannot see signs of the place to which I am leading him from the place that we are in the middle of these hills.

When miraculously we arrive, he sees a strange town on top of another mountain. I drove through this town, quickly, two years ago when I did not want to stop and wait for memory to come. This time I have grown far enough away to go back. I want him to feel what I once felt, but he feels only the circular roads. He sees how I can't find my way back to that place he is still circling this town to find. There are new neighborhoods built around the absorption center and the building I once lived in has been painted with bright flowers. Russian children peer out of what was once Osnat's window. A group of Ethiopians who arrived in between Moses and Solomon still live here. A group of Falash Mura live here now as well. A new group of children have turned the parking lot into a field. I will never know their names.

The fertile earth I once walked through has become stone. The paths I once took from one home to another have become new buildings. The memories live not only in the soil or in the rooms where love was made but also in my sad heart that still believes I can find something I once lost by walking the same terrain. What I expect to find in the land lives only inside me now. He cannot see it in the stone. All he can

see is another woman who once loved another world, who believed in a different dream, who almost took another path that would have led her away from the life that he and I are trying to build.

"So this was our home," I say, leading Steve to the Ma'alot absorption center. "This is where it began."

He sits on a bench. The subtle reminders consume me, that a decade has passed since familiar faces peered from these windows, when it was my cotton shirts hanging on the line to dry. To Steve this is a run-down building with new immigrants hanging worn clothes on the line.

I want Steve to fall in love with Ma'alot the way that I once did. I believe that if he could feel the part of me that thrived here, we would be able to build a future together. I think that if I can make him a part of my past, the past would also become a part of our future.

He has not yet seen the center of town nor the way the mountains look when dusk falls. He reluctantly agrees to stay longer but he is not with me when I drag him up a hill to see the sky or to my favorite falafel restaurant where the proprietor remembers me, where a regular customer remembers when this was my home. Steve is afraid to take me away from my paradise but the darkening sky is a warning.

On the way back to Karmiel, a small town in the Galil where we are staying with friends, we are silent. I wonder to myself: Could I marry someone who doesn't love Ma'alot? Why did I ever leave here? Who have I become? Who is this man I love? He shares my Jewish soul, but does he share my Zionism, the kind that lives still in the dream of the ingathering of exiles, the Zionism that was born in this town?

As we near our destination I realize that although I returned to the place, I have not yet returned to the garden because Osnat and Elad are not with me.

When I awaken drained the next morning I think of Osnat's short poems that she had sent in the spring about triumph, overcoming adversity and not giving up. It isn't until evening that

Steve and I find our way back to each other. He assuages my heaviness with his humor as he tells his friends about the most incredible place on earth, Dina's paradise, a small development town in a northern corner of Israel. I accept the fact that Steve's one hour in Ma'alot won't change his life the way the six months in the town had changed mine. And I know that it is not the place itself that changed me but the lives that were rooted to mine in that soil.

Steve and I make amends but decide to spend the next day apart. We begin our journey together by taking the bus to Haifa, but Steve will tour the town alone while I spend the day with Osnat.

At the station, as we stand in the place where I'm supposed to meet Osnat, I ask Steve, "Would you recognize her from the picture if you saw her?"

"I think so," he says, but as a young woman walks toward us Steve says, "That isn't Osnat—is it?"

I stare at this stylish young woman, study her face until she smiles in recognition. "Yes, that's Osnat," I say, running toward her and throwing my arms around the thin frame of this grown woman. Her hair is neatly tucked into a bun that is a lighter shade of brown from the rest of her hair. She wears black slacks and a sleeveless print blouse from which her black and white checkered bra shows through. I sense that there is an edge to her, a quiet severity, and a new sophistication.

I introduce her to Steve and they shake hands joyfully like old friends yet cautious like the strangers that they are.

"Where do you want to go?" I ask.

"It doesn't matter. Is Steve coming with us?"

"No, he's going to the Baha'i Temple."

"Really?" she asks, pursing her lips together, nervously.

"Yes. There's one near our house that he likes to go to as well."

This bit of information seems to have altered her mood. Perhaps she thought he was going for religious purposes rather than to admire the building and lush gardens. I'm not sure how to bring

her back from her quiet. Her eyes are covered with large, plastic sunglasses.

When we're alone, Osnat blurts out anxiously, "Is Steve Jewish?"

"Yes, of course. We've talked about this before. Why do you ask, because of his light color?"

"No, it's his name... he doesn't have a Jewish name."

"There are many Jews with the name Steve in America. And his Hebrew name is Yisrael." Her tightened lips relax into a smile.

We sit on a bench under a canopy, breathe in salt, and admire the white-capped waves of the Mediterranean.

"We went to Ma'alot the other day," I tell Osnat.

"Really... I can't believe you made it back there, how wonderful."

"I hope that later this month we can go together. You'd be amazed by how much they've built. Do you remember where the absorption center was?"

"Yes, of course," she says, turning her gaze to me.

"Well now they've built another neighborhood below it. There are new neighborhoods everywhere; it feels so much bigger."

"What a pity. I liked it the way it was. Now I won't be able to remember it."

"Oh, no, Osnat. You'll be able to remember it. I also liked it the way that it was, but it's not *that* different. There are still familiar places."

"When I first went away to school after we moved to Rishon, I would take the bus all the way to Haifa thinking we still lived in Ma'alot, forgetting we left and moved to Rishon. In my heart, I still lived in Ma'alot," Osnat says sadly.

Osnat's face shows very little emotion. There is a new deliberateness to her walk, her stilted smile. Her silence is harder to enter, but her words are deeper as she struggles to open her heart.

I don't know if my heart still opens the way that it had when I was her age, when I fell in love with a different version of this country, one that wasn't so Americanized, so split from within. When I landed in Tel Aviv this time only the smell of bus exhaust seemed familiar, sometimes only Hebrew connected me to the

Israel of 1995. The countries themselves seem to be merging together. I can use my American credit card to hear voices from home, place my American cash station card into the slot of any Bank Ha Poalim to receive shekels.

"How's your work going?" Osnat asks.

"It's going well. I'll speak to people next week in Jerusalem to find out more about what's happening in '95."

"What are you finding exactly?" she asks with uncharacteristic directness.

"The book is about ten years in Israel," I begin cautiously. "It is the story of immigrants... from Ethiopia."

I've known for a long time now that my visits are turning into a book, and that she has become a character in my narrative. I have been hesitant to say it aloud, to Osnat, but I know the moment of truth has arrived.

"Also, I want to tell your story." Osnat looks down bashfully. "Is that okay?"

"Of course. Why would that bother me?"

"I want to tell your story because I think it's a success story and important to tell."

"Is it in English or Hebrew?"

"English, of course. Could you imagine me writing a book in Hebrew?"

"I'll have to work on my English in order to read your book."

"Maybe you can help me by telling me what you think. I want to understand more about the differences between life in Israel and life in Ethiopia. You've been here ten years already so maybe you don't think about it," I say, embarrassed by the journalistic tone that I fear has once again entered my voice.

"Of course I think about it. There are many differences in culture and in mentality. One thing I haven't been able to get used to is *chutzpah*. I'm just not like that, and sometimes people take advantage of me because of it."

"That's too bad. But it's not your nature. I think Israelis have a lot to learn from Ethiopians about politeness. What else?"

"The culture is very different from the way it was in Ethiopia. You know, the way people dress." Osnat breaks off and looks away from me and back to the sea.

"So ten years later, are you happy that you came to Israel?" She returns her gaze to me and adjusts her glasses.

"Yes. I have lots of friends…it's good here but I feel that I'm missing something. I've left something behind in Ethiopia. We left a very nice country," she says, straightening her posture.

"But wasn't there famine and drought?"

"No. We came because we were Zionists."

"Why in '84—because you had the opportunity?"

"Yes. Someone organized a group, and we walked to Sudan where we stayed for some months…" Again, she breaks off into silence.

"So you came when you did because you had the opportunity and because you didn't know about the future?"

"Yes, we didn't know about the future."

"But wasn't it different for the people who came with Operation Solomon?"

"Yes. Because of the changing government they had to come."

"Do you think absorption has been more difficult for them?"

"Yes. They live in small groups and don't mix with other Israelis in the caravans. I volunteered again in one recently, in Haifa."

"Really? I thought that caravans had emptied out."

"No, new people are coming in. The Falash Mura," she adds looking down at her feet. "As part of my degree in education at the university, I taught Hebrew to the newcomers, for a small stipend."

As the waves push forward, covering the spaces between our words, I reach into my pack for the woman's journal I had brought for her. In the past I brought her jewelry because she had always admired mine. This time I want to give her something that symbolizes my most recent discovery of her as a poet.

"This is for you," I say.

"You didn't have to get me a gift; you always bring me something," she says accusingly, as if pointing out a bad habit of mine.

"It's no big deal. I saw the book and I thought of you. I remembered that you are always losing your poems. Now you have a place to keep them."

"Thank you. It's very beautiful," she says, leafing through the blank pages with quotes from great women writers.

The afternoon sea breeze gives some relief from the humidity and penetrating sun. It is the hottest Israeli summer in years. Nevertheless, we emerge from our shelter and brave the elements. As we approach the promenade Osnat struggles to fit the book into her purse. I offer to put it in my larger bag, but she doesn't respond. Instead she forcefully stuffs it in her small leather bag, half of it sticking out.

I can't help staring at her long skinny arms. And although she made it clear she didn't want to be taken care of, I can't stop myself from asking,

"Are you eating okay at school?"

"There is so much pressure from exams and studying. When school is over I feel freer, and then I'm not so skinny. "

"So you just have one more year at Haifa University?"

"I want to stay on at Haifa University when I finish my bachelor's and go for my master's degree. I have a lot of friends at Haifa who will be continuing on as well."

"Ethiopians?"

"One Ethiopian and the rest Israeli. I am now working for degrees in both counseling and education. I want to be a counselor in a school."

"That's great. This country needs good role models and good teachers."

She laughs in embarrassment and I believe a little pride.

"So you saw Batya?" Osnat asks.

"Yes. She's finishing high school. She looks great. Elad wasn't home, but I heard he's grown a lot."

"Yes, Elad is so tall," she says laughing affectionately and sounding like the familiar Osnat.

"And Orit moved to Tel Aviv."

"She did? Did she move in with her boyfriend?"

"Yes. What would you and your cousins do without me to tell you what each other is doing? Do you want to eat lunch now?" I ask.

"If you want to. Okay."

We walk past a small park and head for the main street where there are a few houses, gift shops, flowers in buckets but no cafes.

"Why don't we go to Hadera… there are lots of restaurants and it's only a short bus ride away—isn't it? Lunch will be my treat."

"I think we should try to find a place in the station to eat. I'm not sure if we have enough time to go to Hadera. We have to meet Steve at 5:00," she adds nervously.

"We have plenty of time. It's only 2:00 now."

"I don't really know my way around. My friends laugh at me. I've lived in Haifa for two years, but I only know my way from the station to my dorm. I don't know the city."

I follow her to the station. The heat is overwhelming away from the sea, and the thought of eating in the station is unpleasant, but I don't want to push her to go where she isn't comfortable.

"Steve is nice," Osnat says, suddenly cheerful.

"Thank you. I'm glad you think so. Do you still have the same boyfriend?"

"No, we separated during the summer. It was my idea."

"You were together a long time."

"Three years but… he wasn't for me. At first the break up was difficult, but now I'm used to it."

"You didn't want to marry him?"

"I don't think about marriage."

"Good. Do you have a new boyfriend?"

She looks at the ground with a sly smile as if deciding how much to reveal.

"I met someone, but I don't know…he studies with me at Haifa University. English Literature. He can help me with my English! He hasn't been here long. He came with Operation Solomon."

Our conversations spread out along many hours; some begin with a gentle pull of thread and then unravel throughout the day. We approach a subject like her relationship with Daniel or if I want

to marry Steve or not and then it would end. Neither one of us pushes the other beyond what she wants to reveal. We let an idea incubate and then return to it later for completion.

At the station it's impossible to speak and difficult to breathe. The exhaust from buses absorbs what air there is, and the shouts of vendors urging us to come in for falafel drowns our voices. Osnat suggests eating in the cafeteria where there is plenty of room to sit. It's dirty and hot, but we stand in line and wait for plates of hummus and pita.

We dip our bread into sour hummus, and I ask Osnat to take me back to her childhood. She has never taken the long walk back with me, and I was now ready to lead her there.

"What do you remember most about Ethiopia?"

"I remember the sea, the people, the games we played, how it was more fun there. We were all together. Now everyone is at school. Busy. There is little time."

"Do you mean there are more programs… or time is more programmed here?"

"Yes, that's exactly what it is."

"If you had a choice now to move back to Ethiopia, would you?"

"No, I don't want to live in Ethiopia or America…I want to be in Israel," she says adamantly, as though speaking on behalf of all Ethiopians who are tired of such questions and who want to make sure people understand their commitment to Israel as Zionists rather than as refugees.

"Are you a Zionist?" Osnat asks, turning the question to me.

"Yes, I am," struck by the directness of a question I haven't answered out loud in a long time. I assume she's asking if I'm a "lover of Zion" rather than if I'm a political Zionistic who believes all Jews must live in the Land of Israel.

"Dina, do you still want to live in Israel?"

"Yes and no. It's difficult now. If I would have stayed in 1985, I'd be fluent in Hebrew by now. Maybe I'd be integrated into Israeli society. Back when you and I lived in Ma'alot, I couldn't imagine

making my home anywhere but Israel. Yet I also needed to go back
to America, and sometimes I feel that it is only gravity that has
kept me there. And my family, and friends. My work."

"I think the biggest problem for you here would be socially."

"Maybe, but my friends who've stayed haven't changed that
much, but people aren't really Zionists anymore. I still dream of
the Israel of the 1920s...the pioneers...maybe that's the Israel I
still long for."

"Yes," Osnat says capturing me in her deep brown eyes that
suddenly seem darker and wiser. "I know what you mean."

I am surprised by my own words and by Osnat's ability to understand
them. I had written about this longing; I had tried to discuss it with
other friends who stared back at me blankly. Instead they are
enamored of the conveniences of modern day Israel. But Osnat
shares the same dreams of the past with me—Osnat shares my
longing. I had felt this melancholy the first time I led her out of
her classroom and into the library in order to teach her my language.
Now, ten years later, we can talk about it in Hebrew words. And
in some ways, we've transferred that yearning to a smaller place—
Ma'alot. We know that the Israel that Bialik and Buber wrote about,
the land of the ingathering of exiles, where everyone worked the
land and danced in the streets to welcome the Sabbath bride, is
only a distant and in many ways fabricated, dream. And maybe for
every generation the past is a golden age.

Our innocent days in Ma'alot have become our present day
Eden, the Israel we still long for. It is where we were gathered into
the mountains of the Galil, the breasts of Ma'alot. We had been
welcomed home by the land and by our love for each other. Since
we left Ma'alot, our first home in Israel, we've both been wandering.
Osnat moves back and forth between the Israel of her dreams, the
Israel that first welcomed her and the hard reality of daily life,
studying in university. And she travels between the small home
she built in Haifa and her parent's house. And I've drifted back and
forth between America, the Israel I visit, the Israel of ancient
dreams and the Israel where I once began to live my dreams.

"Israel is becoming too much like America." I add.

"Even more so," Osnat agrees. "Does Steve want to live here?"

"Yes and no. He loves Israel but doesn't always have patience for Israelis."

"Israelis aren't that bad," Osnat says, laughing. "They are just the way that they are."

"As I've told Steve recently, I've always wanted a job where I could work half the year in America and half in Israel. I feel that in my heart I live in two places, so I wish my feet could also live on two soils."

"Yes, that would be great. But you are lucky that you get to visit every other year."

"Yes, I have been very fortunate." We wash our half-eaten lunches down with mineral water. I lean back into my chair, aware that we only have a few hours left together.

"Tell me the story of your coming to Israel. Maybe now you can remember more than when you first got here and were so focused on life in Israel."

"Are you saying that we don't look back or think about Ethiopia?"

"No. I'm trying to say that now that you are settled here, now that you are not struggling with daily life, you have more time to reflect on the past."

"Yes, that's true. When I was a child we always spoke about coming to Israel. We followed everything about Israel. We called them our people" She breaks off.

"And then one day your father said, 'we're going to Israel?'"

"I remember very well when he told me that we were going to Israel and that I couldn't tell anyone." She is silent for a while, still sitting upright, looking past me.

"And then you sold your home?"

"No, we didn't sell anything. We walked to Sudan, and we were airlifted into Israel." In her telling she moves from the secret of their *aliyah*, to the long horrible trek to Sudan where thousands died, everyone suffered from exhaustion, starvation and fear of the unknown. She doesn't linger on the journey or the insufferable

months in the transit camps in Sudan. She moves from Gondar to Israel as though airlifting the memory out of her past.

"What did you think when you got here?"

"We were surprised that no one kept the Sabbath."

"You went straight to Ma'alot?"

"Yeah, and we studied and got acclimated."

Her eyes are covered suddenly by a dark veil as if she is overcome by all that had been lost on that journey. I move our conversation to the future, hoping the veil will lift.

"Do you want to go back to Ethiopia to visit?"

"Yeah, there was a group of people from Tigray (1977 arrivals) who went back to visit. They said it was changed, but they had a good time."

"How had it changed?" She tried to tell me a story about the group from Tigray that would have answered my question, but I didn't understand her. Instead of trying harder to explain again she says, "It's not so important."

Strolling along the neighborhoods on our way back to the sea, a cat runs across our path. Osnat laughs while I speak to it in Hebrew.

"You still haven't heard from Jackie?"

"No, I don't know where Jackie is."

This time Osnat's question sends me back to the spring. I had been sitting on the couch in our apartment, and a box that had been turned upside down when my apartment had been broken into was sitting on my lap. It was filled with Jackie's letters from 1985. I had read about her love for Osnat, the love she remembered until it hurt so much she had to stop remembering. I wanted to reach back to tell her who Osnat, Elad and Batya had become. I wanted to tell her about Osnat's volunteer work in the caravan, that she was helping the new immigrants from Ethiopia the way that we had been a decade before. I had wanted to tell her that Osnat was a poet, loved Amos Oz novels the way that we did, that her Hebrew was rich and fluid and soon she would graduate from university. And I had wondered if Jackie would have been proud of the young man Elad had grown up into, his gentleness with

children, the large mischievous smile he still had. I also wondered how she would feel about Batya, who spent her time away from school in front of the kitchen stove? And Yael, a Jerusalemite selling clothes to men at a department store. I knew she would be proud of the way the women have come to embrace their African beauty.

I wondered how she would feel about the fact that I never put away the photographs that she had taken off her wall in 1985. Had she found a way to live in America? What did she do when she heard about Operation Solomon? And, why hadn't I wondered any of this for more than flashing moments over the past ten years?

I had thought of searching for her old number and trying to reach her, but I never did. I remember feeling alone, suddenly, as I neatly put Jackie's letters back in the box. Jackie's letters assured me that the past was real. But sometimes I wondered why it was still so important.

The next morning in April my question was answered when I received letters and poems from both Osnat and Charleen, my former Ma'alot roommate, in one day. I had strained to read the poems that Osnat had sent. Originally in Amharic and rhyming in Hebrew, they were about immigrants walking from Ethiopia to Sudan to be airlifted into Israel. They spoke of triumph and overcoming adversity.

Charleen's poems about lost love, desire, breaking out of her bubble to feel the world around her, were followed by ten neatly printed pages about her daughter Bianca growing up with two parents in separate homes, and the political situation in South Africa where she ended up staying for love rather than pursuing her plan to return to Israel.

Osnat's letter had ended with her wish to visit America that summer and with the words *Don't lose the conecshun*. And I knew that because of these women and the power of memory, I never would.

We settle on our seaside bench. "So, Dina, are you and Steve going to get married?" I don't answer right away, wanting to be truthful, frustrated that I, myself don't know the answer.

"Maybe. He is a wonderful, sensitive man who is spiritual but also on this earth. We are very different, though. Sometimes it's a lot of work to be together. We are old already, set in our ways. When we're ready, we'll get married."

"Yes, of course," she says, with complete acceptance.

The late afternoon sun settles on the waves and illuminates the greens and deep blues of the sea. The white caps grow larger as they crash into the rocks on shore. I lead Osnat as close to the water as we can get without going in. We climb on top of the rocks so that when we sit, our legs hang over the waves.

"Where is Steve's family from?"

"They're from Chicago. When he was nine, they moved to a small town in Illinois, for his father's job. When he was fifteen his mother died. He moved back to Chicago by himself to attend Yeshiva and live near his grandmother."

"Poor thing. Is he still religious?"

"We keep the Sabbath together each week, but no, he isn't observant anymore. What about you, Osnat. Are you still religious?"

"I keep the Sabbath. Just because I wear pants…" she adds defensively, "doesn't have anything to do with my ideology."

"You are right," I assure her. I reach into my bag and pull out the book of poetry I had been carrying around with me all month: Robert Friend's translation of the Hebrew poet Rachel's work. Earlier Osnat told me that although she cannot speak English, she has read Freud and Marx in English for her psychology class. Because of this, I felt confident that she would be able to understand the English translations.

"My friend Robert translated Rachel's poems. Next week he is giving a reading in Jerusalem with Yehuda Amichai. Amichai will read them in Hebrew, and Robert will read the translations."

She reads silently for a few moments.

"Does it remind you of how her poems sound in Hebrew? Are you able to recognize the poems?"

"Yes, it does sound like the Hebrew. They work really well. This is one of my favorites," she says handing the book back to me.

Was it I who bathed in the innocent blue
Under a peaceful sky-
Of my Galilee, my own Galilee?
Was it all a dream? Was it I?

I don't know how to tell Osnat how grateful I am to share poems with her over the Mediterranean. My friends and I spend hours discussing where we've submitted our work for publication, which writers received what awards, or what kind of crisis we were going through in our own writing. I no longer pass around my favorite poems the way I had in Ma'alot.

I think back to the day when Gary, my American friend from Ma'alot and I read T. S. Eliot's poem "Prufrock" to each other in Acre, legs dangling over the sea. And that same summer, translating the American poet Carolyn Forché into Hebrew for Shimon on the border of Lebanon and Israel. Again the sea wild beneath us. And now, Osnat has shown me a corner of the sea that had been hidden from my view, celebrating with me the birth of Robert's new translations of Rachel's poems.

How difficult it is to draw ourselves away from the water. We walk back to the station, laughing at the onslaught of cell phones, and find Steve who is tired from climbing steps and hills and ready to board the next bus. Osnat and I make plans to talk the next week from Jerusalem.

"Here let me give you my phone number, if I could only find a pen".

Osnat hands me her pen with which I will later write down her words.

〰

At the Mount of Olives on Shabbat morning in Jerusalem, Steve and I hold onto each other as we look down at the heavy stone which marks the graves of our heroes. Tears roll down my cheek as an ancient sadness as well as a new and unexplored one overcomes me. There is the obvious sadness that our journey together will

be ending as Steve flies to Europe the next morning for a few days on his way home and I stay in Israel for another week. And there is the despair of indecision, a future that we have not yet claimed. Although we had joked about getting married in Israel, the energy needed to get through each unbearably hot day coupled with our conflicts, prevents us from seriously considering it. Here we stand over ancient tombstones, unable to look the future in the eye.

After watching Steve's taxi drive down narrow Tel Aviv streets the next morning, feeling alone as I remain in front of Duki and Galia's apartment where we spent our last night, I dial the new number Batya had given me the week before. Elad answers in a high unrecognizable voice.

"Batya, is that you?"

"This is Elad, Dina. Are you coming over today?"

"Yes," I say, having made a snap decision.

Patiently Elad explains which buses to take, slowly repeating the numbers from Tel Aviv to Kfar Saba and then to his neighborhood.

"From there you remember—right?"

"Yes, of course I remember."

All I need is an ice-cold bottle of mineral water, a good canvas bag and the correct numbers to lead me to the places I want to go, I think to myself as I board the bus for Kfar Saba. I rummage through my bag for change and find an *assimonim,* a phone token that I brought with me from America. It had become obsolete like my bill with Ben Gurion's face—an artifact.

Now that there are so many cell phones in Israel, so many phone numbers had been given new beginnings, to keep up with the demand for more variations. Even numbers have become tentative, needing to be altered to accommodate postmodern Israel. The reformation of numbers also allows me to connect with those I want to find; I can show up at their doors. With others, I can get lost in the silence between old and new numbers.

As I approach the Yamari's apartment on Masada Street, I see Gaveret Yamari and a young boy with a buzz cut standing in front

of the Azalea bushes. I know that he's too young and unfamiliar to be Elad. Simcha Yamari and I greet each other with kisses, one on each cheek, and then she gives me an unexpected kiss on the mouth.

At home, Elad greets me with a huge smile and kisses on each cheek. "*Ma nishma*," he repeats, pouring me a glass of soda and urging me to sit down. Elad knows all about my visit the week before: what I teach, that my boyfriend was with me, and that I write about Israel. Batya had informed him well.

"Elad, you are so tall; soon you'll be taller than Amnon!"

He laughs shyly. "So how is it going, Dina?"

"Good. I've been traveling all over: Jerusalem, Tel Aviv, the north and...I was in Ma'alot!"

"Wow! My mother said it has changed. How was it?"

"It was good. They've built a lot. I got lost."

"Were you in the *mercaz klita*?"

"Yes, of course. They've planted trees and flowers in front of the buildings where we used to live—it looks really nice, but I liked it better before because you were there and I was there."

Elad smiles sadly, "I didn't want to leave Ma'alot, but we had a small apartment and it was too cold in the winter for my mother's asthma. He pauses and then continues, "Do you remember a woman...she was black like me and fat?"

"Was she a friend of mine?" I ask, not remembering anyone who fit that description.

"I thought I remembered seeing her in your apartment."

"No, I'm not sure who that was."

I wonder, again, how Elad's memories have taken shape over the years. When I saw him in front of the *mercaz klita* in '89, having not seen each other since he was four, he didn't seem to remember me that well. When I showed him a picture of the two of us that had been taken in '85, his memory of me seemed to have returned. As our relationship developed over the years of our brief yet consistent visits, he seems to have formed a deeper memory of me in the past. Or was it the me of the present that he remembered back into the past?

Gaveret Yamari returns from outside with the other boy who it turns out is Elad's cousin. "Hasn't Elad grown?" she says proudly.

"He has, I still can't believe how tall he is."

"He's sweet, isn't he? In Ma'alot he was just a little boy," she remembers.

"He was the cutest child. He sparkled. Everyone loved him." I say.

"Where is your boyfriend? He's very sweet."

"Thank you. He left this morning for America."

Elad returns from the kitchen where he was hiding from too many compliments, "It's a shame that I didn't get to meet him."

Simha Yamari makes coffee from the bean, squats next to the small burner in the corner of the room in front of an outlet. First she empties Ethiopian coffee beans into an electric grinder. When we finish our *injera* and chicken, she brings me a small cup of the sweet but strong coffee that had been brewing during our meal. Simha and I drink together, and I feel a connection to her that I had not felt before. Her Hebrew has improved. With the boys running in and out of the room, there isn't always someone around to translate for us; often we search together for the word we need to finish a sentence.

Simha tells me the story of her son-in-law, her eldest daughter's husband, who was hit by a car when crossing the street. He left behind a wife and five children. Her daughter, who is about my age and from her first marriage, is still trying to sue the driver. I have so many questions about how the family is dealing with this tragedy, but before I can find a way to ask, Batya arrives home. Hot and tired on this ninety-something-degree day, after greeting us she runs straight to the shower and returns refreshed.

Simcha is lost in her embroidery. After telling the story of her daughter's husband, a sadness takes over. I tell her how beautiful her work is and that she should try to sell it in Jerusalem. Batya has already given her the numbers of galleries and shops that we had left for her during our last visit. She thanks me for the

compliment and for the information, but I know that she will never call the numbers.

Everyone looks at each other in surprise at the next knock on the door. Orit walks in with a multicolored Moroccan hat covering her short hair. No one had been expecting her or her new attire: a tight white t-shirt and a Jamaican beaded necklace. Her beige shorts are also skin-tight revealing her strong brown legs, highlighted by her brown cowboy boots with huge wooden heels.

Elad and Batya look pleased to see her, but Simha looks at her disapprovingly. Elad grabs her hand and taunts,

"Did your boyfriend give you that hat...oh. how he loves you..."

"Be quiet, Elad" Orit says, annoyed.

Batya scrutinizes her older sister from head to toe. "What's this?" she asks, referring to Orit's funky outfit.

"What's this?" Orit asks back in the same accusatory tone, staring at her younger sister's blue T-shirt and striped blue and white skirt. The two sisters laugh and lean into each other in a closeness that doesn't seem to have changed since Orit moved to Tel Aviv to live with her boyfriend.

Orit, who now works at a busy pub, unloads gifts: a dress for Mom, a reggae bracelet for Elad, silk underwear for Batya.

"Don't laugh, Batya," Orit chides. "Say thank you."

"Thank you, Orit. Where is your boyfriend?"

"He's at home. Why do you ask?"

"No special reason," Batya replies.

Elad turns to me. "Orit's boyfriend is very nice. He usually comes home with her."

Orit urges her mom to try on the cotton Israeli summer dress. At first Simha looks skeptical but eventually slips on this western-style pastel shift. As she stares at herself in the mirror, Batya says,

"Mom, you look fat." The jovial mood in the room quickly passes as Simha, who hasn't taken this comment lightly, scolds Batya in Amharic with words that sound like stones.

"Okay, mom, you're not fat. The dress looks good on you."

Gaveret Yamari does not look convinced. She quickly changes back into her traditional garb.

"Mom, what did you do to your hands?" Orit asks. We stare at the brown designs that Simha's sister had painted on her hands when she was in Beersheba visiting the week before.

"Is that henna?" I ask.

"Yes," Simha answered, "it's good for your health."

"So they say," Orit says rolling her eyes.

Next to us, Elad and Batya playfully hit each other, laughing. The room fills with the energy and warmth of family dynamics, adjusting to each other's changes and vibrant love.

Batya peers down at my black canvas shoes with thick plastic heels.

"I like those, are they new?"

"I got them in America. They're good walking shoes, and they also make me taller."

"Those are nice," I say looking down at her white crocheted sandals. The room buzzes with talk of shoes, and I feel like one of the sisters. Elad makes fun of Orit's high heels, and she pulls the blue bead around his neck.

"This bead is for good luck," Elad announces proudly, "It's Moroccan."

"No, it's Persian," Batya corrects him.

The cousin Elad's age who up to this point had been mostly silent chimes in, "His Moroccan girlfriend gave it to him."

"Really, he has a girlfriend?"

"No, he's only thirteen," Batya assures me.

"Elad, are you going to have a Bar Mitzvah?"

"Yeah, some day. I'll send you an invitation".

Elad and Batya put their gifts away in the next room. Orit and I talk about where I'm staying in Tel Aviv, her new city. We realize that Duki and Galia live close to her.

"Come visit me. But I'm always at work. Come to the reggae club where I work. It's called Soweto, on Ha Yarakon Street."

The next week, when I suggest to Duki and Galia that we go to Soweto, they laugh. "That place is for teenagers. There's a lot

of sex and drugs and rock and roll," Duki says. "And besides," Galia adds, "we'd be the only white ones there."

I call everyone over for photos and take the first one of the family sitting together on the couch. When I take a second picture of Orit, Batya and Elad standing against the wall, they shout to the camera, "We love you, Dina!"

Batya and Elad walk me down to the bus stop. On the way, Elad says incorrectly in Hebrew, "Batya walks here all day," instead of "Batya walks here every day." Batya and I simultaneously correct him. He seems embarrassed that I am correcting his Hebrew. Elad, especially, wants me to witness their daily lives. He points out their school, post office and friends' homes.

"When are you coming back?" Batya asks me.

Before I have a chance to say anything, Elad says, "She'll be back in two years."

I smile at him, pleased that he's been paying attention to my patterns of return.

"I always tell Batya to write to you but she never does. I'm so happy that you never forget us."

ᘉ

Wherever I travel this summer, my visit is preceded by something exploding or falling from the sky. Steve and I had to cancel a visit to Kibbutz Gesher Ha Ziv on the Lebanese border because Katyusha rockets had landed there before us. We then decided to go to Jerusalem instead, and a riot had broken out in the Christian Quarter less than an hour after our visit. Now I am alone in Jerusalem sitting on a bench in front of the Krystals' home waiting for Mr. K. to arrive with the key to my rented room when the police arrive, clear Ben Maimon Street and ask me to leave my bench. Some hours later I learn that the object they exploded had been two feet away from where I'd been sitting.

"Peace is like war," Osnat had said as we strolled along the Haifa shore. I think about her words as I stroll Jerusalem streets,

never asking where she picks up her slogans. For the first time, I feel anxious to return to America.

I learn from Micah Odenheimer, the director of the Israel Association for Ethiopian Jews (IAEJ), that there will be a protest among the Ethiopian youth against the current educational system and its segregationist policies. My relationship with Micah up to this point has been based on mutual cancellation, but we forgive each other because we know we are both canceling for a good cause and that we share a common purpose.

Micah greets me with a handshake and an appreciative smile as I approach the congress / convention center where the protest is to take place. A large group of police sit around and read the newspaper alongside a handful of Ethiopian teenagers supported by a few Americans.

"They're prepared for action," I say to Micah, nodding toward the police.

"Yeah, when they hear there is going to be a protest, they come in full force." I sit next to him on a stone ledge.

"I understand that my friend Yael was an actor in the play that IAEJ produced. Can you explain to me what it was about?"

"Sure. It was called *The Black Scarf.* It's about a marriage between an Ethiopian man and woman that breaks up in the caravan. The husband wants to leave the caravan, but the wife wants to stay in its protective atmosphere. Later, she compliments another man for his hard work and says that he has what it takes to succeed. Her husband gets jealous and accuses his wife of holding him back. In the end, when her husband finally leaves her, her white scarf turns to black. People loved the play, but the Jewish Agency accused it of being untrue. They said only Christians wear black scarves. As you can guess from the protest, the Jewish Agency is concerned about not making waves, not creating a bad impression. By the way, Yael is a wonderful dancer."

After an hour of sitting under trees and waiting, a bus arrives from Beersheba with young men and a few young women carrying signs that say, "No segregation" and "Give us the *bagrut.*"

They protest against being sent to schools mostly populated by Ethiopians that are known to have low academic standards. And they protest against being put on a vocational track without the option of being placed on an academic track that would eventually lead them to university.

Mostly the protesters sit quietly. When journalists arrive with their cameras, they lift their signs and chant their slogans, moving closer to the convention center where the Jewish Agency is meeting. They want their concerns, which they feel are being ignored, to be put on the meeting's agenda.

The real action begins when the radio station The Voice of Israel interviews the youth along with TV cameras. In unison the students lift their signs until an Ethiopian leader who worked for the Jewish Agency interrupts them. He shouts at the youth in Amharic and at the cameras in Hebrew, that it doesn't look good for Ethiopians to complain. He accuses the IAEJ of pocketing money and presenting naked starving children on their literature. The camera devours images of Ethiopian men yelling at each other and the police physically removing them from the premises, and the leader who was close to a fist fight.

This leader had already broadcast his sentiments the day before on Amharic radio, owned by the Jewish Agency. The message given to the Ethiopian community was, "Stay home. Don't attend the strike. It will only make us look bad." Since this was their only source of communication with the larger community, many obeyed the command. Fortunately, a determined group of students, whose lives were directly affected by the educational system, took the trek from the desert of Beersheba and their words will appear on the front page of the *Jerusalem Post* the next day. Most importantly, the Jewish Agency agreed to meet with Micah and discuss his proposal that suggests ways to improve the structure of education for the Ethiopian youth.

❧

"You are like an Ethiopian," Yael tells me the next day at her apartment at the Canadian Absorption Center, when I refuse to eat another croissant. "Ethiopians never accept food even when they're hungry."

"But I've already had some cola and half a croissant as well as some…how do you say it…watermelon. Yael, you said you had a long hard week. Just sit and rest already, stop preparing food."

"I will," she assures me, returning from the kitchen with our filter coffee.

Every time she leaves the room her sister Ziona buries her head in a magazine. Ziona, who I'd last seen at the Melesa home just after she arrived with Operation Solomon, is on break from school and staying with Yael for a month. She is still shy, but now I can see the way her enveloping smile lights up her face and how much she looks like Yael. I can't tell if Ziona remembers me or not from our very brief visit four years ago when she hardly uttered a word, until she says, "You are much thinner than you were back then."

"No, I am heavier now but thank you."

Yael folds laundry and prepares another load for washing; the swift movement of her hands folding sheets is soothing.

"Guess what," I say bringing her hands to a standstill. "I saw your sister Osnat in Haifa." A huge smile comes over both Yael and Ziona's faces.

"Really?" Yael asks, "At the university?"

"No, she met me at the Haifa station, and we went to the sea."

"You remembered to bring bathing suits?" Yael asks.

"No, we just walked around and sat near the shore. Do you ever see her?" I ask the sisters.

"We see her at the house," Yael answers.

Ziona nods in agreement. While she resembles Yael, she also reminds me of Osnat in her quiet and grace. I assume that like

Yael, Ziona has the same father as Osnat but a different mother who remains in Ethiopia.

When the laundry is finished, Yael settles into the corner of her bed in this one-room studio, eyes glued to the television. I look through her video collection. "Yael, do you have a tape of the play that you were in, *The Black Shawl*? I met with Micah Odenheimer and he told me what a great dancer you are."

"Did he really say that? He is such a good man. He and Simha really help people. Whenever *they* say anything bad about the Ethiopians, Micah takes action. He's a really wonderful person."

"Yes, he is. He told me the story of the play in English, so now I understand what it's about and how it shows the problems that new immigrants are dealing with."

The opening theme of a soap opera blasts through the TV speaker in English. Yael assures me that the entire country is sitting down to watch this show, *The Bold and the Beautiful*. The week before, Galia had dropped everything to watch this same show. I never expected to spend even a moment of my time in Israel like this, but it is relaxing to escape from my own thoughts. The clean laundry folded into piles and Jerusalem hills in the distance, brings comfort after days of running around in the unbearable heat of Jerusalem.

"Next time you come hopefully I'll have a vacation and we can travel somewhere together," Yael says looking directly into my eyes as I prepare to leave. "I wish that I spoke English; it's hard for us to really talk. And I wish I had a home so you could stay with me instead of... outside."

"Someday you will, Yael. Someday you will."

I reach into my bag for my camera and find a bag of fruit that Yaffa sneaked in while I was in the bathroom.

"What's this?" I ask. Yael didn't think I would find it until I returned to my room. She looks embarrassed.

"Thank you, *motek*, sweetheart. You take such good care of me."

Yael walks me outside to catch a taxi back to my room on Rambam Street.

"So, do you want to come to Israel to live?"

"I don't know," I say, tired of this nagging question.

"You are a Jew, aren't you? Well, all Jews should be in Israel."

"It is also possible to be a Jew in other places as well."

"Let me show you something beautiful." She leads me up a path surrounded by trees and flowering bushes. In the distance, the golden light of late afternoon caresses Jerusalem hills.

"Very pretty," I say.

"Very pretty," Yael repeats, mimicking the way my American accent shapes my Hebrew words.

Laughing, we take each other's hands.

<center>❧</center>

I spend my last Sabbath in Israel alone in my room on Rambam Street, doing laundry by hand, reading Alix Kates Shulman's memoir *Drinking the Rain,* eating the fruit that Yael had secretly packed for me and waiting for the phone to ring with Osnat's voice on the other end. I'm frustrated that I still haven't heard from her ,and it's impossible to reach her in her dorm, especially on Shabbat. I left her messages all week with my phone number in Jerusalem.

The phone finally rings at 2:00 a.m., just after I had fallen asleep. It's Steve. He tells me that half of my garden died while we were away, it had been that hot and dry. He assures me we will replant, that it will flourish again when I am home.

I toss and turn the rest of the night: I had planned to leave for Haifa on Sunday to see Osnat, perhaps return to Ma'alot with her. Now I only have two days left in the country. My friend Ayelet, the sociology student who now lives in Haifa, invited me to stay with her. Having still not heard from Osnat to solidify our plans, the familiar questions return. Did I somehow offend her? Is she upset about the book I'm writing? Would I find her in Haifa? What about my friends in Tel Aviv who expect me to return? Or should I stay in Jerusalem? Boaz has offered me his place. What about Petach Tikvah? Eric's wife could give birth any day.

The next morning it becomes clear: I can't leave Israel without seeing Osnat again. I have to travel past her silence to return with her to the garden.

❦

Ayelet greets me in the lobby of her building, carries my bags upstairs, pours me a glass of water and commands me to take a nap. All I want to do is call Osnat. I leave another message with her dorm secretary, this time that I'm in Haifa.

Later that evening, when Ayelet and I return from a seaside cafe, I describe Osnat's dorm for her as a place where students who have almost graduated or who've recently finished school, live. She jumps up suddenly, and points out the window, screaming "It's the building next door!" In the two weeks since I'd last seen her, Osnat was becoming unreachable, yet her home, the home I desperately want to reach, is just outside my door.

When I finally walk up the slight hill to her building the next morning, I don't know what I'll say. I've never confronted Osnat before. I remember a letter that she had sent me the previous spring when I had not written to her for six months. She had wanted to know what was wrong with me, why I hadn't written. She was so worried about me, yet I had just been busy and negligent.

The man at the front desk gives me her room number, and I quickly walk up the four flights of steps to reach it. Out of breath with a wildly beating heart, I knock on the door. There's no answer. A neighbor across the hall peers out from her room and says casually,

"If you're looking for Osnat try room 001—she's usually there."

I go back down the stairs to this basement room. When, again, no one answers, I walk outside and wander around. When I try her door on the fourth floor again, a very thin Ethiopian woman answers. She explains that Osnat is downstairs, in her boyfriend's room. Suddenly I feel like an intrusive parent who has no right to be there. As if reading my mind her roommate says, "No—it's okay, you can go and knock on the door."

"It's okay. I'll come back in an hour. Tell her to wait for me."

An hour later her roommate invites me to wait for Osnat to finish her shower. I study her walls; she seems to have left Michael Jackson behind. The magazine cutouts of white models and photographs of cars are incongruent. The only familiar object to me is the poem that her sister Marta had written for her when she left home. On her shelves are psychology textbooks with the journal I gave her stuck in the middle.

Osnat enters the room with a towel on her head and a huge smile,

"Ma nishma, you look great—what a cool outfit," she says approving of my short shorts and funky leather sandals I had just bought in Jerusalem. I am so happy to see her that at first I forget how long it has taken to reach her. Her roommate returns to her desk as Osnat combs out her hair, complaining about all of the exams they had that week and how difficult it is to master English.

"I know how it is," I say. "Every day I struggle with my Hebrew—to find the right words."

"Dina, you are doing very well, especially for someone who doesn't live here," Osnat says like a teacher watching my progress.

"Let's go for a walk and give Ora some quiet time to study."

"Good idea," Osnat says, grabbing her leather pouch.

As soon as we are out the door I blurt out, "I called you so many times and left messages from Jerusalem so that we'd be able to plan a trip to Ma'alot together. When I didn't hear from you I thought that maybe you didn't want to see me."

"What nonsense! On Saturday night I got home very late. I was going to call you Sunday, but I got home at 2:00 in the morning. I was so frustrated that I kept missing your calls and couldn't get back to you—I had hoped that we could go to Ma'alot together, but now you're leaving tomorrow."

"Well, where have you been?"

"One night we went to a friend's apartment in Haifa, and last night we went to listen to music and got home so late..."

I follow her up a hill. I don't know where she will take me, but I don't really care. I am amazed, suddenly, that in the middle of our lives, while Osnat is taking exams and hanging out with her boyfriend, waiting to return home for the Sabbath to her baby brother Baruch who she misses desperately, and while I was traveling from city to city to the homes of friends, letting go of some connections and reviving others, gathering some people's words and other people's numbers, we find ourselves living next door to each other again, if only for a day. My building is just down the hill from her building.

Osnat leads me into a forest, lush for early summer. The rains stopped months before. We walk for a while and then settle on a bench. Heavy clouds darken the sky.

"It isn't going to rain, is it?" I ask her.

"Of course not, it never rains in summer. Sometimes I come here to read a book. The only sounds I hear are the birds singing. It reminds me of the forest in Ma'alot."

"I was thinking the same thing." I had been remembering the walk Osnat and I had taken the day after Jackie's departure, how we had strolled hand-in-hand through the Ma'alot forest as an Israeli family stared at us from their picnic table.

"Will you come to Israel to live?" Osnat asks like the refrain in a prayer that needs to be repeated every year at the same time.

"Maybe someday" I say, wanting to change the subject. We had already spoken of this, of how we long for an ancient Jerusalem or a Zionism of 1948.

I had already spoken of how I live in one country and dream in another. And perhaps she is waiting for a better answer, but I can't give her one.

"I got a call from Steve last night, and he said that while we were away half of my garden died."

"Wasn't there a neighbor who could water the flowers?"

"Yes, they were watered, but it wasn't enough. The plants aren't in the earth—they are in temporary pots—they need so much water to keep them alive."

"When you get home maybe you can replant them," Osnat offers.

I have not planted my garden in the real earth in America. I have not made room for the plants to spread their roots. I fly off instead to the gardens of Israel where I live in many rooms but have no house that is mine. When I return to America, I think to myself, I want to plant a garden in the earth, I want to plant a tree.

Osnat and I do not return to Ma'alot together. We do not walk on the land that would remind us that the paths we once walked on together have been buried under new cement buildings. Instead, we walk in Osnat's forest where she leads with confidence, where I follow.

Nonetheless, on parting I say like a prayer, "Maybe next time we'll go to Ma'alot." We stand in the place between our two buildings the way we would often stand in Ma'alot between her absorption center and mine. We look at each other a long time.

"I'll walk you home." She leads me to my building, and says with unexpected emotion, "I'm going to miss you so much. Please come back to live."

"Oh, I will, I will, I'll always come back to live."

Pockets of Hope
(1996-1998)

*Water marks the boundaries
of oases. Between one tree
and another, there is all the thirst
of the earth.*

—*Edmond Jabès*
from The Book of Questions

July 29, 1998

Osnat,
Ma'alot *is where the tree was planted but our lives have
grown together in dorm rooms in Haifa, the forest in Romema,
bus stations, the town on the sea, the new Ma'alot, and now,
the ancient city of Caesarea. And because we live in our own
history, the short time in Ma'alot that tied our lives together
over a decade ago now, this time we do not need to return to
"the place." We look, instead, at the ruins of an ancient city
while you hold my daughter in your thin arms, wipe away
her tears, sing her name like a song you've known all your
life. In Caesarea where you played once as a girl, we walk the
stone fortresses, sun glistening on water. You have brought my
daughter a new dress. I've brought you myself, without so many
questions.*

Winter 1996

Steve and I, newly married, are in Israel for a brief visit on our way back from Vienna where a composer put to music my poem, "Say a Prayer but the Sea Wind Blows Them Out," about Shimon's family in Ma'alot. After the musical performance, I read more poems about Israel to an audience of closed Austrian faces. It is a relief to leave the wintry Vienna streets where I'd felt mostly the absence of Jews, for a sweltering Tel Aviv and a visit with Osnat.

I had not been in touch with Osnat since our walk through the forest more than a year before. This time, when I speak to her within hours after I land, she describes herself as not having felt like Osnat for a long time. She is overwhelmed by problems: her grandmother who lived in Netanya has died; the university won't let her graduate until she completes an additional English course, and her father returned to Ethiopia in order to try to bring to Israel the children from his first marriage.

While her husband is away, Osnat's mother, who still doesn't speak Hebrew, is working at a hummus stand in order to support the family. She is also taking care of the youngest children, Tovah and Baruch, who are still in school. Baruch, the youngest, does not speak Amharic; he talks to his mother in signs.

When Osnat tells me of her father's return to Ethiopia, she admits for the first time what I have already known: she and Yael have different mothers. The children who Mr. Melesa went to help

are siblings of Yael and Ziona. Their mother is not Jewish, and so they could not immigrate to Israel under the Jewish Law of Return. I'm still not sure how Yael and Ziona made their way to Israel. Yael would never admit to me that she is not a Jew. This was why she didn't have a Bat Mitzvah with the other girls in 1985 and why she felt so uncomfortable roaming around the Ethiopian Coptic Church with me in Jerusalem in 1993. Yet I still couldn't explain why she had lectured me the year before about how all Jews should live in Israel.

The morning after our arrival in Israel we pick up Osnat from her new dorm room in Kiryat Yam, and head east. In the back seat of our rented car, as we turn the corner to reach the road to Ma'alot, Osnat returns to herself. With beaming eyes she tells Steve, "This is the most beautiful road in the world."

When we arrive in Ma'alot, Osnat and I jump out of the car and like the girls that we once were together, run through town arm in arm.

We stand in front of the absorption center and stare at the bold flowers painted on our buildings, the newly planted trees. Osnat stands on her toes, peers into the window of her former apartment where Ethiopian and Russian faces look back. "Poor things," she says. She stares into the window for a long time, as if she could return to what used to be her life.

Later in the week, when Steve and I meet Osnat and her boyfriend, Zennemen, for dinner, we are no longer the girls we once were but two women on a double-date for New Year's Eve. After returning with Steve to Ma'alot, he and Osnat feel like old friends, and Zennemen, who arrived with Operation Solomon and speaks more English than Hebrew, has become our fast friend. Instead of asking when I'm getting married, Osnat wants to hear all about our June wedding, which she wishes she could have attended.

Our buoyant mood celebrating old and new friendship dampens after hours of waiting in line to get a table at a local restaurant. Soon we notice others who arrived after us, being seated. Osnat

and I grow frustrated and finally enraged. Zennemen seems to be telling her in Amharic to relax. Steve also doesn't want to make a scene. When another group of four who arrived at least an hour after us is seated, I confront the waitress. She shrugs her shoulders and five minutes later seats us. None of us utter what becomes more obvious as the evening wears on. Osnat and Zennemen are the only Ethiopians in the restaurant, and our party is the last to be seated. We try to enjoy our toast and cheese when it arrives after another long wait, but a shadow has fallen across the table.

I realize that although in many ways Osnat's life is like that of other Israeli college kids, sometimes the attitudes of others must make her still feel like an immigrant girl peering out the window, toward the future.

Summer 1998

This year is the 50th anniversary of the founding of the State. In the Chicago university where I've been running the Jewish Studies program for the year, I brought the Israeli writer Batya Gur to campus to give us a fifty-year perspective. She dwelled on what was gained, the development of the state, the obvious problems and overwhelming accomplishments. But as I stand in Jerusalem this summer with my husband Steve and our baby daughter Sarina, looking across at Robert's mulberry tree that is no longer dropping fruit, I can't help dwelling on what has been lost. Burger King has taken over the Café Atara. Writers like Scholem Aleichem and Bialik are only street names, no longer the major poets taught in the schools. Jewish writers sit at home behind computers, reach each other through electronic mail.

And, most painfully, the first English language poet, my dear friend Robert, died on January twelfth. On his grave, which we climb a small hill and many thin roads to find, it is written, *Your gift survived it all.*

Lost, too, is the era of the founding fathers running the country. In November 1995, Prime Minister Yitzhak Rabin was assassinated

by an extremist Jew, and six months later, Benjamin Netanyahu became prime minister. The integrity and idealism left over from the previous government has been drowned out by bus exhaust and empty rhetoric.

Around the same time, all of the disappointment, rage, disillusionment, confusion and victimization felt by the Ethiopian community culminated in their response to what had come to be called "the blood tossing." The Ethiopian community discovered that blood donated by their soldiers was later secretly discarded. Officials said they did not want to insult the Ethiopian soldiers by refusing their blood, so they drew it but didn't feel they could use it in medical emergencies because of the high incidence of HIV-positive blood among the Ethiopian community.

This incident brought about the largest and most violent strike among the Ethiopian community. Thousands of people showed up for this event. In 1985, when the community protested against the rabbinate's decision to have the entire male population re-circumcized, they did so by quietly walking across the country. In '95 students had quietly protested against segregation in education. They were so hurt and fundamentally changed by the blood-tossing incident that their elegant silence turned to desperate shouts of rage.

In 1998, their rage can still be felt. According to Asher Elias, a *sabra* Ethiopian whose father immigrated to Israel as a teacher in 1965 among the first Ethiopians in Israel, an entire generation is losing its way.

In 1995 when Asher saw the IAEJ drop-in center in the "Ethiopian Ghetto" in Tel Aviv where high school dropouts and other lost youth hang out, he felt compelled to become involved in the Ethiopian community. He was shocked to discover young teenagers separated from their families, on drugs, and involved in crime. After spending a few hours in this run-down center Asher could no longer believe the problems were temporary. Micah Odenheimer convinced Asher to work for his association. Days after Micah's

offer, Asher quit his job in marketing and became budget manager for IAEJ as well as director of international relations.

In his office in the center of Jerusalem, Asher paints for me the bleak picture of 1998.

"The educational initiatives that you ask about are not working. If anything, the dropout rate is higher. The students get a sense of the situation early, that they aren't getting the help they need, that no one really cares if they succeed or not. There were 2,000 dropouts this year, a high rate of criminal activity, drugs, and prostitution in slum areas of cities and in places like Hadera—even among ten-year-olds."

"Some of the problems are segregated schools. They aren't sure where the money is going from the Ministry of Absorption or the Ministry of Education. The money isn't getting to the schools or to the kids. Each school gets a certain amount of money per Ethiopian head, but the money is not getting to the kids. As a result, many of the kids are on vocational tracks. They feel like underdogs in bad schools in bad cities where the teachers have very low expectations of them. Eighty percent of the Ethiopian students are in boarding schools. There is also a problem with those who stay in their own communities because no one knows what to do with them. There is no follow-up on those who stay home from school."

"Asher, is there any hope?" I ask, demoralized.

Laughing sadly at my question he continues, "There have been a lot of programs aimed at improving the education of the Ethiopians, but there has not been enough real help. People are writing theoretical proposals, but nothing is being implemented. There are too many individual organizations that conduct research and come up with plans, but they don't have the wherewithal to get these programs into the schools. Organizations need to work together. IAEJ designed an initiative that involves working with computers and with small groups of students at a time, and Joint Distribution is carrying it out. Micah and I both believe that this has gotten off the ground because the two organizations are

working together. It is moving very slowly but the places where the program has been implemented are showing success.

"I also believe that there would be more hope if the Ethiopian immigrants would take more responsibility for their own lives and advocate their own leaders. For too long they have relied on others and that has proven dangerous."

᪐

Most of the Ethiopian immigrants who arrived with Operation Solomon in 1991 are now out of the caravans. Those who remain are without family or have a disability that prevents them from getting work. The mortgage program of 1995 moved some families to development towns where they could afford to buy homes, but generally did not move people to integrated or thriving communities. Those who had been in the caravans for so many years did not master Hebrew or develop skills for employment. So while the *olim* are now out of their mobile homes, they are still mostly in remote corners of the country amongst themselves, struggling to get by.

When you drive through Hasrat Yasaf, the largest caravan in the north of Israel where Osnat tutors new immigrants, it feels as though it is still the aftermath of Operation Solomon. The main road is crowded with men and women walking home from class with large plastic notebooks in their arms. Old women sit in the scant shade of young trees. The only difference from 1991 is the large white *kippot* on the heads of every male. These are the Falash Mura, the converts, who have been filtering in slowly over the years after government scrutiny of their Jewish roots.

The caravan social worker who speaks only Hebrew laughs at my questions like "What are the differences between Operation Solomon and the *aliyah* of the Falash Mura?"

"The Beta Israel came because they were Jews. These people (Falash Mura) came because they were separated from a family member or because they had to. The *vatikim*, veteran, Ethiopians resent the Falash Mura because in Ethiopia, they didn't choose to

be Jews. Many even ridiculed Jews and now that it's convenient to be a Jew, they come back. In fact, they are even more religious than the Jews because they were forced to go through a strict conversion process. They are required to take an exam about what it means to be a Jew and they are required to go to the *mikvah.*

"The major difference in terms of life or preparatory time in the caravan is that this time we are encouraging the new *olim* to do things for themselves and to keep a strong sense of family. What was happening before was the family would send the kids away to school and then not follow up. They were not used to relying on telephones to stay in touch, and their children's schools were often far from the caravan sights. Other family members were in the army, and it was as if the government were separating and raising each family member individually but without the proper provisions. Everything was done for them. Families broke up, and when they no longer received help from other sources, they didn't know how to do anything for themselves.

"Now a caravan worker will take the *olim* to the clinic, for example, for a period of time and then encourage an aunt or another family member to come along. Eventually the family will learn to help each other in situations such as this. If the family is strong, they can help each other, follow up on kids in school."

I ask about hope and am given numbers and proposals for future programs. But for me the real pockets of hope are still in the lives of my families.

🌿

Osnat and Zennemen, her boyfriend now of several years, live in an apartment in Kiryat Yam. Zennemen will soon finish his army duty, a desk job not too far from their home. He is also working toward a degree in international relations at Haifa University where he and Osnat first met. This gentle man, who looks about thirty, speaks English very well but still struggles with Hebrew. Osnat teaches Ethiopian children in a development town. She graduated

from Haifa University and still hopes to attend graduate school in counseling.

I learn from Osnat that Yael still lives at the Canadian Absorption Center in Jerusalem, works in a clothing store in the new mall and studies theater and performance. Joint Distribution gave fellowships to all of the actors in her troupe to study at the Jerusalem Theater for a year, a dream come true for Yael. Another dream of hers has also come true. After not having seen her for fourteen years, her mother finally arrived in Israel—for a visit. Friends and family from around the country travel to Yael's apartment in Talpiot to pay their respects to this woman who has not seen her daughters since they were young. But when her tourist visa runs out, Yael's mother will return to Ethiopia because she is not a Jew.

Elad wears silver earrings in each ear and three long braids hang down his back. He still has a sparkle, a mischievous grin but there is something new—a certain restraint. He is a tough Israeli teenager but still escorts his mother to the store and helps her carry the groceries up four flights of steps to their Kfar Saba apartment where an Ethiopian stamp remains on the door.

The hearth in Kfar Saba is still filled with family. Elad, Simcha and Batya pass my baby daughter from arm to arm like a blessing. Amnon finished the army and works in a factory. Elad has one more year of high school and hopes to become a paratrooper in the army. Batya works in the market in town and is engaged to the college student she had met some years before. He, too, lives with the Yamari family. When Batya brings me in the next room to change Sarina's diaper, she shows me the beautiful ring he gave her, and we hug.

The eldest two children, Orit and Shlomo, are both married and live outside the family home. Orit married her boyfriend of many years who is part Russian and part Yemenite. Elad describes their three-year-old baby boy as "mocha." They live near her husband's family in Hadera, where the Yamaris often visit for Shabbat. Shlomo, the son who had arrived with Operation Solomon, married an Ethiopian woman and they,

too have a baby boy. Simha Yamari is a proud grandmother of sabra Israelis.

When I look into Osnat's eyes at twenty-six, Batya's eyes at twenty-two and Elad's eyes at sixteen, I still see a trace of youthfulness, a strong sense of self as both Israeli and Ethiopian. There is also sadness, the unspokenness of what had been lost: Elad's father who returned with another wife, Yael's mother who will return to Ethiopia, Osnat's childhood and her dream of what a Promised Land would be.

As I've witnessed the poverty of families in the "Ethiopian ghettos," listened to stories about racism, the stigma of AIDS, segregation in the schools and now the ever-increasing dropout rate and lost generation turning to drugs and crime, I've also witnessed two families growing and thriving against all odds. They are home because what they've left behind has been integrated into who they've become, in the soil where they have planted new roots.

I once dreamed of Israel as a place where I could gather fruit from trees. On Kibbutz I pulled lime from bushes and planted almond trees on the border between Ramat Rachel and an Arab village. Later I planted trees on the outskirts of Jerusalem through Karen Kayemet for the births of children, for the death of my mother.

And I have planted a tree in America. It is a lot of work to make it grow, to nurture the garden around it. Even if I still dream in Israel, I've cultivated my life on American soil. But as I carry my daughter through Jerusalem streets, place her into the open arms of the people whose lives I've watched grow up here, I know that these lives and this landscape can be traced in the lines of my face.

Spring 2002

A year ago I gave birth to a son and named him Ilan, Hebrew for tree. I named him after my mother who died three weeks after our return from Israel in 1998. Having another child and naming

him after my mother is a way of blessing her memory and an act of belief in the future. These days it is more difficult to believe in the future, but my baby son laughing and my young daughter waving her flag in celebration of Yom Ha'atzmaut, Israel Independence Day, force me to.

Sarina cherishes baskets made by Ethiopian Jewish women. When she was a baby she sat in the caravan watching them spin the thread into patterns and shape clay into the sculptures that sit on our shelves. "Of course Ethiopian Jews live in Israel," my daughter tells her preschool class, "I can't believe that there was a time when Israel *wasn't* their home."

At home she looks at a crack in our ceiling that makes a funny shape.

She tells me it looks like Israel. When I ask her why she says, "Because Israel is breaking."

She wants to go and help fix it. I wonder how such a young heart can absorb this ancient longing. If I could speak I would say, "My dear partner in waiting, our return will come soon."

Home: Twenty-five Years after Operation Moses (2009)

(What is taught by the branches
men in turn teach
to the branches. What is sung by the sea
men in turn sing
to the sea.
All this joy,
this being at home:
Is there nothing we have spared?)

—*Edmond Jabès*
from The Book of Questions

The tall, slender Ethiopian man with Rastafarian braids who served as a paratrooper in the army rushes into his apartment in Kfar Saba and weeps. Among his wife, baby son, sister and her children, is an American woman and her family who he thought he had lost through the difficulty of language and the passage of time. He hugs her with all his strength and kisses her children, shakes hands with her husband and father before apologizing for being late and dirty from being outside. He asks for permission to shower so he can greet them properly.

When the day before, his wife, Devorah, told him she'd stopped by, he didn't believe her. He'd been asking about her, wondering about her, suffering over his inability to reach her. He thought he had mastered her patterns of return: every two years. Now it had been more than a decade. Recently he had come upon a photo of her from their last visit, her very white daughter in his mother's black arms.

She would return every few years and infuse his memories and bring gifts from America. He never had enough language to tell her what it meant to him, and her Hebrew seemed more and more limited the older he got. Yet she would say what she needed to through her presence, her returns.

When a decade passed without any visits he began to get friends to help him, and he said to Devorah, just months ago, "I have to find her." So when Devorah told him she stopped by when he was

at work installing security cameras all over the country, he didn't believe her.

This tough, Israeli paratrooper, father, husband, installer of security systems, breaks down again when he returns from the shower and tries to greet her. When he leaves the room again, his mother explains that he's embarrassed by his own tears. When he returns he kisses her three times on the cheek, and kisses her children and sits next to her and tells her how he had looked for her and then she appeared.

The man is twenty-eight-year-old Elad, and the woman, of course, is me. There is no other way to describe the emotion of our reunion after eleven years, twenty-five years after Operation Moses.

Before Elad's dramatic return home, my father, husband, children and I had been sitting with Simha Yamari who was wrapped in her traditional garb, having just returned from the Ethiopian *shul* in their neighborhood. When Batya heard from Devorah that I'd be coming on Shabbat, she gathered her family who now live in a settlement in the West Bank, and took a bus to Kfar Saba. On the Sabbath, she explains to me, her husband usually takes the kids since she is with them all week while he works long hours as a plumber. We met him briefly when we first got to town, and then he went off with the two youngest to visit friends, while the two eldest, eight and six, stayed to see the American visitors.

Batya is radiant in her long white skirt, long-sleeved white t-shirt and green head covering on this unbearably hot summer day. When I tell her how beautiful the different shades of green are in her scarf, she says, "Just like your eyes." Standing in the kitchen, Simha Yamari, who up to this point had been blowing kisses and saying "*Ma nishma*," begins to speak to me in Amharic and Devorah translates, "I can't speak much, but you are deep in my heart, and I'll never forget you. In the future, when your children come by themselves to Israel, they can stay here." On the refrigerator,

there is a photo I'd taken of Batya and Elad standing next to *injera* in their kitchen, in 1991, just after Operation Solomon.

I am grateful for this Sabbath because the television is off and everyone is home from work. We take turns holding Elad's eight-month-old son, Ori. The stillness allows us to speak to each other, to find the words we need. Elad doesn't absorb the stillness like the others do. He wants to take us to the orange groves we've been gazing at from their *marpeset*. My eight-year old son, Ilan, wants to stay behind with Simha, Batya and Batya's daughter, Shira. Elad gives my father an umbrella like their elders carry to protect them from the sun and fills bottles with water. Finally, my father, Sarina, Steve, Elad, Devorah, and Batya's eight-year-old son head out with baby Ori in his stroller.

A hot wind comes off the fields that separate Kfar Saba from the Arab village of Kekillya. First we pass the rows where during the right season, they pick watermelon and squash.

"When you were a child," I remind Elad, "you used to steal squash and watermelon."

"Sometimes I did," he agrees, with his mischievous smile, "but later, after they picked the fruit, they'd leave out some extra, and we'd come and gather it."

"That was very nice of them."

"Well you know how it says in the Bible that you should always leave a corner of your harvest for those who need it."

Elad stops to make sure everyone drinks water and looks down at me.

"Dina, I can't believe you found your way here, that after all these years you remembered where the house is."

"It was Steve who looked at the map on our way out of the Dead Sea and realized it goes through Kfar Saba. All I had was the name of your neighborhood and the name of your street and the number seven. Steve led me to your home."

"All the honor," Elad says to Steve who is trailing behind, not quite understanding our Hebrew.

Elad continues, "It is so good to see you, I can't express it."

"I feel the same way. I am just in shock, to see you as a father."

When Devorah comments on his overflow of emotion he says, "She is like my sister."

After we walk for a while in the hot wind of the fields Elad asks if we still want to make our way to the oranges, a little further on.

"Well we've come this far," Steve answers.

"Dina, I'm taking you here because I want you to remember this day. I don't want you to forget me."

"Elad, I've found you after eleven years. Do you think I'd forget you? Never."

"I know. But I want you to know that this is your home. I don't want to have to tell you. I just want you to know."

When we reach the groves Elad takes my daughter Sarina to a far corner where she can find the ripest oranges, a place the stroller can't reach. I carry baby Ori while Devorah waits in the shade, speaking fluent English with my father. My daughter and Batya's son run through the groves together, bite into the sticky tartness. As I watch them I think to myself, *this is the future.*

Back at the hearth in Kfar Saba, Ilan is asleep on the couch. Simha asks who wants *injera* and Sarina is the only taker. I explain to them that it is her favorite meal and about the Ethiopian restaurant in our town and how I want her to taste the real thing. We all gather around as she relishes the taste of their food, leaves only the spicy beans in the center.

"I remember when Elad was little," Mrs. Yamari says laughing, "and he'd invite you to our home for *injera*, but you wouldn't come."

"Well, he was only four, and I didn't know if it was okay or not. I didn't want to just appear at the dinner table."

Batya joins her in laughter.

As we prepare to leave Batya says, "I love you Dina."

"I love you too, Batya."

"I'm older now, so I will be better at staying in touch."

Elad and I exchange emails and cell phone numbers and he says, "I will come to see you before you leave the country."

An hour outside of Kfar Saba and my cell phone rings with Elad's voice at the other end.

August 2009

Dear Osnat,

We do not apologize this time for the decade that has passed between us. You sent my daughter a book for her birthday. I sent you a note about my son's birth.

When I last tried to call you were in Thailand with Zennemen who you now laugh about saying, "I was so young." You seemed more and more out of reach.

When I got to Jerusalem none of the old numbers worked. When I finally reached your sister Liat who gave me your number and I heard your voice, there were children crying in the background. I couldn't believe they were the cries of your daughters, ages one and two. Later I say to my husband, "The children of Operation Moses now have their own children, with Hebrew names, curly hair and beautiful dark eyes."

A week later I carried Elad's son through fields of oranges the way you carried Sarina through fields of sand in Caesarea the last time we were here. Now we tell time by our children. Sarina was exactly the age that Elad's son Ori is now, the time of our last visit.

From our room in Jerusalem, I invited you to my poetry reading. It took you a long time to understand what I was saying. I was only two days in the country and my Hebrew wasn't flowing. This was my above-ground-reading, unlike in the old days when I read in bomb shelters and basements. This was at T'mol Shimshom, named after Agnon, against Jerusalem stone, and in front of the English speaking poets of Jerusalem. I wanted you to be there, but you said it was too hard with the kids and all. I read the poems that were born here as well as the

poems of my life in America. My poems now live side by side with each other, like peaceful countries.

As soon as I heard your voice this time I knew that something was wrong. When I asked how the family was you said, "Half good and half difficult." You finally told me that your sister Marta was dead, and to make sure I understood you repeated, "She is no longer alive." My heart sunk into my stomach. When I asked what happened, and you said you didn't know, I began to imagine the worst. The night before, my friend Eric who you met long ago in Ma'alot, and who drove in from Beit Shemesh to see me, told stories about Ethiopian men killing their wives because they couldn't tolerate the shifting dynamics. Such stories circulate, but your family is different. And anyway Marta wasn't married, you finally tell me. And when I meet her son, I see from his light brown skin and straight hair that his father was white. When I later asked your cousins, who hesitated to tell me of her death until Batya insisted, they said it was from high blood pressure, eight days after the birth of her son. You later told me it was three days after his birth.

You came back from Haifa where you'd lived since college, to help your parents take care of Marta's son Yoseph in their home in Ramat Eliyahu. Now you have your own daughters, but you let go of them when three-year-old Yoseph needs to be held.

"If I could live anywhere I'd live in Jerusalem," you tell me when I am finally sitting next to you again in your mother's home. "But I have to be here; I can't leave Marta's son."

Jerusalem still feels most like home to me, too: the sense of history, the stone against which I rest my forehead in prayer, can sit with poet friends old and new and find an immediacy and intimacy no matter how much time passes between us. It is a place I keep returning to the way I return to you, and you to your mother's home.

You asked us to meet you in your mother's home instead of your own, five minutes away, on the other side of town. You explain that you're here all of the time, and that you live in

temporary housing only because you and your husband Ilan, are about to buy a home of your own.

You tell me I never change and yet I feel so different inside that I can't believe it doesn't show on my face. My generous poet friend Betsy says it is a deeper quality of beauty although I am heavier and older: it is something from inside.

I haven't come this time to ask questions of home. Maybe that is the peace that has settled in my once awkward posture. Home is something we've come to take for granted. We are at home in ourselves and in the world.

Both you and Elad, and Simha Yamari, your aunt, feel at home enough now to tell me your home is mine. You've both commanded that from now on when I arrive in this country, I come straight to your apartments instead of to hotels and kibbutzim. Nothing more needs to be said.

You are a Jew living among Ethiopians, working among Israelis, mother to Sabra daughters. Your children will understand the world from where you came because you wear it in your graceful posture, the way your mother, in her tired eyes, wears it across her shoulders like a Shamma.

Your mother's sadness is palpable. When she speaks of Marta she is stricken with pain.

And when she speaks of Yoseph.

When I ask how your father is you say fine and then stare at me so I don't go any further. I don't know if he still lives in this house or not. But in all of the tumult of your children climbing and my kids devouring the cake your mother put out for them and your sharp stare—I swallow my questions, I let them go.

When I tell you you look the same you say no it can't be, that you are not the same because it is difficult with two young children, your long hours of work in a bank, helping to raise Marta's son, the sadness that has joined your family like an extra child. These are the struggles of any Israeli, any citizen. But in some ways, hair pinned back, t-shirt and jeans, glasses that give you an intellectual look, you are the same. When I

am sitting next to you in the corner of your mother's home you are easy to find, easier than I remember, as we chat with the intimacy of old friends.

On the wall are wedding pictures your mother has had enlarged. It takes me awhile to recognize you with your straightened hair and stark white dress. Your husband looks older, not like your former boyfriends Daniel or Zennemen. It isn't until I see your smile in the photo that I think about old promises. When I left you as a twelve-year-old girl I said, "I always want to keep in touch, know when you get married." Neither of us would have believed you'd wait until your mid-thirties like I did.

Why didn't you tell me you got married, became a mother, lost your sister?

Your life has been full. You haven't had the luxury to wonder if I'd ever return.

I can see from the pictures that Liat was also a beautiful bride and Ziona, who came with Operation Solomon, married a Russian. You laugh when you try to describe the color of their children. You don't say much about Yael, still single in Jerusalem, working in a clothing store.

I give you a copy of my poetry book, Apples of the Earth, and you put it in your purse and vow to work on your English. If I'd known you had daughters I would have brought you dresses as well.

It is difficult to understand just how much time has passed between us the way it is difficult to understand distances between countries by moving through the sky. But when you look at my eleven-year-old daughter who you carried as a baby, you understand. You tell me you enlarged the picture I sent you ten years ago of her in your arms and hung it in your home. People have asked if she is your own child. And it is from looking at your Sabra siblings and your mother's house that I understand the passage of time: Baby Baruch is in the army,

little Shai is a grown man, Tova is twenty and living in your parent's home, helping with Yoseph.

And I would not have recognized the family home had you not led me there. I remember it as a single home next to open fields, garlic drying in a tub on the lawn. Now it is surrounded by other buildings, run down, and I realize it is an apartment. Inside it is darker than I remember, the shades drawn, the sadness in the walls.

Your daughters keep climbing all over you, and I know it is time for their bath and bed so I prepare to leave, anxious to return to our kibbutz. They ask for "abba" but he doesn't get home until ten p.m. They are also drawn to my Steve; they prefer men you explain.

You are a good and modern mother. No sweets, juice only on the Sabbath, no television. They get spoiled with all of these things at Savta's house, you explain. On the street you kiss and shake hands with elders, an uncle, a friend. You live amongst each other.

We agree this time that there is no need to return to Ma'alot. "It was fun, but now everyone is gone so there is nothing," you say. My family and I drove through anyway so my children could see my first home here. "Look at my view," I kept saying, pointing to the mountains.

On the way from the sea to the Kinneret, I found another place in the Galil where I could imagine building a home. It is a village on the way from Nahariya to Ma'alot that runs on solar energy and windmills. We went there to see a woman who sells Ethiopian crafts. She rescued the women from the San Jen caravan when it emptied and the government stopped supporting their art because it wasn't profitable. She brings clay to the apartments, scattered throughout Israel, where these women have settled, clay the color of the dirt they used near the rivers where they bathed in Ethiopia. They still make their

sculptures and pots and she fires them, sells them and brings them the money.

There was a peace surrounding her home that I haven't found anywhere else, a lemon tree, an open porch looking out at Galilee Mountains. It was even more beautiful than Ma'alot because we were inside the mountains instead of admiring them from a distance.

She told stories about the history of your people, the way you washed in rivers, bathed when you came in contact with strangers, drew yourselves from the pure waters of your Judaism to find Jerusalem. It is in the stories and silences of your people, the stone of Galilee hills and Jerusalem buildings that I am most at home, in the idea that your home and Elad's home is also now home to my children.

I know your people suffer still from poverty, AIDS, disenfranchisement and all of the old evils. But you and your family remain my hope that for future generations Israel will be a gentler home.

Osnat, I think the dream has come true, although dreams change color when you touch them.

Acknowledgments

The traveling, gathering and living that has become this book spans decades.

My gratitude goes out to so many who have lived some of it with me, contributed their knowledge or gave me shelter in Israel while I researched and wrote parts of *Drawn from Water*.

Special thanks to the "first responders," as writer Gary Shteyngart so eloquently put it, those who read the first tentative pages a long time ago: Brenda Berman, Alvin Rosenfeld, Charlene Schlager and Sandi Wisenberg.

Thanks for the generosity, honesty, thoughtfulness and sustaining friendship of those who read early drafts of the entire manuscript: Galia Englemayer, Bernard Friedman, Cha Johnston and Judy Schwartz.

A profound thanks to the later responders: Amy Davis for asking thoughtful questions and who with a critical, gentle and generous eye helped me make this a better book.

Ben Furnish, editor extraordinaire, who asked me to revise with my poet's hat on. To the others at BkMk, Susan Schurman and Maureen Hirthler who have created a true home for *Drawn from Water* and for your editorial and artistic acumen.

Thank you to all those who shared their knowledge along the way: Shoshana Ben Dor, Chaim Rosen, Yossi Har El, Yehuda Weintraub, Shai, Barbara Ribakove Gordon, Shlomo Gronich, Micah Odenheimer, Asher Elias, the Israeli Association for Ethiopian Jews, the Jewish Agency, and the Ministry of Absorbtion.

Thank you Rosellen Brown, Yossi Klein Halevi and Sue William Silverman for your support.

Thanks to those who provided a sense of home in Israel during the gathering and writing of this: Azriel Har-Lavan, Elana Gabai, The Kedem family, Duki Dror, Galia Englemayer, Shimon Shiri, SVK, and Robert Friend, of Blessed Memory. Thank you Robert, also, for permission to quote from your poems.

A special thanks to Hilai, artist's colony in Israel, the Ragdale Foundation in Lake Forest, Illinois and the Writer's Workspace in Chicago where large chunks of the book was written and revised.

Thanks Cha Johnston, my Ma'alot roommate, for thirty years of friendship from across oceans, for taking, keeping and sharing beautiful photographs of Ma'alot, including the cover photo for this book.

Thanks Henny Wenkart editor of the *Jewish Women's Annual* for publishing excerpts of the book in 1995 and 2013 and to Philipe Kafka for publishing excerpts of it in her anthology *Lost on the Map of the World* (Peter Lang).

Thanks to the Illinois Arts Council for two fellowships that allowed me to return to Israel and that gave me time to write, to the Evanston Arts Council for a cultural grant, and to the Jewish Federation of Chicago for a grant to get back to Israel to write the essay "Five Years after Operation Moses," which ultimately turned into this book.

The deepest gratitude goes to my Ethiopian families, especially Elad, Osnat, Batya, Jaffa and Amnon, for sharing your stories, for opening the door.

To my father, Gilbert Elenbogen for believing in me and in the book from the beginning, for endless support insight and wisdom. And to my mother of blessed memory, Irene Kaplan Elenbogen and my sister Beryl Elenbogen for a life time of support.

Deepest gratitude to my son, Ilan for technical assistance and for being wonderful.

To my daughter Sarina for joining me on the journey and becoming my partner in crime in 2014. And to my husband Steve for love, patience, reading maps and being my traveling companion.

Dina Elenbogen is author of the poetry collection *Apples of the Earth* and recipient of two fellowships and an award from the Illinois Arts Council. Her work has been published in numerous magazines including *Prairie Schooner, Poet Lore, Tikkun, Bellevue Literary Review, Paterson Literary Review, New City Chicago* and numerous anthologies. She holds a poetry MFA from the University of Iowa and teaches creative writing at the University of Chicago's Graham School. She lives in Evanston, Illinois, with her husband, Steve Siegel, and their two children, Sarina and Ilan. For more information, visit her at www.dinaelenbogen.com

DRAWN FROM WATER

Dina Elenbogen

Interviewed by Sabrina Veroczi

Q. *When you move to Chicago after living in Ma'alot, you write that you "don't know, spiritually, how to be a Jew or a poet in this country." How has that feeling changed for you over the years? Do you still feel like Israel is your home as a Jew and a poet?*

A. That sentence came straight out of my journal after my return visit in 1989, after having been away from Israel for five years. I was in my twenties living alone in an apartment in East Rogers Park, teaching part-time at several universities. I was not part of a Jewish community. I was not settled with the fact that I was living in the United States instead of Israel. I still felt like a crucial part of myself as both Jew and poet was more alive and belonged in Israel. The urgency that came into my work in Israel, partly dictated by circumstances, did not pervade my American poems.

This feeling has changed over the years as the circumstances of my life have evolved. I have found a fulfilling way to be a Jew in America. When I got married and had a family, I joined Beth Emet, The Free Synagogue in Evanston, and sent my children to a private Jewish day school. I felt like I was growing and thriving as a Jew in America. Both my children's school and one of the institutions where I taught, Spertus Institute of Jewish Studies, were on a Jewish calendar and allowed me time off for holidays. This helped us build Jewish lives for our children and deepened our

sense of community. Our children speak Hebrew and read Torah. We have Shabbat with family or friends every week.

I don't worry so much anymore how to be a poet in America. I write poetry. I have poet friends. I try to go to poetry readings when I can. I teach creative writing, so I am always talking with my students about literature.

Having said that, although I do live a satisfying Jewish and literary life in America, I still feel that Israel is my spiritual home that offers me something deeper as both a Jew and a poet. Poetry is in the air there. Jewish life permeates. Cities still come to a standstill for the Sabbath. But life there has also become more complex. I am less naïve, and the country is less idealistic. It isn't the same country I fell in love with in 1977 and 1984.

Q. After writing an article containing the "composite voices of all the different people" you have interviewed about the Ethiopian Jews, you say that "the reporter is taking over so the poet can rest." This book seems to require that the reporter and the poet collaborate. Can you discuss the balance between the two sides and the process of writing this book?

A. When I first started writing about the Ethiopian Jewish community I felt a certain responsibility to tell the story factually. I tried to be a good journalist in the first articles I wrote on the subject. I sensed back then that my personal stories with Elad and Osnat were an important part of the narrative, and so sometimes I interspersed journal entries into more factual writing. On my first and subsequent return trips to Israel, as I say in the book, I was trying to find the truth about their absorption into Israeli life. This led me to the offices of anthropologists and sociologists. In the early drafts of the book, these voices competed with each other. There were too many interviews and too much personal material. I also sensed that Elad and Osnat's families were not typical. In order to tell the whole story I needed to find out how Ethiopian

communities were faring throughout the country. The search for the larger picture led to a more journalistic voice.

I knew I wanted to work with Ben Furnish at BkMk after he read a draft of the book and asked me to revise with my poet's hat on. I had been looking for permission to write from my own perspective, a poet's perspective, for a long time. When Yossi Klein Halevi read my book and said that the Ethiopian Jews had found their poet, I knew that I had achieved my goal.

Q. At times, the language barrier between you and the Ethiopian Jews keeps you from understanding the complexities of their journey, yet it also seems to provide you with a deeper connection to the families that you work with. How has your time in Israel and your study of Hebrew affected the ways that you use language?

A. One of the things I share with my Ethiopian friends is the way we consider language to be sacred. As they speak their most profound truths in parables, I speak mine in poetry. We try not to waste words, to speak aimlessly or to speak dishonestly. Israelis are direct in their speech and do not hide behind language the way that Americans sometimes do. I have become a more direct and sometimes *chutzpahdik* communicator from living in Israel. I am a more delicate speaker from being among the Ethiopians. I love speaking Hebrew because of its conciseness and the poetry inherent in the language. I hope I have picked up some of the rhythms of Hebrew in my poetry.

Q. Of all of the relationships that you have in Israel over the years, why do you think that Elad and Osnat remained so important to you?

Some of it has to do with timing. Osnat and Elad are the first Ethiopians I met and the first children I fell in love with. It was a magical time in our lives. As newcomers to a completely different world than the one they knew, they noticed and cherished the small miracles of daily life. Israel, and especially

Ma'alot, was also a new world for me, although not in as extreme a way it was for them. Discovering each other and our otherness added to the miracle. Elad was such a cute child; he sparkled. I loved his mischievousness, and I felt his sadness that he couldn't articulate. I assumed it had to do with what took place on his trek and his time in Sudan. I knew it had to do with his father who remained in Ethiopia. I just loved him, and love him now and have taken pleasure in watching him grow up into a true mensch.

With Osnat it was similar. Because she was older we shared more with each other. As I write in the book, I think we recognized something in one another—our quest for learning, love of language, our sometimes shy and quiet natures. Our relationship has evolved over the years, and she has become the one who takes care of me when I visit Israel. Now she is the Israeli who has her own home and family that my family visits. I am constantly amazed by her inner and outer beauty. During my most recent visit, I felt that same connection with Elad's sister Batya. She has come to feel like family the same way that the others do.

Q. *Can you discuss the title,* Drawn from Water?

A. *Moses* or *Moshe* literally means *the one drawn from water.* My Ethiopian families came to Israel with Operation Moses. In Ethiopia they washed all of the time, particularly when they came in contact with strangers. They think of water as purity, and bathing in water as purification. I think of them as having been drawn from the purity of their religious practice in Ethiopia to a practice in Israel that has become less pure because of what they've had to abandon. One of those rituals is the mikvah where women purify themselves after menstruation and giving birth. In Ethiopia they bathed in rivers and lakes. In Israel they looked for natural bodies of water but had to settle for mikvahs in town or nothing at all.

Q. *Early in the book you meet Yossi's mother, a scientist from Vienna who supports your decision to teach the Ethiopian Jews. You write that "Unlike her son, Ora understands that home is not always about comfort." What is your understanding of "home"?*

Home is where one can truly be oneself. It is where we are loved and honored for who we are and pushed to reach our potential. As far as the immigrants are concerned, I believe they are at home when they are able to hold onto the customs that are dear to them, to their essence, and at the same time benefit from their new culture and become productive and thriving citizens.

DISCUSSION QUESTIONS

1. Why does Dina go to Israel? What hopes does she have when she first arrives at the kibbutz? How is the experience different from what she expected?

2. Why does Dina decide to move to Ma'alot? What is she looking to find in the new community? What are the challenges she faces?

3. What does Dina realize when she returns to America? How has her perception of America changed? What rituals does she create or enact to honor her time in Israel and remember the people she has befriended?

4. What does Dina learn from the artist Alemu Eshtie and his paintings? What does she discover about him when she visits his home? In what ways might it be easier to tell a story through painting, music or poetry?

5. Dina writes that what she "love[s] most about Ma'alot and in Israel in general is the richness of daily life." What do you think she means by this? How is this different from life in America?

6. What role does food play in *Drawn From Water*? How can food help define a culture and community? What examples can you find of the various rituals that are centered around meals?

7. When Dina visits Osnat's room at Haifa University, what important discovery does she make? In what ways does Osnat use her writing to connect with her Ethiopian culture and her experiences in Israel? In what ways can literacy preserve heritage?

8. What does Dina learn about the Ethiopian Jews from the

professor at Hebrew University? Would you consider him to be an objective source? How does Dina respond to his "sadness, anger, and disillusionment"? What challenges do journalists face when conducting interviews?

9. Dina writes that "The Ethiopian community still speaks in whispers, protests in silence but more and more voices could now be heard in song and in other forms of expression. Over time, the singers, dancers, artists and artisans have found ways to express their struggles, their history and their identities through their art." What does Dina discover by watching Shlomo Gronich's concert? What does Gronich tell her in his interview?

10. What role does poetry play in *Drawn From Water*? In what ways do you think the voice of the poet was present in the narrative? In what ways can prose and poetry intersect?

11. What does Dina realize when she tries to share her experiences of Israel with Steve? What questions does it raise for her about their relationship?

12. Why do you think Dina ends the book with a letter to Osnat? What does the letter say?